WOMEN AND RELIGION IN THE WEST

What is the relationship between women and secularization? In the West, women are abandoning traditional religion. Yet they continue to make up the majority of religious adherents. Accounting for this seeming paradox is the focus of this volume. If women undergird the foundations of religion but are leaving in large numbers, why are they leaving? Where are they going? What are they doing? And what's happening to those who remain?

Women and Religion in the West addresses a neglected yet crucial issue within the debate on religious belonging and departure: the role of women in and out of religion and spirituality. Beginning with an analysis of the relationship between gender and secularization, the book moves its focus to in-depth examination of women's experiences based on data from key recent qualitative work on women and religion. This volume addresses not only women's place in and out of Christianity (the normal focus of secularization theories) but also alternative spiritualities and Islam, asking how questions of secularization differ between faith systems.

This book offers students and scholars of religion, sociology, and women's studies, as well as interested general readers, an accessible work on the religiosity of western women and contributes fresh analyses of the rapidly shifting terrain of contemporary religion and spirituality.

THEOLOGY AND RELIGION IN INTERDISCIPLINARY PERSPECTIVE SERIES IN ASSOCIATION WITH THE BSA SOCIOLOGY OF RELIGION STUDY GROUP

BSA Sociology of Religion Study Group Series editor:
Pink Dandelion and the publications committee

Theology and Religion in Interdisciplinary Perspective Series editors:
Douglas Davies and Richard Fenn

The British Sociological Association Sociology of Religion Study Group began in 1975 and provides the primary forum in Britain for scholarship in the sociology of religion. The nature of religion remains of key academic interest and this series draws on the latest worldwide scholarship in compelling and coherent collections on critical themes. Secularisation and the future of religion; gender; the negotiation and presentation of religious identities, beliefs and values; and the interplay between group and individual in religious settings are some of the areas addressed. Ultimately, these books reflect not just on religious life but on how wider society is affected by the enduring religious framing of human relationships, morality and the nature of society itself.

This series is part of the broader *Theology and Religion in Interdisciplinary Perspective Series* edited by Douglas Davies and Richard Fenn.

Other titles published in the BSA Sociology of Religion Study Group Series

Reading Religion in Text and Context
Reflections of Faith and Practice in Religious Materials
Edited by Elisabeth Arweck and Peter Collins
ISBN 978-0-7546-5482-7 (Hbk)

Materializing Religion
Expression, Performance and Ritual
Edited by Elisabeth Arweck and William Keenan
ISBN 978-0-7546-5094-2 (Hbk)

A Sociology of Spirituality
Edited by Kieran Flanagan and Peter C. Jupp
ISBN 978-0-7546-5458-2 (Hbk)

Religion and the Individual
Belief, Practice, Identity
Edited by Abby Day
ISBN 978-0-7546-6122-1 (Hbk)

Women and Religion in the West
Challenging Secularization

Edited by

KRISTIN AUNE
University of Derby, UK

SONYA SHARMA
University of British Columbia, Canada

GISELLE VINCETT
University of Edinburgh, UK

ASHGATE

Published by
Ashgate Publishing Limited
Gower House
Croft Road
Aldershot
Hampshire GU11 3HR
England

Ashgate Publishing Company
Suite 420
101 Cherry Street
Burlington, VT 05401-4405
USA

Ashgate website: http://www.ashgate.com

British Library Cataloguing in Publication Data
Women and religion in the West : challenging secularization. – (Theology and religion in interdisciplinary perspective)
1. Women and religion – Western countries 2. Women – Religious life – Western countries 3. Women in Christianity – Western countries 4. Women in Islam – Western countries 5. Secularization
I. Aune, Kristin II. Sharma, Sonya III. Vincett, Giselle IV. British Sociological Association. Sociology of Religion Study Group
200.8'2'091713

Library of Congress Cataloging-in-Publication Data
Women and religion in the west : challenging secularization / edited by Kristin Aune, Sonya Sharma, and Giselle Vincett.
    p. cm. — (Theology and religion in interdisciplinary perspective series in association with the BSA sociology of religion study group)
  ISBN 978-0-7546-5870-2 (hardcover : alk. paper) 1. Women in Christianity. 2. Women and religion. I. Aune, Kristin. II. Sharma, Sonya. III. Vincett, Giselle.

BV639.W7W6154 2007
200.82—dc22

ISBN 978-0-7546-5870-2

2007021338

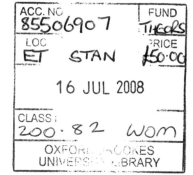
Printed and bound in Great Britain by MPG Books Ltd, Bodmin, Cornwall.

Contents

List of Figures and Tables

List of Contributors

Kristin Aune is a Senior Lecturer in Sociology at the University of Derby. Her research focuses on gender and religion, especially gender in evangelical Christianity. her publications include *Single Women: Challenge to the Church?* (Paternoster, 2002), *On Revival: A Critical Examination* (coedited with Andrew Walker, Paternoster, 2003) and several chapters and articles in books, journals and reference works.

Stef Aupers is a postdoctoral researcher in sociology at Erasmus University Rotterdam, the Nnetherlands. He participates in the research program *Cyberspace Salvations: Computer Technology, Simulation and Modern Gnosis*, funded by the Netherlands Organisation for Scientific Research (NWO). He has published widely on New Age and in 2004 defended his Ph.D. thesis *In de ban van moderniteit: De sacralisering van het zelf en computertechnologie* [Under the Spell of Modernity: the Sacralisation of Self and Computer Technology] (Amsterdam: Aksant).

Sarah Bracke holds a Marie Curie postdoctoral fellowship based at Utrecht University (Gender Studies) and affiliated with the University of California Santa Cruz (Anthropology). her work explores questions of religion, modernity, secularism, subjectivity and gender in a European context. Her doctoral dissertation looks at women involved in religious movements that challenge secularization. Her current investigation engages with notions and epistemologies of the (post)secular. She has published in, among others, *Tijdschrift voor Genderstudies*, *Tijdschrift voor Humanistiek, Ethiek en Maatschappij*, *Andere Sinema*, *European Journal of Women's Studies* and *Multitudes*. She is part of various feminist groups and networks, including the transnational European feminist research and activism network NextGenderation.

Dick Houtman is an associate professor of sociology at Erasmus University Rotterdam, the Netherlands, and a member of the Amsterdam School for Social Science Research (ASSR). His principal research interest is cultural change in late modernity, with a focus on its political and religious ramifications. His latest book is *Class and Politics in Contemporary Social Science: 'Marxism Lite' and Its Blind Spot for Culture* (Aldine de Gruyter, 2003) and he is currently preparing a book that is provisionally titled *Beyond Faith and Reason: New Age, Postmodernism and the Disenchantment of the World*.

Serena Hussain completed her Ph.D., 'A Statistical Mapping of Muslims in Britain' at the University of Bristol, the first Ph.D. to be financially supported by the Muslim Council of Britain. Her research, analysing data from the 2001 national Census, was the first to confirm that Muslims experience greater levels of disadvantage compared with all other faith groups in England and Wales. The findings will be published as *Muslims on the Map: A National Survey of Social Trends* by IB Tauris. She is currently a Research Fellow at the University of Leeds. Her main areas of interest are Muslims, social justice, disadvantage, minority communities in Britain, faith and faith-based NGOs.

Penny Long Marler is a Professor of Religion at Samford University in Birmingham, Alabama, where she also directs the concentration in congregational studies. she has co-authored two books, *Being There: Culture and Formation in Two Theological Schools* (Oxford, 1997) and *Young Catholics at the New Millennium* (Dufour, 2001), and over 30 articles on religion and religious institutions. She has received major grant funding for research and programmatic initiatives and currently directs the Resource Center for Pastoral Excellence, funded by a $2 million grant from the Lilly Endowment.

Rubina Ramji is Assistant Professor of Religious Studies in the Department of Philosophy and Religious Studies at Cape Breton University, Canada. Her research has focused on images of Islamic women in the media. She is the author of a variety of chapters in books, including *Globalization, Religion and Culture* (Brill, forthcoming), *Mediating Religion: Conversations in Media, Religion and Culture* (T&T Clark, 2003), *God in the Details: American Religion in Popular Culture* (Routledge, 2001), and articles in the *Journal of Religion and Film*. She is working on issues of identity and religious belief amongst second generation Canadian Muslim youth.

Siân Reid has been conducting research on various aspects of contemporary paganism since 1990. she is the editor of *Between the Worlds: Readings in Contemporary Neopaganism* (Canadian Scholar's Press Inc., 2006). She has also contributed chapters on pagan themes to a variety of other collections, including *Magical Religion and Modern Witchcraft* (Lewis, 1996), *The Oxford Handbook of New Religious Movements* (Lewis, 2002) and *Religion and Canadian Society* (Beaman, 2006). She is the lead researcher on the Canadian Pagan Survey Project, and teaches in the Sociology and Anthropology Department at Carleton University.

Garbi Schmidt is a senior researcher at the Danish National Institute of Social Research, Copenhagen, where she coordinates the ethnic minorities research initiative. She is a member of the steering committee of the Academy of Migration Studies in Denmark and co-founder and president of the Danish Forum for Islamic Studies. She has carried out research among immigrant Muslim communities in the United States, Sweden and Denmark. Key publications include *Islam in Urban America: Sunni Muslims in Chicago* (Temple University Press, 2004) and 'Dialectics of Authenticity: Examples of the Ethnification of Islam among Young Muslims in the United States and Denmark', *The Muslim World*, 2002. Besides continuing her work on Muslim immigrants in the western context, her research projects include perspectives on transnational marriages among Pakistani and Turkish immigrants living in Denmark.

Sonya Sharma is a Postdoctoral Research Fellow with The Family Food Practices research program at the University of British Columbia, Canada. She is exploring how local food cultures, social class, and family context interact, and intersect with gender, race and culture to produce everyday food practices. She is also a researcher on the project 'The Negotiation of Spiritual and Religious Plurality in Healthcare' (Trinity Western University, Canada). Her doctoral thesis (Lancaster University) explores the impact of young women's Protestant church involvement on their sexual identities. An article co-written with Kristin Aune, 'Sexuality and Contemporary Evangelical Christianity', appears in *Negotiating Boundaries? Identities, Sexualities, Diversities* edited by Clare Beckett, Owen Heathcote and Marie Macey (Cambridge Scholars Press).

Marta Trzebiatowska is Lecturer in Sociology at the University of Aberdeen. Her doctorate (University of Exeter) investigated the social construction of gendered subjectivities in contemporary Polish convents. Her article 'Habit Does Not a Nun Make' ('Habit Zakonnicy nieCzyni') was published in Leszczynska and Koscianska (eds) *Women and Religions* (Nomos, 2006). Her research interests include religion, gender and sexuality, migration, and social theory.

Giselle Vincett is a Postdoctoral Research Fellow at the University of Edinburgh. Her current work investigates the religiosity of young Scottish Christians in Glasgow. Her doctoral thesis (Lancaster University, UK) entitled 'Feminism and Religion: a Study of Christian Feminists and Goddess Feminists in the UK' was based upon qualitative work with Christian and contemporary Pagan women in the UK. A paper based upon some of her Ph.D. research, entitled 'Quagans: Fusing Quakerism with Contemporary Paganism' will appear in the forthcoming volume *The Quaker Condition: the Sociology of a Liberal Religion* edited by Pink Dandelion and Peter Collins (Cambridge Scholars).

Linda Woodhead is Professor of Sociology of Religion at Lancaster University and Director of the AHRC/ESRC Research Programme on Religion and Society. She has written on the decline of the churches and the rise of alternative forms of spirituality in the West. She is currently involved in an EU funded research project on the Muslim veil in the UK, and is writing on religion and emotions, and on religion and gender. Recent books include *The Spiritual Revolution: Why Religion is Giving Way to Spirituality* (with Paul Heelas, Blackwell, 2005) and *An Introduction to Christianity* (Cambridge University Press, 2004).

Women, Religion and Secularization: One Size Does Not Fit All

Giselle Vincett, Sonya Sharma and Kristin Aune

Introduction

This volume arises from several core questions concerning women's religiosity in the West: Why do women predominate numerically in religion? Given this, why are many disaffiliating? And when they leave, where are they going and what are they doing? These developments in women's religiosity have occurred in parallel with – but without much reference to – a major and enduring debate in the sociology of religion: secularization. Secularization refers to the process whereby the sacred loses its significance and can occur on several levels: societal, individual and within a religion itself (Dobbelaere 2002; Casanova 2006). In this book we attempt to bring women's religiosity into dialogue with secularization theories.

We take it as a given that in the western world, secularization is a fact even in countries (such as the United States) where church participation is still high. Secularization is a modern phenomenon: it arises when certain events and ways of thinking associated with modernity come together. By this, we do not mean to suggest (as some have) that a given culture *must* secularize as it modernizes.

Historical overview

Secularization theorists often point to the schism of the churches in the West, which began with Luther in the sixteenth century, as the first of the multiple threads that led to secularized modernity. It is not that Luther, Calvin and others *caused* secularization so much as that they represented a particular way of thinking which has come to be typical of modern western societies. That is, they questioned the authority of what had previously been unquestionable: the Catholic Church, its Pope and its priests. The separation of what became the Lutheran Church from the Catholic Church gave rise to many and varied schisms. Rather than there only being one Church, very quickly there was a multitude of churches to choose from; which was the *true* church depended on where you stood. Similarly, the rationalist philosophy of the eighteenth century is also key to the development of the modern mindset. Philosophers began to question the authority of God and elevated the rational or the mind over 'feeling'. As a result, the church came to be associated with *irrationality*; God did not make sense. Descartes' 'I think therefore I am' is a radical break from the long held beliefs of the Nicene Creed: 'I believe in one God, the Father Almighty, Maker of heaven and earth, and of all things visible and invisible'.

The industrial revolution which occurred in the West in the late eighteenth and nineteenth-centuries undoubtedly sped up the process not of secularization per se (church attendance in the late nineteenth-century was as high as perhaps it had ever been, as Marler shows in this volume), but of particular ways of experiencing and thinking about the world. Industrialization involved urbanization, which led to the separation of work from home (for men, and for some women). The terrible working conditions of many meant that the home came to be idealized as a haven, which further promoted the split between the public and the private. If work was in the public realm, and home was the private, where did this leave the church? Depending on the country, the church was more or less bound up with the state, but the state was taking over many church functions, such as welfare and schooling. More and more then, the church came to be seen as part of the private realm. Meanwhile, between industrialization and the First World War, men were increasingly feeling alienated from the sacred. The sacred and the profane, like the public and the private, became compartmentalized, and many men spent most of their time in the awful conditions of the profane. This had two consequences. The horrors of the Second World War drove many back to the church: it was familiar and comfortable, it united communities torn apart by war, and it provided stability in a world that desperately craved it. Nevertheless, the rebellious children of the Baby Boom generation saw the church as old-fashioned and irrelevant and many turned away from it.

There are several things to note about this brief summary. First, it gives the impression of an inexorable and uniform process (across class, gender, nation and religion). Second, it does not explain the rise and continued health of certain forms of Christianity. Third, it is a theory that only fits a certain segment of western populations; that is, it fits white men, and especially white, Protestant men in Europe. We will return to these issues after briefly examining some of the theories of secularization that attempt to nuance the argument.

Critiques

David Martin (2005a, 2005b) has pointed out that some forms of Christianity have fared quite well and have even grown under secularization: he argues that secularization, rather than being uniform, is better thought of as two (or more) streams that exist alongside each other. Evangelical and charismatic Christianity, which until very recently were the only growing forms of Christianity in the West, parallel the flight from the rest of the churches. This is what Woodhead and Heelas (2000) have called 'co-existence theory'. Similarly, taking into account geographical differences in secularization rates by looking at, among other things, the links between church and state in different countries reveals that in states where the church has been strongly tied to a repressive state, church attendance levels are often low. Where state and church have long been separate, at least officially, church attendance levels tend to remain high, such as in the United States (Martin 2005b). This theory is refined by factoring in levels of industrialization and postindustrialization: in countries that are postindustrialized, attendance levels tend to be lower (Norris and Inglehart 2004).

The general critique of secularization theories is well known. A large group of theorists have pointed out that rather than secularizing, western societies are actually showing signs of (re)sacralization. This means that people return to thinking about the sacred and relocate the sacred in a newly holistic manner. The rise of alternative spiritualities, now the fastest growing religious form in the West (Berger et. al. 2003; Reid, this volume), has led some to highlight this trend. Indeed, one of the original proponents of secularization theory, Peter Berger, is now one of the strongest voices arguing the case for (re)sacralization (1999).[1] Derationalization is an important feature of sacralization. Where religion came to be seen as backward and anti-modern, in late or post modernity – with the rise of alternative spiritualities in particular – questioning begins of the dualistic tendencies that once defined modernity and a new holism emerges.[2] Other key features of (re)sacralization are: *deprivatization*, or the public sphere's reenchantment with religion (Casanova 1994) – seen, for example, in the growing involvement of religious groups in public policy and welfare service provision as well as the incorporation of subjective wellbeing spiritualities into the culture as a whole (Heelas 1996; Heelas and Woodhead 2005); *religious growth through conversion* – for example, the conversion of western non-believers to Islam or evangelical Christianity; and *intensification* through the radicalization of previously less committed believers – for example, growing support for forms of more radical or fundamentalist religion (Woodhead and Heelas 2000: 429–475; Berger 1999).

In taking Europe as a model that is then applied globally or at least to the rest of the West, secularization theory is often Eurocentric (Davie 2002).[3] Secularization has largely been propounded by white, male Judeo-Christian (in culture or faith) academics (Berger 1999: 2) and has tended to be blind to the experiences of other groups. In part, the lack of attention to religions other than Christianity is understandable: forms of religion which have central bodies of organization, such as the Vatican, and clear physical and public meeting points (i.e. churches), are easy to count. But religious formations which are diffuse with no central organization, or which are opposed to centralized organization, or those with small, regular non-institutionalized meetings, such as holistic spirituality, Wiccan covens or Jewish Friday night Shabbat meals, are harder to count (Heelas 2006). As Hussain notes in this volume, Tietze (2000) has shown how the standard ways of measuring religiosity have arisen from the rationalization of religious traditions, which is a symptom, he argues, of secularization itself. Exactly how non-Christian religions like Islam fit with the secularization paradigm is a long-overdue question (Chambers 2006).

---

[1] Berger (1999: 12) also refutes what he calls the 'last-ditch thesis' of sociologists of religion such as Bruce (2006). This thesis says that resurgence only shows a last-ditch defence or dying gasp of religiosity, which cannot last.

[2] For more on the changes associated with late or postmodernity, and their implications for religion see: Flanagan and Jupp 1996; Heelas 1998; Woodhead and Heelas 2000.

[3] Occasionally these analyses are helpfully nuanced by gender: for instance, Bernice Martin (2001) points out the growth of Pentecostalism amongst women in South America. Her findings are not foregrounded here, however, because of this volume's concern with the postindustrial West.

Gender

The gendered, or feminist, critique of secularization is less well known – that is, what happens when women's experiences are taken as the standpoint from which to examine secularization. This question was notably raised by Linda Woodhead (2001, 2005), whose arguments have informed this essay and who, with colleagues at Lancaster University,[4] organized the 2005 British Sociological Association Sociology of Religion Study Group conference *Religion and Gender*, from which several chapters in this volume originated. This volume gives room for the first time for an extended discussion of this theme.

Some theorists of women, religion and secularization featured in this book accept the secularization theses, but others do not. This means that while some are concerned with refining the theories so that they take account of secularization's impact on women, others challenge the theoretical premises of secularization from the perspective of women's experiences; this second group tend to endorse the arguments of sacralization theorists and add to sacralization theory the experiences of women. This volume takes account of both perspectives, and some writers express a combination of the two.

Callum Brown's (2001) book *The Death of Christian Britain* represents an important attempt to explore women's relationship with secularization. Brown shows how, between 1800 and 1963, religiosity was driven by textual, media and literary discourse about personal identity available through Christian novels, magazines, obituaries and tracts. Life stories were entwined with constructions of gender and Christianity. Religiosity was identified with femininity, while men were represented as irreligious or reluctant believers, and this impacted rates of churchgoing. When people's gendered identities were tied to Christianity, religiosity remained high, particularly among women. But when representations of personal identity shifted away from Christianity from the 1960s (Brown pinpoints 1963 as the key date), secularization advanced. The liberalization in sexual attitudes and behaviour and the advent of feminism issued major blows to Christian religiosity. In the industrial period women had been identified as the main carriers and supporters of religiosity, so when women accepted feminism and sexual liberalism as alternative resources for identity construction, this was a significant setback for the church. Church attendance declined sharply, and femininity ceased to be associated with piety.

Brown is not without critics (Percy 2001; Morris 2003; Gill 2003[5]), but two important points can be drawn from his work. First, within industrializing modernity, the period identified with secularization, secularization occurred differently for women and men. An important facet of institutional or structural differentiation relates to the division of society into public and private spheres. While men became occupied with the public world of work and (for the middle-classes) governance, women's

---

[4]   The organizing committee comprised of Linda Woodhead, Paul Heelas, Sevgi Kilic, Sonya Sharma and Giselle Vincett.

[5]   For example, Percy (2001) ponders the viability of calling the industrializing West's religion 'feminized', given the dominance of men at its leadership and governmental levels. He and others also dispute the extent to which Christian Britain can be said to have died.

activities took place largely in the domestic arena (Elshtain 1981; Davidoff a 1987; Tilly and Scott 1987; Pateman 1988; Poovey 1988; Seccombe 1992, Clark 1995).[6] The core characteristics of secularizing modernity – rationaliz ....on, separation of church and state, bureaucratization, industrialization, capitalism – were mainly driven forward in the public arena by men. The division of women and men into 'separate spheres', coupled with the privatization of religion as it lost its social influence, feminized religion, connecting it with women's activities in the private sphere. It is difficult to know exactly how this feminization contributed to men's declining attendance or women's increasing attendance, but it is clear that these changes occurred, and that the existing preponderance of women as churchgoers is connected to this.

Second, Brown's work highlights that women's disaffiliation from traditional forms of religion is vital to understanding patterns of religiosity, secularization and sacralization. Women's move into paid employment, together with their quest for more egalitarian sexual relationships and the right to make choices about their lives, changed the gendered construction of the private/public boundary and the stability of religion in the private realm. Marler's contribution to this book maps this quantitatively across the US and UK. These crucial two points crystallize to form a key paradox explored by this book: women are both the most religious[7] *and* are disaffiliating from religion in significant numbers, so much so that their changing social position is seen as a key cause of secularization.

But if Brown stands with those who believe that secularization has occurred, others consider secularization a totalizing metanarrative that has had unfortunate consequences for women. Bracke writes in this volume of the problematic way in which secularization theories have upheld a norm of masculine rationality. Modern men's experiences are taken as the norm and model for the future of religion: when men leave religion, religion is said to be dying, regardless of its continuity in women's lives. Measuring religiosity is difficult, but existing measures continue to find that women's religious involvement exceeds men's across different nations, religions and types of society, and that in western postindustrialized and Christian/ post-Christian contexts this gender imbalance is particularly pronounced (Inglehart and Norris 2003: 49–72). Often women's continued religiosity is viewed as marginal to the 'main event' of male secularization; evoking a series of binary oppositions

---

[6]   The separate spheres family remained unattainable for many working-class people. Low wages paid to working-class men made it unviable economically and working-class women and men worked as servants in middle-class families (Seccombe 1992, 1993; Clark 1995). In equating ideal gendered behaviour with middle-class values, separate spheres discourse was oppressive towards the working classes, who were expected by religious, medical, legal and literary ideologues to attempt to conform to middle-class ideals of full-time motherhood despite their lack of economic resources.

[7]   For example, in 2005, women constituted 57 per cent of English churchgoers (Brierley 2006: 12.3). The US Congregational Life Survey produced a figure of 61 per cent (see Marler, this volume). Alternative religions are harder to count. Berger et al. (2003: 27) found 64.8 per cent of adherents were female in the US and Heelas and Woodhead (2005: 94) found that 80 per cent of those involved in the holistic milieu (an inclusive term that includes New Age and alternative spiritualities) in Kendal, UK, were women.

that feminist theorists have long critiqued (de Beauvoir 1953; Friedan 1963; Daly 1968), women are positioned as the irrational others of secularizing modernity. This, we believe, must be exposed and replaced by the argument that totalizing theories of secularization collapse in the face of women's experiences. Women's experiences instead point to a different 'truth' about religiosity in contemporary times.

Women's religious experiences prompt some additional challenges to secularization theories. These concern the problem of measuring women's religiosity and the neglect of non-Christian religion and spirituality when theorizing women's beliefs. Conventional measures of gender and religiosity often relate to attendance at places of worship, frequency of prayer, study of religious texts and adherence to religious doctrines or beliefs (e.g. Argyle and Beit-Hallahmi 1975; Walter 1990; Loewenthal *et al.* 2002; Inglehart and Norris 2003: 49–72[8]). But measuring women's religiosity by attendance at places of worship can be inaccurate. This is because religious obligations for men and women are sometimes different, with women's involvement in domesticity and childrearing considered a more important expression of faith than attendance at a place of worship – this seems especially so for Jews and Muslims. Additionally, some religious bodies forbid women entry to public places of worship when they are menstruating. Others deny women admittance altogether – for instance, women are currently unable to enter half the UK's mosques on the basis of their gender, and are encouraged to pray instead at home (*Dispatches: Women-only Jihad*, 2006, London: Channel 4). It seems, therefore, that existing measures work better for Christian women's religiosity than for other religions, as chapters in the Islam section of this book show. Indeed, some of the existing work exploring reasons for women's dominance in religiosity treats religiosity as synonymous with Christianity (for example, Walter 1990; Davie 1994: 117–138; Walter and Davie 1998).

'New Age' or neo-pagan spiritualities – which might prompt one to attend yoga classes, invoke the goddess or seek out various alternative therapies – is not conducive to conventional measures of religiosity either, and since women predominate in alternative spiritualities (Heelas and Woodhead 2005: 94–107), not measuring alternative spirituality is particularly problematic. We take issue with the belief (as expressed, for example, in Bruce 2006: 42) that there is no community in alternative spiritualities and that therefore they are difficult to count. Casanova (2006: 18) points out that most theories of secularization assume that the processes of modernization ultimately 'make community inviable', but he argues instead that modernity simply makes new forms of community possible, especially 'voluntary associations'. Alternative spiritualities are based upon such new forms of community, especially small voluntary groups. The gender gap in alternative spiritualities leads us to ask whether these forms of community are particularly appealing to women.

It is worth saying a few words about the apparent exclusion of men's experiences from this book. It might be argued that in focusing on women specifically, rather than gender in general, we are neglecting half of the population. Our response to this is

---

[8]   Some studies take account of the need to conceptualise religiosity differently across different traditions – for example, Miller and Stark (2002) include keeping kosher and lighting Sabbath candles as measures of Jewish religiosity.

first that secularization theories have thus far mainly been about men's religious and/or secularizing behaviours. This is the case in so far as explanations for secularization have been related to the changing nature of work, which during modernity was a predominantly male activity. We believe that the impact of secularization on women needs to be considered. Additionally, men's behaviour has often been taken as the norm from which generalizations can be made about the general population. We believe that this is a mistaken move. Not only does women's spirituality fail in some cases to conform to the male norm, but it often challenges the validity of these norms. So in addressing women's place vis-à-vis secularization we aim to redress a long-neglected balance.

Feminism

Significant to women and secularization is the feminist movement. During the rise of second-wave feminism from the 1960s, most secular feminists rejected traditional religiosity as irredeemably patriarchal. Looking back however, even Christian feminists like Elizabeth Cady Stanton, who published *The Women's Bible* in 1898, felt that traditional Christianity had largely discounted women's contributions to church life. The tireless efforts of first-wave feminists, many of whom possessed a Christian background, paved the way for future feminist theologians during the 1960s and 1970s who would pick up from where Stanton finished, articulating the marginalization of women associated with patriarchal Christianity. Scholars have generally considered women's departure from traditional religion during second-wave feminism an example of secularization (Brereton and Bendroth 2001). Subsequently, mainstream feminism has given little coverage to women's religiosity. Leela Fernandes (2003: 9) argues that 'feminist theorists and organizations tend to relegate spirituality to the local "cultural" idiom of grassroots women (usually in "other" places and for "other" women), acknowledging it in the name of an uneasy cultural relativist tendency of "respecting cultural difference."'

Furthermore, the many women who have left traditional religion have not necessarily experienced secularization, but have acquired other, non-sexist spiritualities. Women's turn to other forms of spirituality and religiosity means that they are not rejecting modernity as much as they are undertaking a complex series of negotiations with modern culture, constructing reciprocal forms of accommodation and resistance (Brereton and Bendroth 2001: 215). As is apparent in this collection, women's responses to secularization differ. Some leave traditional church (Aune; Sharma); others join alternative spiritual communities (Vincett; Reid; Woodhead); while others reclaim and/or renegotiate traditional religion (Trzebiatowska; Bracke; Ramji; Schmidt). These in-depth qualitative studies are particularly successful in representing these different meanings and (re)formations of women's individual and collective spirituality, bringing a novel contribution to feminist knowledge.

Communities

One of the givens of this book is that secularization exists in some form and all individuals in the West must engage with that backdrop. Whilst adherents of religions that are connected with immigration into predominantly Christian countries remain religious, they appear to be so in part because of secularization. David Martin (2005b) has suggested that high levels of religiosity amongst such communities reflect their desire to differentiate themselves from their (nominally) Christian neighbours by building strong religious communities. Although differentiation and identity remain important factors in second-generation religiosity remaining high, Ramji and Schmidt indicate that second generations are reacting to other factors. Second generation Muslim Canadians, argues Ramji, think of themselves as fully Canadian; what they assert through their religiosity is their difference from the dominant secular context. Bracke's research indicates that in western countries where religion was forcibly separated from the state, high levels of religiosity amongst young Muslim women signify an assertion of an identity distinct from the dominant order, and a contemporary and progressive version of the religion of their grandmothers. Similarly, conservative forms of Christianity actively try to counteract secularization by differentiating themselves from society and engaging in mission. Adherents of alternative forms of spirituality, and especially of political forms such as feminist Wicca, are also differentiating themselves from the dominant orders, both in their formation of a (re)sacralized worldview and against male hegemony. In all of these cases then, religion becomes a way of expressing one's identity and agency against the context of secularization.

Space

This siphoning off of religion into the private realm may go some way to explaining why there appears to be less evidence of secularization among Muslim than Christian women. Their holistic conceptualization of society disaffirms any notion of a public/private split. Martin similarly identifies Islamic societies' tendency to see religion as 'a complete system co-extensive with society' (2005b: 28). Hussain makes this point in this book, noting that British Muslims are considerably more likely than other groups to say that religion impacts how they live their lives. Indeed, it is ethnic minorities, especially Muslims, who have brought new fervour to religion in Britain in recent decades.

The essays in this book on Christianity suggest that when women move away from traditional roles as housewives and mothers they become less – or less conventionally – religious. But does this apply to Muslim women? Hussain, Schmidt, Ramji and Bracke all argue that young women live out their religiosity in public, not just private, contexts, and that young Muslim women's religiosity depends on their late modern context for its vibrancy. Their religiosity is constructed, even enhanced, through technology, especially the internet, and the educational opportunities available to them in an individualistic liberal democracy. In fact, the quest to display 'authentic' or 'real' Islam encourages them out of the private family to practice their religion through study groups, academic reading and internet forums in the more public arena. Some of the most radical consider their parents' more 'cultural' or traditional Islam inferior to their own authentic version.

But there may be specific contextual reasons for young Muslims' radicalization that do not extend beyond the immediate local or national milieu. In the British context, as Chambers (2006: 337) puts it, the marginalization of Muslims by some in the media and political realms 'appear[s] to be strengthening, rather than weakening, minority self-consciousness and, by extension, religious consciousness.' It seems, as several of our authors comment, that the broader international context of anti-Muslim sentiment since 9/11 has been a significant factor in this radicalization.

Women react differently to the challenges of late modernity, but where they are attracted to religion, it is generally because it reinforces or helps them cope with their negotiation of daily life. Religion can break down the dualistic split of public/private and create a 'thirdspace'. The term 'thirdspace' has been used by various theorists, notably in the field of geography.[9] We use it to mean those spaces (physical, mental, social) which may be described as both/neither spaces; that is, spaces which are not easily categorisable as, for example, entirely public or private spaces. A theme of this book is that such spaces are particularly prevalent for women and the women who use them often conceptualize them in this way even when others might not.

Woodhead (2005; see also Marler in this volume and Hakim 2000: 158) employs a typology of three groups of women to explain women's different attitudes to religion. The first group consists of women whose primary role is in the home. Some may engage in part-time employment, but if they do, their jobs tend to be in the caring sector. The second group is termed 'jugglers' or 'adapters'. These women combine paid employment with caring for their family. The third group is work-centred. They are primarily committed to paid employment, often in traditionally male fields.

The first group, home-centred women, Woodhead claims, is most often found in traditional religion, especially Christianity. They are least likely to abandon traditional religion because it validates and reinforces their position. However, the situation is probably not so clear-cut. Women who are full-time wives and mothers may not perceive their position as 'private' in the way some have viewed it. For them, it is a locus of both public and private: where friends and relations meet,

---

[9]   Bhabha has employed this term in his work in postcolonial studies to denote the cultural practices (culture is primarily spatial for Bhabha) of hybridized populations (specifically immigrant and displaced populations) in making their new space home. The identities of immigrant and displaced persons are composed of both a new identity and their old identities and so are both and neither – hence they create spaces that may be called 'third space' (Papoulias 2004: 55, Bhaba 1990a and b). Soja is a geographer who has also used the term, notably in his 1996 book *Thirdspace: Journeys to Los Angeles and Other Real-And-Imagined Places*. Latham (2004: 272) summarizes Soja's very different use of the term as referring to both a 'spatialized trialectic' method of analysis and 'the particular texture of everyday lived spaces that exceeds the compartmentalized knowledges of the conventional social sciences'. In both cases, the definition of 'thirdspace' remains slippery. We choose to use the term 'thirdspace', rather than 'third space' as we think it more reflective of the experience of intersecting boundaries.

where tradespeople visit, children constantly cross boundaries, and where they move around in 'public' spaces of their community such as school, shops, etc. (Rose 1993). It is not, then, that religion here is privatized, so much as that religion is able to accommodate these women's differing experiences of public and private. Morgan (2002) and Wright (2002) have suggested that the church is a third sphere, both public and private, where women often do 'feminine' work (cleaning, decorating, pastoral care etc.). We contend also that traditionally religious women are likely to only comply with traditional religion so long as they are content and able to conform to its ideal construction of women's place as wife-and-mother, as Marler, Aune and Sharma show in their chapters; Bhopal (1998) has found something similar in the case of Hindu, Sikh and Muslim women. For example, although many women desire to become wives and mothers, the gender imbalance in churches renders this an impossible ideal. Women who remain in traditional religion thus assert their agency in that choice, and some are actively reshaping their religion according to their own ideas of authenticity.

Women who 'juggle' the public and private, who work both outside and inside the home, are the most likely to insist upon forms of religiosity that reflect their experience of intersecting boundaries. Alternative forms of spirituality do this very well. Even the title of Síân Reid's recent book (2006), *Between the Worlds: Readings in Contemporary Neopaganism*, reflects the neo-pagan preoccupation with creating various forms of thirdspace. However, those women involved with liberal Christianity may also be reshaping religion to suit their experience, as in Vincett's chapter on 'Fusers'. These religions, being less rigid in dogma and praxis, may be more amenable to incorporating 'spirituality' than other forms of traditional religion. It is perhaps these women who most challenge secularization theories in that they are not doing the expected either when they leave the church or when they stay – that is, they are blurring boundaries between what have been treated as fixed categories: religion/spirituality, public/private, religious/secular. For the traditional and the juggling women, the home blurs distinctions between religious and secular by incorporating meditation or shrine rooms or space, and having church groups or religious classes meet in the home.

The women least likely to be involved with religion, and thus most secularized, are those for whom the construction of public/private is strongest. They are the women most likely to be involved in full-time and professional careers. These women are least likely to blur the boundaries between home and work (as do the 'jugglers') or to experience their homes as anything other than 'private' (as women that are more 'traditional' are apt to do). These women are least likely to inhabit thirdspace.

Security and embodiment

Danièle Hervieu-Léger contends that 'it has become clear that belief proliferates in proportion to the uncertainty caused by the pace of change in all areas of social life' (2006: 59), which is another way of summarizing the differences we see between the religiosity of different groups of women. Similarly, Norris and Inglehart argue that people who feel least secure, whether there are threats to their personhood, family or community, are the most likely to be religious (2004, 2006). These theses fit quite well with women's situation. Western women's detraditionalization – their transition from home-making to self-making – requires them to grapple continually with issues surrounding their personhood (as Marler and Woodhead show in this collection). Even women who seem least threatened, such as traditional stay-at-home mothers, must still negotiate these issues. Several studies (Houtman and Aupers, Reid, Vincett) indicate that where a woman lives a counter-cultural life or has counter-cultural politics, such as lesbians or spiritual feminists, she may be attracted to alternative spiritualities, to help her cope with and to reaffirm her position (see Houtman and Aupers in this book). Her lifestyle and politics may become bound up with her religiosity, so that, once again, the distinction between boundaries is fuzzy.

For women the notion of boundaries is charged in another important way. 'Woman' is not an abstract concept. Women are embodied, and their experiences of embodiment are bound up with spatial experiences and boundaries. For example, when a woman is excluded from certain positions or spaces in a church or mosque, she experiences her position through her body – and her body may be given as the reason for her spatial position. As Kim Knott points out, we all negotiate boundary issues in our everyday embodiment: our bodies are 'at once subject, object and tool, a means by which we engage with things' (2006: 133). Where, for example, do our bodies end and the world begin? This is a question particularly charged for women who have been associated with the natural and whose embodied independence has often been subverted by dominant constructions of 'woman'. But women have also written positively about their experiences of blurred embodied boundaries, in making love, or in pregnancy and breastfeeding, (Miller-McLemore 1992) and some feminists have attempted to write theo/thealogies based upon such blurred boundaries (Miller-McLemore 1992; Raphael 1996; Heyward 1989).

Women's embodiment and boundaries reappear throughout this text. Women's bodies are central to their religious and spiritual experiences, and are 'often the conflicting site of both giving in to, as well as resisting, dominant constructions' (Thapan 1997: 11). A woman experiences her body, sexuality and identity as a social being located within a certain cultural context with its dominant values and norms (Thapan 1997). Sharma shows in her chapter that the traditional Christian message that church communities inscribe on women's sexuality results in embodied experiences of shame and guilt for young women who challenge this message and become sexually active. Such is the case in Aune's chapter on single Christian women who confront marriage and family as defining norms for women who join the church.

Moreover, women's bodies are material realities that are made meaningful through social relations, interactions, practices and spaces. How women choose to live out the realities and meanings that their bodies present are threaded through the narratives of the women in these empirical studies. The moves women make to live out their embodied religious and spiritual subjectivities, nevertheless, exist between subversion and compliance, and always in relation to prevailing social constructions. Woodhead demonstrates in her chapter how women's work of care that creates holistic spiritual practices is lived through the body creating spiritual connection and community with other women. Likewise, Vincett and Reid illustrate that the female body is vital to the rituals, images and experiences of neo-paganism, Goddess Feminism and fused spirituality, challenging mainstream masculine imaged monotheism. The embodied spiritual experiences of these women confront the dualisms that have often defined traditional Christianity. Jackson and Scott argue that women's embodied subjectivities 'entail embodied selves engaged in embodied social activity and embodied interaction…the body is inseparable from the totality of the self' (2001: 19). The papers in this volume suggest that the non-separation of the body, the spatial, the social and the religious is a major theme in women's spirituality.

Whether the habit, hijab or niqab, women's religious clothing is another way that women embody and mark sacred differentiation in their lived contexts. Significantly, both Muslim and Christian women's clothing is a way that they mark their religiosity and embody sacred space. By publicly marking their sacred difference they challenge conventionalities concerning bodily appearance, revealing the tensions that are present within western society when religion is lived on and through the body. Moreover, women's bodies are sites where boundaries blur, where tradition and non-tradition are lived out, where the secular and the sacral converge.

Outline and summary

Penny Marler's chapter sets the scene for the empirical section on Christian women. Her quantitative analysis demonstrates how changing family, social and work contexts have affected women's involvement with and participation in traditional church. Due to the process of secularization and the turn to individualization, Marler perceives woman's role as moving 'from home-making to self-making', impacting women's affiliation to the church (they are attending less) and the places where they cultivate self and spiritual care.

Kristin Aune reveals the tensions between traditional gendered roles in church and single women's desire to be considered as equals in the evangelical church. In her ethnographic study of a congregation, she contends that single women's status is an 'abnormal' standing in the face of church values that endorse marital and familial roles as normative. Single women's attempts to negotiate these norms often result in their marginalization, causing many to disaffiliate from church.

Sonya Sharma shows how a marital-confined sexuality is a Protestant Christian ideal that can conflict with young women's developing sexual selves. Through interview data she captures how young women negotiate and confront sexual desire and experiences whilst involved in conservative church communities. Some remain within the church, but those who decide to leave do so because the church's traditional ideals for sex and gender no longer fit with their evolving sexual identities.

Marta Trzebiatowska's chapter focuses on women who subvert secularized feminine norms of marriage and family to join religious orders in Poland, whilst at the same time the traditional gendered roles within their families equip them for a convent lifestyle. Becoming a nun is a distinct life path, a woman's shaping of her own life. The religious identities that these women choose to adopt confront the secularization that surrounds them and marginalizes them.

Evident in these chapters is women's varying relationship to the church because of the impact of secularization: secularization permeates into women's religious identities. Women's religious identities are no longer synonymous to their relationship with a husband or children; a woman can be self-identified (Webster 1996). The options women have to create a life of their own means that they no longer have to give way to a feminine piety that clashes with their vocational and personal goals. On the one hand, women are prompted to seek sources outside of traditional church to have their spiritual and personal needs met, while on the other, women are looking for opportunities within traditional religion to fit with their evolving selves and life change. An underlying question of this section is whether the church can adapt to women's changing lives.

The section of this book entitled 'Alternative Spiritualities' looks at gender and the rise of neo-paganism and holistic spiritualities. Dick Houtman and Stef Aupers provide evidence of the spread of spirituality into the mainstream and link it to the detraditionalization of women's lives. This helps to explain the gender gap in alternative spiritualities, in that alternative spiritualities attract those – women – whose identities are shifting most rapidly. Houtman and Aupers refute the claim that the New Age is so diverse as to be a kind of pick-and-mix religion; they point out that it may be individualized but it still comprises shared beliefs.

Síân Reid argues that feminist spiritualities such as feminist Wicca and Goddess Feminism offer women a route toward the 'reenchantment' of secularized modernity: 'Individuals who are dissatisfied with this fundamental divorce must find a way to re-embed moral relevance into the process of living'. Further, religious communities, praxis, myth and symbolism found within alternative feminist spiritualities revalue women's experiences in late modernity. She argues that this positive revaluation in large part explains the growth of such spiritualities.

Giselle Vincett presents her research on a group of (mainly) women she calls 'Fusers'. This group fuses neo-paganism with Christianity, and as such, represents one way that women who stay within Christianity are changing the religion to positively incorporate their experiences and values. Those who fuse from outside of Christianity demonstrate a way to retain links with Christianity despite leaving the churches. The Fusers are an example of a religiosity based upon the crossing and fusing of normally segregated forms of religion.

Linda Woodhead examines the changes that have occurred in women's lives in the West since the 1960s and argues that these changes have often been 'confusing and contradictory'. Women who work outside the home, continue to be the primary caregivers *and* shoulder the majority of domestic work are the segment of the population most likely to be involved with holistic spiritualities to offset the stresses of juggling multiple and sometimes conflicting responsibilities.

These authors argue that although the flight from Christianity exists, women do not necessarily cease to believe or practice. They also take issue with the view that alternative spiritualities are too individualized to be coherent and too diffuse to be significant. Taken together, the three chapters suggest that women's religiosity in alternative spiritualities, although formed within the context of secularization, differs from traditional constructions of a secularized worldview, perhaps because of differing gendered experience. As such, they contend, women involved with such spiritualities challenge the gendered, dualistic and Christocentric construction of secularization theories.

Serena Hussain's chapter opens the Islam section with quantitative data from recent UK surveys. Muslim women are more likely to be married, to have more children, and to be primarily occupied in the home rather than in paid work outside it. Muslim women's religiosity can therefore be linked to their role in the domestic arena, where they teach faith to their children, and where Islam 'provides a strong enough alternative and forum against the disenchantment resulting through exposure to the public sphere'. Yet evidence also suggests that when women's exposure to the public sphere increases, their religious commitment remains, even strengthens; indeed, younger, educated women's embrace of the hijab can be understood as an attempt to assert a strong Islamic identity in the public realm.

Like some others in this volume, Sarah Bracke is critical of the secularization paradigm as one which upholds masculine rationality and 'does...poorly in accounting for religious women's lives and subjectivities.' Where theorists have equated religion with irrationality and marginality, Bracke explores how young pious Muslim women in Kazan negotiate the discourses of secularization. Presenting themselves as modern, knowledgeable, 'real' Muslims they challenge hegemonic notions and binaries associated with secularization and religion.

Some of the themes in Hussain and Bracke's chapters recur in Rubina Ramji's. Ramji challenges the earlier reading of second generation immigrant Muslims as simply adapting to western culture and in the process secularizing. Based on research with 58 young Canadian women whose parents had migrated to Canada before their birth or during their early childhood, Ramji reports a significant religiosity among many of them. Second generation immigrants, she says, engage in 'not a process of assimilation, but rather of negotiation'.

As a consequence of secularization, those who have been most religious have generally been those most involved with the private realm – women. But it is also true that women's religious activities pose a challenge to the assumed absence of religion from the public sphere. This is the case for Muslim women, whose expressions of religion may begin at home but often move into the public realm. Garbi Schmidt describes the way Muslim women in the United States work to enlarge the public spaces available to them for religious practice, for example by defending their faith and working for women's rights in non-domestic spaces, by embracing the veil (marking them as free from the western preoccupation with appearance) and by creating internet sites showcasing their progressive work for Muslim women's participation.

Conclusion

Further work needs to be done in the sociology of religion in theorizing women's religiosity. We offer this volume as contributing to the first steps in gendering one of the key concerns of the sociology of religion. Considering ways to analyse and report the degree of women's spiritual and religious activity – and disaffiliation from religion – are areas where more research is needed. With respect to secularization, future scholars might investigate how secularization and sacralization are impacted not only by gender but also by ethnicity, social class, sexuality, ability and age. The gendered nature of secularization or sacralization within other world religions should also be taken forward. The study of 'men *as* men' and their specific, gendered relation to secularization and religion will be a useful topic for exploration. This is the case not least because men's departure from the Christian churches has been at least as great as women's. One of the themes of this book concerns the spatial location of women, another under-explored area in the sociology of religion. Closer examination of the interconnections between politics, gender and secularization/ sacralization is an area we hope others will take forward.

Finally, it is worth restating the key theses of this book. Secularization occurs but at different levels and contexts. It is strongly related to women's changing roles in western societies. Traditional religiosity survives especially among women whose lives take place principally in the domestic arena, while women who have entered professional careers are least likely to stay traditionally religious. Between these two extremes lie women who might be called 'jugglers', who integrate the domestic and public domains. These women are most likely to move into new forms of spirituality and religiosity.

The modes of belief of the women in this volume are neither secular nor sacral, but both. Women are leaving the churches but are also numerically dominant in various forms of religion, especially the newer forms of alternative spiritualities. It is therefore important to recognize the simultaneous appearance of manifestations of decline and of growth or transformation; this means it may be as appropriate and significant to speak of sacralization as of secularization. This is core to secularization debates, but takes specific forms when women's religious experiences are considered. Moreover, this tension is related to our central paradox: women are the majority of religious adherents, but women's disaffection from religion is also an important social phenomenon.

Women, to lesser or greater extents, live in and create what we have termed 'thirdspace'. In this sense – that women do religious work within the public sphere; that religion refuses to be confined to the domestic arena – religious women's faith-inspired activities seem to be questioning the idea that secularization renders public religiosity insignificant. Women pose a challenge to secularization theories: we must go beyond one-size-fits-all theories to understand the complex interconnections between women, religion and secularization in the West.

References

Argyle, Michael and Beit-Hallahmi, Benjamin, *The Social Psychology of Religion* (London: Routledge & Kegan Paul, 1975).

Berger, Helen, Leach, Evan A. and Shaffer, Leigh S., *Voices from the Pagan Census: A National Survey of Witches and Neo-Pagans in the United States* (Columbia, SC: University of South Carolina Press, 2003).

Berger, Peter (ed.), *The Desecularization of the World: Essays on the Resurgence of Religion in World Politics* (Washington: Ethics and Public Policy Centre; Grand Rapids: Willam B. Eerdmans, 1999).

Bhabha, Homi K. (ed.), *Nation and Narration* (London: Routledge, 1990a).

Bhabha, Homi K., 'Interview with Homi Bhabha: The Third Space', in J. Rutherford (ed.), *Identity: Community, Culture, Difference* (London: Lawrence & Wishart, 1990b).

Bhopal, Kalwant, 'South Asian Women in East London: Religious Experience and Diversity', *Journal of Gender Studies*, 7(2) (1998): 143–156.

Brereton, Virginia. Lieson and Bendroth, Margaret Lamberts, 'Secularization and Gender: An Historical Approach to Women and Religion in the Twentieth Century', *Method & Theory in the Study of Religion*, 13 (2001): 209–223.

Brierley, Peter, *UKCH Religious Trends No. 6 2006/7* (London: Christian Research, 2006).

Brown, Callum, *The Death of Christian Britain* (London: Routledge, 2001).

Bruce, Steve, 'Secularization and the Impotence of Individualized Religion', *The Hedgehog Review: Critical Reflections on Contemporary Culture: After Secularization*, 8(1&2) (2006): 35–45.

Casanova, José, *Public Religions in the Modern World* (Chicago: University of Chicago Press, 1994).

Casanova, Jose, 'Rethinking Secularization: A Global Comparative Perspective', *The Hedgehog Review: Critical Reflections on Contemporary Culture: After Secularization*, 8(1&2) (2006): 7–22.

Chambers, Paul, 'Secularisation, Wales, and Islam', *Journal of Contemporary Religion*, 21(3) (2006): 325–340.

Clark, Anna, *The Struggle for the Breeches: Gender and the Making of the British Working Class* (Berkeley, CA: University of California Press, 1995).

Daly, Mary, *The Church and the Second Sex* (Boston, MA: Beacon Press, [1968] 1985).

Davidoff, Leonore and Hall, Catherine, *Family Fortunes: Men and Women of the English Middle Class, 1780–1850* (London: Hutchinson Education, 1987).

Davie, Grace, *Religion in Britain since 1945* (Oxford: Blackwell, 1994).

Davie, Grace, *Europe: The Exceptional Case* (London: Darton, Longman & Todd, 2002).

Davie, Grace, 'Is Europe an Exceptional Case?', *The Hedgehog Review: Critical Reflections on Contemporary Culture: After Secularization*, 8(1&2) (2006): 23–34.

de Beauvoir, Simone, *The Second Sex,* trans. Howard Madison Parshley (London: Jonathan Cape, [1949] 1953).

Dobbelaere, Karel, *Secularization: An Analysis at Three Levels* (Bruxelles: Peter Lang, 2002).

Elshtain, Jean Bethke, *Public Man, Private Woman: Women in Social and Political Thought* (Oxford: Robertson, 1981).

Fernandes, Leela, *Transforming Feminist Practice: Non-Violence, Social Justice and the Possibilities of a Spiritualized Feminism* (San Francisco: Aunt Lute Books, 2003).

Flanagan, Kieran and Jupp, Peter C. (eds), *Religion, Sociology and Postmodernity* (Houndmills: Macmillan, 1996).

Friedan, Betty, *The Feminine Mystique* (New York: Dell, 1963).

Gill, Robin, *The 'Empty Church' Revisited* (Aldershot: Ashgate, 2003).

Haddad, Yvonne Yazbeck, Smith, Jane I. and Moore, Kathleen M. (eds), *Muslim Women in America: the Challenge of Islamic Identity Today* (Oxford: Oxford University Press, 2006).

Hakim, Catherine, *Work-Lifestyle Choices in the 21st Century: Preference Theory* (Oxford: Oxford University Press, 2000).

Heelas, Paul, *The New Age Movement: Religion, Culture and Society in the Age of Postmodernity* (Oxford: Blackwell, 1996).

Heelas, Paul (ed.), *Religion, Modernity and Postmodernity* (Oxford: Blackwell, 1998).

Heelas, Paul, 'Challenging Secularization Theory: the Growth of "New Age" Spiritualities of Life', *The Hedgehog Review: Critical Reflections on Contemporary Culture: After Secularization*, 8(1&2) (2006): 46–58.

Heelas, Paul and Woodhead, Linda, *The Spiritual Revolution: Why Religion is Giving Way to Spirituality* (Oxford: Blackwell, 2005).

Hervieu-Léger, Danièle, 'In Search of Certainties: The Paradoxes of Religiosity in Societies of High Modernity', *The Hedgehog Review: Critical Reflections on Contemporary Culture: After Secularization*, 8(1&2) (2006): 59–68.

Heyward, Carter, *Touching Our Strength: the Erotic as Power and the Love of God* (San Francisco: Harper & Row, 1989).

Inglehart, Ronald and Norris, Pippa, *Rising Tide: Gender Equality and Cultural Change* (Cambridge: Cambridge University Press, 2003).

Jackson, Stevi and Scott, Sue, 'Putting the Body's Feet on the Ground: Towards a Sociological Reconceptualization of Gendered and Sexual Embodiment', in Kathryn Beckett-Milburn and Linda McKie (eds), *Constructing Gendered Bodies* (Houndmills: Palgrave, 2001).

Knott, Kim, *The Location of Religion: A Spatial Analysis* (London: Equinox, 2006).

Latham, Alan, 'Edward Soja', in Phil Hubbard, Rob Kitchin and Gill Valentine (eds), *Key Thinkers on Space and Place* (London: Sage, 2004).

Loewenthal, Kate Miriam, MacLeod, Andrew K. and Cinnirella, Marco, 'Are Women More Religious Than Men? Gender Differences in Religious Activity among Different Religious Groups in the UK', *Personality and Individual Differences*, 32(1) (2002): 133–139.

Martin, Bernice, 'The Pentecostal Gender Paradox: A Cautionary Tale for the Sociology of Religion', in Richard K. Fenn (ed.), *The Blackwell Companion to Sociology of Religion* (Maldon, MA: Blackwell, 2001).

Martin, David, 'Secularisation and the Future of Christianity', *Journal of Contemporary Religion*, 20(2) (2005a): 145–160.

Martin, David, *On Secularization: Towards a Revised General Theory* (Aldershot: Ashgate, 2005b).

Miller, Alan S. and Stark, Rodney, 'Gender and Religiousness: Can Socialization Explanations be Saved?', *American Journal of Sociology*, 107(6) (2002): 1399–1423.

Miller-McLemore, Bonnie, 'Epistemology or Bust: a Maternal Feminist Knowledge of Knowing', *Journal of Religion*, 72(2) (1992): 229–247.

Morgan, Sue, 'Introduction: 'Women, Religion and Feminism: Past, Present and Future Perspectives', in Sue Morgan (ed.), *Women, Religion and Feminism in Britain, 1750–1900* (Basingstoke: Palgrave Macmillan, 2002).

Morris, Jeremy, 'The Strange Death of Christian Britain: Another Look at the Secularization Debate', *Historical Journal*, 46(4) (2003): 963–976.

Norris, Pippa and Inglehart, Ronald, *Sacred and Secular: Religion and Politics Worldwide* (New York: Cambridge University Press, 2004).

Norris, Pippa and Inglehart, Ronald, 'Sellers or Buyers in Religious Markets?', *The Hedgehog Review: Critical Reflections on Contemporary Culture: After Secularization*, 8(1&2) (2006): 69–92.

Pateman, Carole, *The Sexual Contract* (Cambridge: Polity, 1988).

Papoulias, Constantina, 'Homi K. Bhabha', *Key Thinkers on Space and Place* (London: Sage, 2004).

Percy, Martyn, *The Salt of the Earth: Religious Resilience in a Secular Age* (London: Sheffield Academic Press, 2001).

Poovey, Mary, *Uneven Developments: The Ideological Work of Gender in Mid-Victorian England* (Chicago: University of Chicago Press, 1988).

Raphael, Melissa, *Thealogy and Embodiment: the Post-Patriarchal Reconstruction of Female Sacrality* (Sheffield: Sheffield Academic Press, 1996).

Rose, Gillian, *Feminism and Geography: The Limits of Geographical Knowledge* (Cambridge: Polity, 1993).

Salomonsen, Jone, *Enchanted Feminism: The Reclaiming Witches of San Francisco* (New York: Routledge, 2002).

Seccombe, Wally, *A Millennium of Family Change: Feudalism to Capitalism in Northwestern Europe* (London: Verso, 1992).

Seccombe, Wally, *Weathering the Storm: Working-Class Families from the Industrial Revolution to the Fertility Decline* (London: Verso, 1993).

Soja, Ed, *Thirdspace: Journeys to Los Angeles and Other Real-And-Imagined-Places* (Oxford: Blackwell, 1996).

Stanton, Elizabeth Cady, *The Woman's Bible*, abridged ed. (Edinburgh: Polygon, [1898] 1985).

Starhawk, *Circle Round: Raising Children in Goddess Traditions* (New York: Bantam, 1998).

Thapan, Meenakshi, 'Introduction: Gender and Embodiment in Everyday Life', in Meenakshi Thapan (ed.), *Embodiment: Essays on Gender and Identity* (Mumbai: Oxford University Press, 1997).

Tietze, N., 'Managing Borders: Muslim Religiosity among Young Men in France and Germany, in A. Salvatore (ed.), *Muslim Traditions and Modern Techniques of Power. Yearbook of the Sociology of Islam 3* (Hamburg: LIT Verlag, 2001).

Tilly, Louise A. and Scott, Joan W., *Women, Work and Family* (London: Methuen, 1987).

Walter, Tony, 'Why Are Most Churchgoers Women?', *Vox Evangelica*, 20 (1990): 73–90.

Walter, Tony and Davie, Grace, 'The Religiosity of Women in the Modern West', *British Journal of Sociology*, 49(4) (1998): 640–660.

Webster, Alison, 'Revolutionising Christian Sexual Ethics: A Feminist Perspective', in Adrian Thatcher and Elizabeth Stuart (eds), *Christian Perspectives on Sexuality and Gender* (Leominster: Gracewing Fowler Wright, 1996).

Woodhead, Linda, 'Feminism and the Sociology of Religion: From Gender-Blindness to Gendered Difference', in Richard K. Fenn (ed.), *The Blackwell Companion to Sociology of Religion* (Maldon, MA: Blackwell, 2001).

Woodhead, Linda, 'Gendering Secularisation Theory', *Køn og Forskning* (Women, Gender and Research), 1–2 (2005): 24–35.

Woodhead, Linda, 'Why So Many Women in Holistic Spirituality?' (Lancaster: unpublished paper, 2005).

Woodhead, Linda, and Heelas, Paul (eds), *Religion in Modern Times: An Interpretive Anthology* (Oxford: Blackwell, 2000).

Wright, Sheila, '"Every Good woman Needs a Companion of Her Own Sex": Quaker Women and Spiritual Friendship, 1750–1850', in Sue Morgan (ed.), *Women, Religion and Feminism in Britain, 1750–1900* (Basingstoke: Palgrave Macmillan, 2002).

PART 1
Christianity

Chapter 1

Religious Change in the West: Watch the Women

Penny Long Marler

The thesis of this chapter is that religious change in the West – particularly the rise and decline of Christian denominations and congregations – is strongly influenced by long-term and largely unexamined changes in women's lives. These changes stem directly from the demographic transition accompanying the industrial revolution and the gendered division of labour that supported it. Important to this transition and accompanying socio-economic and religious changes was the northwestern European or 'nuclear' family ideal. As the family moved from a unit of production to a unit of consumption, the woman became the primary (re)producer of children and religious piety in the domestic or private sphere. In this way, women's unpaid domestic – and for single or poorer women, paid domestic or manufacturing work – supported the wage economy. At the same time, women's unpaid religious work supported the expansion of religious institutions. Care for others at home and church was the province of women and self-mastery through work the province of men.

As western economies shifted away from manufacturing to technology and service, a number of important social and cultural changes affected the family and especially women. In twentieth–century Europe and North America fertility rates fell as a result of rising economic and educational aspirations among the middle-class, expansion of tertiary employment sectors, increased public and private support of working families, and the contraceptive and equal opportunity revolutions. Women's paid work became an integral part of the postindustrial consumer economy. Care for others at home and church increasingly conflicted with work schedules and career demands; older ideals of feminine piety and domesticity clashed with new concerns for vocational fulfillment as well as spiritual and physical self care. Such changes inevitably affected women's religious involvement, and by consequence of socialization, the religious identification of their children. Despite the fact that religious elites continue to be predominantly male, as the women go, so goes the church.

Several observations are important here: first, women's greater involvement in religious congregations has been generally taken for granted and/or accounted to natural differences[1]; and second, when women are studied more often than not

---

[1] The understanding employed in this essay reflects Haraway's (2001: 49–75) analysis of gender as both socially and politically constructed. Nevertheless, some US and British studies have found that feminine traits among men and women are linked to spirituality

the focus is on their role as clergy. Excluded from power in mainstream Christian denominations, women have been largely overlooked as important research subjects. Indeed, as women have aspired to or achieved those positions, they have become more interesting (see, for example, Carroll, Hargrove and Lummis 1983; Lehman 1985; Lawless 1988; Wallace 1992; Lehman 1993; Nesbitt 1997; Zikmund, Lummis and Chang 1998; Chaves 1999; Ingersoll 2003). Only very recently have studies examined lay women's groups and parachurch (or transdenominational) movements (Davidman 1991; Kaufman 1991; Winter, Lummis and Stokes 1994; Griffith 1997; Brasher 2001). Not surprising from this perspective, such research appears at an acknowledged low point for traditional institutional religion in the West.

This chapter focuses primarily on the cases of the United States and the United Kingdom. As liberal societies that moved in a postindustrial direction earlier than other European nations, the UK and the US provide important illustrations of new developments in women's family, work, and religious experience.[2] Inasmuch as the argument examines the relationship between labour market change and religion, this chapter also follows the recent work of Hochschild (2003) and McGee (2005) and proposes a neo-Weberian treatment of the subject. The Protestant ethic that birthed the spirit of western industrial capitalism is now a postindustrial and global capitalist ethic animated by the spirits of evangelical Christianity on the right and feminist spirituality on the left. Moreover, the primary carriers of expressive (post)Christianity – either in the differentiated sphere of home, hearth, and church or in the dedifferentiated reality of the twenty-first century work lifestyles and holistic spirituality – have been women.

Demographic transition in the West

The development of the West from a pre-industrial through an industrial to a postindustrial economy reflects the classic stages of demographic transition (see Fig. 1.1).[3] Despite high birth rates, sustained population growth prior to the seventeenth century in Europe was checked by a combination of war, famine, plagues, and epidemics. During the seventeenth and eighteenth centuries, however, public sanitation improved and better

---

and religiosity and masculine traits, as Thompson and Remmes (2002) conclude, 'thwart' them. While such research tends to support physiological or psychological explanations for differential participation in religion, these findings do not eliminate socialization or social location explanations (Miller and Hoffmann 1995; Francis et al. 2001; Francis and Wilcox 1998; Robbins et al. 2001; Stark 2002; Thompson and Remmes 2002).

[2]   Both the US and the UK are laissez faire economies with relatively unregulated markets (Hakim 2000: 17–19).

[3]   There is considerable variation between western nation states in the timing and pace of industrialization. As a consequence, the relationship between labour market and other demographic changes is less direct than is predicted by the classic theoretical model. Where convergence in labour market structure and other demographic changes such as lowered fertility, decreased nuptiality, and the increased presence of women in the workforce is most notable – regardless of the 'take off' and timing of industrialization between western nations – is from the 1960 onward in the West. Stolte-Heiskanen (1977: 251–253) notes that while the UK industrialized first and fastest among European nations, up until the mid-twentieth century birth rates remained higher in the UK than in France, Belgium, and Sweden but lower than in Italy and Belgium.

transportation increased access to food supplies. Disease was reduced; mortality declined; and life expectancy rose. Because birth rates remained high, first, Europe, and then, North America, realized dramatic population growth (*Population Bulletin* 2004: 6).

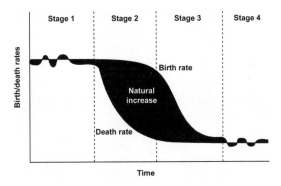

Figure 1.1   The classic stages of demographic transition

In the nineteenth century birth rates began to fall in the developed countries. From the eighteenth to the twentieth century, the birth rate in the US dropped from an average of seven to four children per woman. Urbanization, industrialization, later age at marriage, economic growth and rising class expectations all contributed to this decline. During the world economic crises of the 1930s, the total fertility rate fell further to about two children per woman in the United States and dropped even lower in Europe. In the fifties and sixties post World War II 'baby boom', US fertility rates temporarily rebounded to turn of the century levels, while in Europe the rate climbed to 2.8 children per woman. The protracted fertility declines in the West after 1970 in both the US and Europe coincided with social trends especially affecting women and families. Consequently, the total fertility rates in many European countries fell below 2 children per woman by 1980, signaling the beginning of real population decline and what population experts call a 'second demographic transition' (*Population Bulletin* 2004: 7).

This chart shows the declines in fertility rates for major world regions in the 1950s and in 2003 (see Fig. 1.2).

As described, both North America and Europe witnessed rather steep declines in fertility from the immediate post-war period to the present. Reported fertility rates in less developed regions are higher but also show decline. What is important to note is the fact that the first demographic transition from pre to postindustrial economies in Europe and North America occurred much more slowly. Because of advanced capitalism in and global corporate expansion from the West, the demographic transition in developing countries has occurred at a more rapid rate.[4] The global

---

[4]   For example, in nearly all developing countries, there has been a substantial increase in age at first marriage which has been linked empirically to increased education among women (in all but sub-Saharan Africa) and theoretically to the decline in arranged marriages, an increase in marriages based on mutual attraction, the deficit of available men, the rise of dowry costs in South Asia, changes in the legal age at marriage, and a change in global norms about the desirability of early marriage for women. The increasing cost of establishing a

expansion of advanced capitalism insures that western consumerist *and* Christian, especially evangelical and neo-Pentecostal, values are exported.[5]

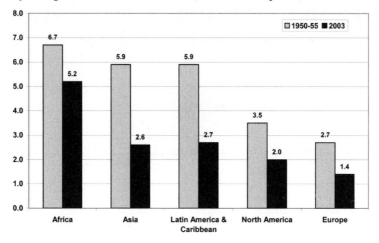

Figure 1.2   Fertility levels in major world regions: 1950s and 2003

The next chart provides a closer look at the total fertility rates in the US and the UK from 1960 to 2000 (see Fig. 1.3).

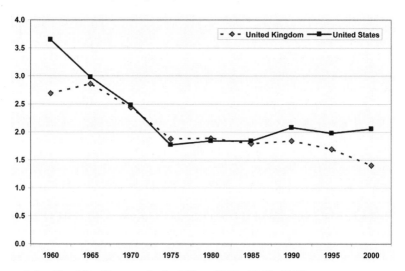

Figure 1.3   Total fertility rate in the US and UK: 1960–2000

household in developing countries is also thought to contribute to the postponement of marriage among men (Mensch, Singh, and Casterline 2005: 1–7, 28–29). For a fuller discussion of the acceleration of the demographic transition in developing countries, also see Tiano (1987).

    5   For an overview of the phenomenon of the 'globalisation of charisma' and the 'charismatization of the global' – and particularly for the history of North American conservative Protestantism and its late twentieth century neo-Pentecostal ('health and wealth') expansion into developing countries in Africa and Latin America – see Coleman (2000: 17–71, 234).

As compared with the US, fertility rates in the UK had been lower, longer.[6] While the US experienced a larger increase in its post-World War II fertility rate than did the UK, the decline thereafter was very similar (Kupinsky 1977). Total fertility rates for fifteen European Union nations echo this trend with Ireland starting and ending at a higher level (3.76 in 1960 to 1.87 in 1995), Germany exhibiting the lowest levels (2.37 in 1960 to 1.35 in 1995), and Finland, Sweden, and the UK falling in between and near the EU average (Drew 1998: 14–15).

Recent fertility differences between the UK and the US are largely due to immigration. As Hakim observes, similarity in steep declines in both countries – and the West, generally – reflect responses to the contraceptive and the equal opportunity revolutions. Increasingly, older cultural and religious conventions about gender roles are giving way to increased diversity and 'choice' from the standpoint of individual women as to their family and work behaviours and commitments (Hakim 2000: 1–83).[7]

The nuclear family ideal

According to Peter Laslett, the four aspects that combined to create the western family ideal included: a large proportion of nuclear households with kin composition restricted to parents and unmarried children, a late age of maternity, a narrow age gap between spouses, and a high incidence of servants (Laslett 1977). That this family ideal was realized only at certain junctures and among middle and upper classes is clear, and that its emergence varied across western nations is also clear. This nuclear family image functioned as both a socio-economic ideal and a Christian one: 'for a man shall leave his mother, and a women leave her home …' (Smith 1993: 399).[8]

In the UK, the nuclear family ideal was demographically realized among the upper classes prior to the twentieth century. From the turn of the century until World War II, the older family wage economy declined, the family consumer economy emerged, and the middle-class expanded greatly. Tilly and Scott (1987) observed that in the early decades of the twentieth century, the numbers of married women 'at home' increased as a result of the contraction of economic sectors traditionally employing women such as the garment trade; the overall increase in men's real wages which made the single, male breadwinner

---

[6] British population studies, in fact, show that nuptiality fell sharply in the last quarter of the nineteenth century as a result of rising age at first marriage and fewer marriages. Changing marriage patterns, moreover, acted as a break on fertility. Indeed, up until the 1980s variation in fertility was closely tied to marital fertility in Europe (Woods 1996: 315–319; Anderson 1996: 225–241, 385).

[7] Not surprisingly, Hakim's social psychological 'preference theory' and particularly her description of diverse work-lifestyle choices for women in the postindustrial West has been critiqued from conflict, structural, and feminist/critical theoretical perspectives (see, for example, Breugel 1996; Crompton and Harris 1998; Crompton and Lyonette 2005; Ginn et al. 1996; Proctor and Padfield 1999). The interest in Hakim's work here is principally her documentation of the presence and prevalence of three distinct patterns of work-lifestyles among women in the West and especially in the UK and the US.

[8] For a review of the ways in which this nuclear family ideal mutes or obscures women's work patterns and primarily functions to legitimate the gender division of labour in industrializing nations, see especially, Bose (1987: 267–285) and Stolte-Heiskanen (1977: 255–257).

model more widely available; increased life expectancy, especially of men; a decline in family size; and the prolonged residence of working children in the household. The socialization of children also became the principal concern of married women as investments for the future. Indeed, turn of the century autobiographies are testaments to the social, economic, and emotional importance of the 'mum' in British family life.

In North America, the expanse of land and the availability of 'unfree' domestic labour – at first, indentured servants and increasingly African slaves – made the nuclear family pattern more generally available and at an earlier time.[9] Neo-local as contrasted with combined households proliferated in pre and early industrial America, and age at first marriage was considerably lower than in northwestern Europe (Smith 1993). The result was rapid population growth, especially as mortality rates declined and life expectancy increased in the nineteenth century. As urbanization escalated in the later half of the nineteenth century, large scale immigration from Europe provided a boon to the economy; a trend toward increased age at marriage made single women available for manufacturing jobs; men went to work; and married women, especially white married women, remained at home (Kupinsky 1977). According to Bose (1987: 278–279), the availability of surplus labour and the rise of the 'cult of true womanhood' largely explain women's exclusion from the paid labour force in the US. Ironically, during the depression era of the 1930s, the lack of available jobs also spurred a revival of the feminine domestic ideal, much as it did after World War II, because of the perceived threat to men's jobs.[10] Otherwise, the initial pattern across the twentieth century among married women who worked outside the home was a staged one: single women worked prior to marriage and childbearing; interrupted work after marriage to bear and rear children; and resumed work after their children were weaned, started school, and/or left home. This is a pattern similar to the long-term experience of women in the most developed countries in Europe (Stolte-Heiskanen 1977).

Despite a longer period of decline in nuptiality in the UK as compared to the US, during the post World War II period the proportion of nuclear family households converged.[11] This chart shows a similar pattern of decline in the proportion of households 'married with children' and an increase in non-family households, especially the category 'living alone' (see Fig. 1.4).[12] Over the last thirty years, this

---

[9]   The availability of land for neo-local or nuclear family households may account for disproportionate population growth in the US through frontier settlements in the nineteenth century and suburban development in the mid-twentieth century. High fertility, nuptiality, and the proliferation of nuclear family households occurred at both times and both periods coincided with religious revivals.

[10]   See also Griffith (1997).

[11]   For example, from 1902–1910 the mean age at first marriage in Scotland was 27.5 for males and 25.6 for females, and the figures for England and Wales were only marginally lower. Between 1941 and 1971, the age at first marriage continued to decline to a low in England and Wales of 23.2 for men and 21.3 for women. By 1991, median age at first marriage was 26.5 and 24.6 for men and women, respectively. By 2002, the age at first marriage for women below 50 in Western Europe as a whole was 28 years (Mensch and Casterline 2005).

[12]   These data were compiled by the US Bureau of Labor Statistics from national population censuses, household surveys, and other sources. For the US, data are from the March (2003) Current Population Survey and for the UK, 1994–95 figures are from the household survey, data for all

shift in household configuration is largely a result of the postponement of first marriage and childbirth as well as increased cohabitation prior to or instead of marriage (Festy 2000; Cliquet 2003). These trends reflect a move away from the nuclear family ideal.

The trend toward a diversity of family forms emerged first in the Nordic countries which have tended to be precursors of European wide patterns. For example, common-law couples constituted only one per cent of all couples in Sweden in 1960. By 1975, that figure rose to 11 per cent, and by 1996, 23 per cent of all Swedish couples were in consensual, common-law unions. The UK followed a similar but lagged trend line: by 1996, 11 per cent of all couples were in common-law unions. In the US, the proportion of adults of the opposite sex living together rose from one per cent in 1970 to three per cent in 1980, to five per cent in 1988, and to seven per cent in 1996. Living together is particularly prevalent among the young. In late 90s Sweden, 70 per cent of couples aged 16 to 29 lived together. In the UK, the figure was 53 per cent and in France, 41 per cent. Even in Ireland, Spain, and Italy where overall cohabitation rates were low, the rates for young couples were much higher – 29, 12, and 11 per cent, respectively. In the US, 23 per cent of all couples under 25 years of age who were living together were unmarried (Martin and Kats 2003: 11).[13]

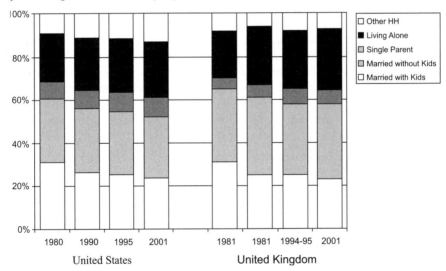

Figure 1.4   Household distribution in the US and UK: 1980–2001

The nuclear family ideal is challenged in the late twentieth and early twenty-first centuries by increases in divorce. Since 1960, divorce rates tripled in both the US and

other years are from population censuses. For the US and the UK, in addition, some unmarried cohabitants are included in the 'married couples' category while some are in 'other households', depending upon respondents' self-classification. If unmarried cohabitants were included in US figures for 'married couples', that category would increase by 2 percent in 1980 and 4 percent in 1999 – bringing the proportions between the UK and the US even closer. Also noteworthy is the fact that 'same-sex' couples were explicitly enumerated in 2001 in the UK; they are, however, not included in 'married couples' here for comparability with the US (Martin and Kats 2003: 12, 28).

[13]   See also Drew (1998: 24–5).

Europe. By 2002, the divorce rate in most western European countries was nearly 30 per cent. The divorce rates in Scandinavia, the UK, and the US, were at least 20 percentage points higher, down somewhat from peaks in the eighties and nineties (Festy 2000: 4; Cliquet 2003: 6). Recent stabilization of divorce rates in Northern Europe, the UK, and the US are generally attributed to the rise in cohabitation and lower rates of remarriage among the divorced (Drew 1998: 18–21).

Births to unmarried women also increased dramatically. By 1994 in Sweden the percentage of live births outside marriage reached 51.6 per cent compared with Greece and Italy, both below three per cent. Trend data from the US and the UK present an interesting contrast with other European data. In 1980, the US had higher levels of births outside marriage. By 1990, however, the percentage more than doubled for the UK and continued to rise thereafter. In 2001, nearly 40 per cent of all live births in the UK were to unmarried women – a figure similar to that of France and rivaling 1995 levels in Norway (Drew 1998: 18–21) (see Fig. 1.5). Differences between the UK and US largely reflect the fact that in Europe the majority of non-marital births are to unwed parents living together. Births to unwed teenage mothers in the US, on the other hand, are much higher than in any industrialized nation (Martin and Kats 2003: 12).

One consequence of the contraceptive revolution is voluntary childlessness, another challenge to the nuclear family ideal. In a wide-ranging survey of research in the US and Europe, Hakim concludes that 20 per cent is the stable plateau for childlessness in the majority of prosperous modern societies. Whereas that level is not unprecedented historically, the fact that twenty-first century childlessness is more often a choice rather than a result of a wartime shortage of men or poverty and poor nutrition is something new. 'Childless women today,' Hakim observes, 'are typically sexually active, often married or cohabitating, and not the unmarried spinsters that were so common in earlier decades with low marriage rates' (Hakim 2000: 53–56).

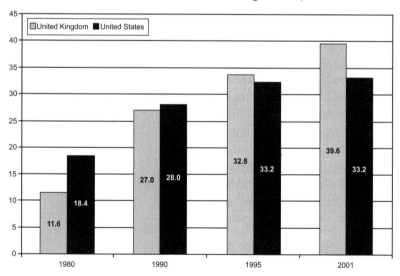

Figure 1.5   Births to unmarried women as a per cent of all births in the UK and US: 1980–2001

Another important feature of changed women's lives in the West is the increase in women's labour force participation, particularly in the last several decades. This general trend is influenced by the demands of a postindustrial economy, the needs and economic aspirations of individual households, and increased education and career commitments of women (Meyer 2003). This chart illustrates the similar rate of and increase in female labour force participation in the US and the UK since 1980 (see Fig. 1.6). The Nordic countries in Europe have the highest female employment rates, ranging from 64 per cent in 2000 in Finland to 73 per cent in Norway. Southern European countries, with the most traditional family forms, were at about 40 per cent in 2000; the rest of Europe, including France and Germany had a female employment rate in the fifty percentile range (Boeri, Del Boca and Pissarides 2005: 13).

Since female labour force participation has been historically higher in the UK than in the US, similar and slightly higher rates in recent decades are especially noteworthy.[14] Overall labour force participation rates, moreover, obscure an important difference: in the US, a higher proportion of women are presently in full-time, continuous employment. Women in full-time jobs, further, tend to hold less traditional attitudes than homemakers and part-time workers (Hakim 2000: 99–102).

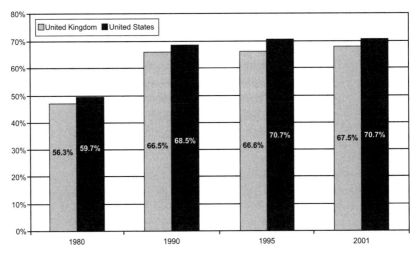

Figure 1.6   Female labour force participation rates in the US and UK: 1980–2001

Finally, studies in the US and the UK show that despite increases in married women's roles as workers, their roles as carers, both in terms of expectations and behaviours, persists (Hattery 2001; Dex, Walters and Alden 1993). Research in the eighties and nineties documents the pressures of the 'second shift' or the 'double [or triple] time bind' for women, whether secondary earners or full-time careerists (Hochschild 1989, 1997). More recent research shows a 'lagged adaptation' in work/home gender role

---

[14]   From 1900 to 1950, the percentage of women working in the UK ranged from 32 to 34 per cent, after which it increased rapidly; in the US, by contrast, only about 20 per cent of women worked in 1900, a rate which rose gradually to 31 per cent by midcentury (Kupinsky 1977: 190; Stolte-Heiskanen 1977: 261).

behaviours (Gershuny and Robinson 1988; Artis and Pavalko 2003). While married women still outpace their spouses in gender typed housework and child-care, time spent in such activities is decreasing due to increased participation by men.

Whether because of methods that emphasize central tendencies or theoretical assumptions that presume a zero sum relationship between homemaker and career preferences among women, Hakim (2000) argues that most research hides that women's employment and lifestyle options are increasingly heterogeneous. She documents an emergent gendered division of labour structured around three types of work-lifestyles among women in the West: 1) 20 per cent of women are 'home-centered' and benefit from a marriage market that continues to offer equal or better chances of social prestige, investment in motherhood, and economic success; 2) an equal percentage are 'work-centered', whether childless or mothers, and benefit from a labour market that is still the primary route to competitive achievement in a capitalist economy; and 3) the remainder, about 60 per cent, are 'adaptive' and attempt to balance family and employment as secondary earners in the tertiary or 'pink collar' work sectors (2000: 158). It is among the adaptive that 'second shift' pressures are most felt, among the work-centered that family responsibilities are increasingly shared by husbands and paid child care experts, and among the home-centered that self, child, and home 'makeovers' provide status and identity (McGee 2005: 165–168).

Religious change in the United Kingdom: watch the women

How do changes in women's lives in the West relate to religious trends? Bruce's analysis of religious change in modern Britain as well as cross-national research on religious belonging conducted by Hadaway and Marler (1997) is consistent with the argument advanced here. According to Bruce (1995), the shift from established church to dissenting sect began after the Reformation and was complete in the nineteenth century. Church-state separation eroded the taken for-granted status of the Anglican Church and increased the sectarian appeal of nonconformists and immigrant Catholics. Employing a number of sources, Brown (2001) argues that the results of the 1851 census revealed a 'historically high' incidence of worship attendance at approximately 40 per cent of adults. For a number of reasons including the lack of churches in upland and island areas of Scotland, rapid urban and population growth, and the relatively slow pace of new church construction, attendances from 1800 through 1850 were likely lower (2001: 161–162).

According to Brown (2001, 2006), increased pluralistic competition in the religious economy twinned with burgeoning industrialization created a new market, a 'salvation economy', which legitimated and promoted a gendered division of labour. In the late Victorian and Edwardian periods, the discursive engine that drove that new economy was the pious wife and mother.[15] Women became the spiritual and moral guardians of home and hearth, and congregations grew as women rearranged

---

[15]   Brown associates discursive Christianity explicitly with the industrial era and defines this form of Christian religiosity as 'the peoples' subscription to protocols of personal identity which they derive from Christian expectations, or discourses, evident in their own time and place' (2001: 12).

their Sunday worship schedules (and that of their mostly female servants) to accommodate family needs and religious requirements (Brown 2001: 149–155).

As a response to changed labour demands during and following the two World Wars, women increasingly engaged in a 'staged' pattern of work not dissimilar to their 'staged' religious involvement. Oral histories examined by Brown indicate that women tended to be involved in church as children and teenagers but that they stopped going after they married and started their families (2001: 143–144). Whereas motherhood interfered with work it also tended to interfere with church activity. Different from work patterns – and perhaps exacerbated by them – returning to active church participation after children departed became less likely. While the salvation economy and the 'discursive Christianity' that supported it sustained some momentum, church membership and especially church attendance declined. That women continued to mediate religion is evidenced by upsurges in the forties and fifties in the enrollment of children in Sunday school and in religious rites of passage such as marriages and baptisms that women traditionally orchestrated. The effect was that religious identity in Britain 'thinned', preparing the way for precipitous declines in both church membership and attendance in the 1970s (Brown 2001: 162–169).[16]

This chart shows the strong correlation (r=.84) between best estimates of religious membership change in Great Britain and the birth rate from 1901 to 2001 (see Fig. 1.7).

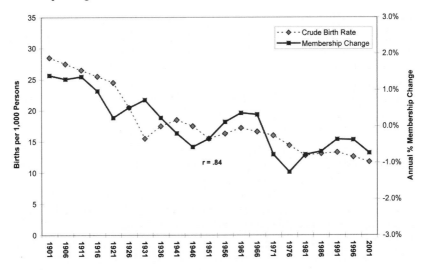

Figure 1.7   Crude birth rate and per cent religious membership change in Great Britain: 1901–2001

---

16   In an essay on the post-war generation and establishment religion in England, Barker (1995) concludes that late twentieth century religious decline was, in part, a result of family formation change. She reported that from the fifties to the seventies, the percentage of 'religious' ceremonies dropped from two thirds to one half of all marriages. By the 1981 European Values Survey, only 14 per cent of British respondents and 16 per cent of Europeans considered faith an important value to develop in children.

The results illustrate a close tie between religious membership change and the birth rate. The birth rate, in turn, is influenced by marital and family formation patterns which are also related to labour market shifts. As expected, the growth and decline of religious bodies parallel the demographic transition in the UK (Bruce 1995: 40). Industrialization is accompanied by growth in religious institutions and the transition to a postindustrial economy is reflected in the deinstitutionalization of religion.[17]

British women (and men): believing or belonging?

Brown's (2001, 2006) analysis provides both support for and evidence against Grace Davie's (1994, 2000) widely debated contention that contemporary British religiosity is characterized by 'believing without belonging'.[18] As for support, Brown demonstrates the presence of a strong discursive Christianity in Great Britain from about 1800 to 1960. Moreover, that discursive Christianity endured in spite of a longer-term erosion of church membership and a simultaneous, though steeper, decline in church participation: many continued believing without actively belonging.

Through an examination of popular literature, oral histories, and autobiographies, Brown documents the generational and gendered sources of this transition. In sum, such rhetoric moved from heroic narratives of the individual journey to salvation in which the woman as wife and mother was the primary mover to nostalgic narratives of Christian community where the woman as wife and mother was the principal guardian. Post-sixties generations (both women and men) are largely inarticulate about conventional Christianity. Their parents' nostalgic religion of loss – the 'moral museum' as opposed to the 'moral hero' narrative of their grandparents – is quite literally lost on them. According to Brown, these discourse changes signaled the 'death of Christian Britain': in effect, neither believing nor belonging.[19] Now, the

---

[17]   Growth in religious adherence and practice during Britain's nineteenth century urbanisation, Brown (2001: 166–9) argues, is evidence against a traditional secularization narrative. Moreover, he explicitly ties the dissolution of conventional Christian identification and practice to the 'the distinctive growth in the 1950s of women's dual role in home and work' which created 'a new stress about which model defined a women's "duty," upsetting the salience of evangelical protocols, and rendering women part of the same religious "problem" as men' (2001: 179).

[18]   Voas and Crockett (2005) summarize Davie's (1994, 2000) 'believing without belonging' thesis in its 'strong' and 'weaker' versions. The 'strong' version of the Davie thesis maintains that Europeans continue to believe in God and have religious sensibilities despite the fact that they cease traditional practice. Despite Davie's insistence that much of the belief that persists is unorthodox, 'optimistic' observers of religion in Europe maintain that the Christian faith endures despite all appearances to the contrary. A 'weaker' version of the Davie thesis grants that the belief which persists may be 'non-Christian, vague, and even non-religious' and may, in fact, be a transitional phase toward secularity rather than a constituent characteristic of it.

[19]   Brown (2001: 186) admits that autobiographies from the sixties forward are 'few' and 'elite' and demonstrate 'antagonism toward conventional Christianity' and experimentation with 'eastern mysticism'. Yet what is most remarkable to this historian is the relative 'silence' in the discourse. He concludes that 'the evangelical narrative has decayed' and 'gendered discourses on religion have withered' (2001: 196).

search for a personal faith is largely relegated to 'the "New Age" of minor cults, personal development, and consumer choice' (2001: 196).

Recent empirical research confirms the generational sources and overall linear direction of institutional religious decline in Great Britain. In three important quantitative analyses, Voas and Crockett demonstrate that religious decline in twentieth-century Britain has been continuous, affecting affiliation, attendance, and beliefs (Voas and Crockett 2005; Voas 2006; Crockett and Voas 2006). Examining the best available evidence from the major British social surveys, they conclude that the primary source of this decline is intergenerational transmission rather than period or age effects (Crockett and Voas 2006). In a study of religious decline in Scotland, Voas (2006) found that whereas a majority of post World War II children ('baby boomers') were raised in a religion, it was this generation whose disaffiliation was primarily responsible for the precipitous declines that Brown described.[20] This same generation, then, is responsible for the much lower levels of affiliation of their own children.[21]

Crockett and Voas (2006) examine theoretical 'counterforces' to decline, especially the influence of immigration and ethnic minorities. They found that although the non-white ethnic minority immigrant population is more religious than the white population, rates of intergenerational decline between immigrant parents and their children are nearly as high as for the white population.[22]

Such research confirms the impact of parents' and mother's religion on faith transmission and the continued difference between women's and men's religious affiliation. For British young adults aged 16 to 30 in 2000 whether both parents, one parent, or neither parent has a religious affiliation strongly influences their own affiliation as well as their attendance and the salience of religious belief. Crockett and Voas conclude that 'As one would expect the child's affiliation is usually to a parental denomination (with mothers appearing slightly more influential than fathers), though there is an approximately eight per cent chance of the child moving to another group, irrespective of whether one or both parents, or neither, have an affiliation' (2006: 577). They find that when both parents are religiously affiliated,

---

[20]   In an analysis of twenty years of British Social Attitudes survey data (1982 to 2002), Crockett and Voas tie overall declines in rates of religious affiliation to cohort change from an affiliation rate of more than 80 per cent among those born in the early 1900s to less than 40 per cent among those born in the 1970s. Similar differences between early and later twentieth century generational cohorts occur for having 'no doubts' that God exists (50 per cent versus less than 20 per cent) and for reporting regular worship attendance (30 per cent versus less than 15 per cent) (2006: 570–573).

[21]   Of particular interest is the fact that the proportion of individuals raised in no religion in Scotland increased from about five percent in 1905 to nearly half the population by 2000. This growth, Voas (2006: 111) found, was largely at the expense of those raised in the Church of Scotland who dropped from over seventy per cent to less than thirty per cent over the same period.

[22]   In an examination of female fertility by regularity of church attendance in the British Household Panel Survey, Crockett and Voas (2006) found no significant differences, although this longitudinal survey spans slightly less than a decade and the steepest declines in fertility occurred prior to this period. Although Voas found that 'evidence from the British Household Panel Survey suggests that people who attend church have completed family sizes one third higher than those who do not' (2006: 116).

there is about a 50 per cent chance of adopting a religious affiliation; when there is only one religious parent the chance is slightly less than 25 per cent.

In an analysis of birth cohorts from the early twentieth century to the present, Crockett and Voas found that females continue to outpace males in their religious affiliation, church attendance, and religious belief. While the overall proportional decline for both men and women was similar, more systematic analysis uncovered interesting differences. For example, female respondents born between 1900 and 1919 were 51 per cent more likely to attend church than their male peers, and those born between 1960 and 1970 were only 39 per cent more likely to attend. On the other hand, the gender gap between the corresponding cohorts on the certainty that God exists increased slightly from 32 to 36 per cent (2006: 583n). The gender gap in religious affiliation also has increased but Crocket and Voas conclude that this is not particularly surprising given that affiliation was 'nearly universal' in the earliest birth years (2006: 574). These findings are consistent with Brown's conclusions about the differential salience of religion between men and women, historically, and the more recent erosion of religious piety among women – especially between older and younger cohorts – and gives evidence of the 'de-feminisation of piety' (2001: 192).[23] The tantalizing finding, on the other hand, of an increase in belief in God points to a more complex dynamic than the 'de-pietisation of femininity'.

De-feminizing religion and feminizing spirituality?

Heelas and Woodhead (2005) explored a hypothesized 'turn' from 'theistic' religion to 'subjective-life' spirituality in Great Britain and the US. In addition to a review of literature, they examined the extent of involvement in both the congregational domain and the 'holistic milieu' in the town of Kendal in England.[24] Like Voas and Crockett (2006) and Brown (2001, 2006), they found that traditional religious practice has declined but unlike them – and perhaps in support of Davie (1994; 2000) – they documented growth in the production and consumption of alternative forms of spirituality. Heelas and Woodhead (2005: 49–76) concluded that involvement in religious congregations declined from a high of approximately fifty per cent in 1850 in Britain to its current level of eight per cent and from 40 per cent in 1950 in the US to its current level of approximately 20 per cent.[25] In the holistic milieu, they found

---

[23]　The English 2001 Church Life Profile, moreover, reinforces observations of religious decline and underlying generational and gendered patterns of disaffiliation. According to Cameron and Escott (2002: 6–7), current UK church attenders are much older than the UK population, and women continue to be over-represented (65 per cent as compared with 51 per cent in the general population).

[24]　Subjective-life spirituality consisted of 'sacred activity' grouped together under terms such as 'body, mind and spirit', 'New Age', 'alternative' or 'holistic' spirituality. They included yoga, reiki, meditation, tai chi, aromatherapy, paganism, rebirthing, reflexology, and wicca, among others (Heelas and Woodhead 2005: 7).

[25]　Whereas the level of current religious participation in the UK is less than half of that in the US, the pace of change (here, decline) has occurred at a faster rate and over a shorter period of time in the US.

that involvement in both Britain and the US was at low levels in the seventies and has increased steadily to the present.[26]

Perhaps most interesting is the demographic profile of contemporary 'spiritual' practitioners and consumers in Britain. According to Heelas and Woodhead (2005), they are predominantly female, middle aged, and well educated. Many are (or were) employed in 'pink collar' caring professions like nursing, teaching, and social work. The majority are married.[27] Based on their interviews in Kendal, Heelas and Woodhead provide a composite profile of such women and compare it with one of their mother's generation. They describe a young woman born in the fifties who becomes a nurse, motivated less by explicit Christian values about gender (although, these may linger from her Sunday School rearing) than by the fact that as a woman she regards a network of personal relationships as a 'key source of significance'. 'As the years roll by', they say, she becomes disillusioned by the 'iron cage of bureaucracy' in the healthcare workplace that emphasizes efficiency rather than subjective well-being. In order to address her frustration at work, her need to 'go deeper and become more authentic', she may be drawn to practitioners and groups in the holistic milieu (2005: 103).[28]

If this woman had been born in the thirties, Heelas and Woodhead argue, her Christian faith and idealism, reinforced at church and in Christian literature, might have led her to a career in nursing. After she met 'the man of her dreams', she likely would have given up work to raise her children and take them to church 'as her parents had taken her' (2005: 117). This especially well-socialized mother as 'moral guardian' might have spent her later years in volunteerism through the Mother's Union at church and Girl Guides in the community. As Brown (2001) found while many women born in the interwar period retained a strong sense of Christian identity their actual church participation declined.[29]

Perhaps the twentieth-century narrative of nostalgia about religion and women's roles that Brown described was particularly ill suited for intergenerational

---

[26] Heelas and Woodhead found that nearly eight per cent of Kendal's population was active in religious congregations and close to two per cent in the holistic milieu. Review of similar data in the US and Britain yielded an estimated ratio of congregational practice to involvement in alternative spirituality in Britain at five to one; based on similar but less conclusive data, they estimated a ratio in the US as high as ten to one and as low as three to one (2005: 45–48; 59–60).

[27] Survey respondents in Kendal revealed that 80 per cent of those active in the holistic milieu of Kendal and environs are female; 78 per cent of the groups are led by women; and 80 per cent of the one to one practitioners are women (Heelas and Woodhead 2005: 94)

[28] This transition, Heelas and Woodhead found, may be facilitated by 'downsizing' work involvement, for example, moving from a full time to a part time position or from a more routinized to a less routinized job. They may even become holistic milieu practitioners. It should be noted, however, that their stage of family formation may also facilitate such down-sizing: many of these women, aged 40 to 64, are beyond the childbearing and early childrearing stages (2005: 93–94).

[29] As Crockett and Voas (2005) document, clear differences in religious identification and involvement persist, especially between pre and interwar cohorts and the post World War II generations.

transmission. Thirties mothers retained their identity, took their children to church but gradually ceased regular practice; the Sunday school faith of their fifties children neither extended to adult identity nor practice, and they did not take their own children to church. The result was the generational downward spiral in religious involvement in the UK described by Brown and documented by Voas and Crockett. As Heelas and Woodhead found, many women retained an interest in spirituality if not traditional religion. Passing on this new 'faith' to a younger generation is made difficult by mid-life conversions to non-traditional spirituality as well as the holistic milieu's client centered structure and self orientation.

Religious change in the United States: watch the women

Industrialization in the West, particularly in the UK, preceded widespread industrialization in the US. The recorded peak in church membership in Great Britain also preceded that in the US, and both membership trend lines roughly parallel that of the birth rate (see Fig. 1.8). The primary difference in these empirical trajectories is that church membership in Britain declined more slowly over a longer period of time.[30] It took only thirty years for the US to realize the kind of church membership decline that occurred in Great Britain over a century. In both cases, church membership fell sharply around 1970.

The dominant religious trend since the settlement of the US has been growth and geographic expansion. Fueled by immigration, a high birth rate, and a large proportion of 'unchurched' persons, reaping a bountiful religious harvest was relatively easy in the American context. Gathered in through the revivals of the Great Awakenings and a near pervasive evangelical zeal among American churches, religious denominations grew (Hadaway and Marler 2006). Records show that church membership increased from 42 million in 1916 to 55 million in 1926, and to 72 million by 1942 (Kosmin and Lachman 1993: 46).

The pace of church growth was not constant. After the stock market crash of 1929, the thirties witnessed a 'birth dearth' as fertility rates dropped, and in the fifties, a postwar 'baby boom' as birth rates surged (Ahlstrom 1975: 445; US Bureau of the Census 1975: 49; Crispell 1992: 43). Church membership statistics followed a similar trajectory. For example, while the Presbyterian Church (USA) grew more slowly than the general population from 1924 to 1935, it grew at about the same rate from 1935 to 1945. As for other US denominations, Presbyterian growth outpaced the national population from 1950 to 1960 (Hoge, Johnson and Luidens 1994: 5).

---

[30] As models of secularization a la Martin (1978) suggest, the longer-term rise and fall of UK's Anglican monopoly might be expected to result in the long, slow erosion of religious identity – despite a mid-nineteenth century and largely evangelically-driven increase in churchgoing. By contrast, the timing, pace, and character of religious change in the much younger and more pluralistic US would be expected to be different. Whether that difference is a sustained and creative, religious pluralism 'loosely' held together by an optimistic Christian (and Protestant) mission or simply a delayed secularization schedule due to its geographic expanse and immigration patterns as well as the pace and timing of its own demographic transition, viz. a viz. industrialization, is a matter of debate (compare, especially, Martin 2005 and Bruce 1999).

This growth among Presbyterians was due to two factors: a) from 1953 to 1956 the Presbyterian infant baptism rate was over 40 per cent higher than the birth rate for white Americans and b) the number of adult baptisms among Presbyterians rose to its highest recorded level at 51,840 in 1955 (General Assembly Missions Council 1976: 99, 103). The fortunes of American religion at mid-century were tied to those of the nuclear family (Marler 1995).

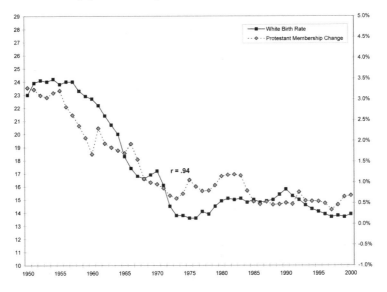

Figure 1.8   White birth rate and per cent membership change in the US: 1950–2000

My mother's (and grandmother's) church

In an analysis of the 1960 National Election Survey, Roozen (1979) reported the percentage of respondents with children among all Protestant church attendees at 42 per cent which was close to the distribution of this family type in the general population (see Fig. 1.9).

Two regression analyses of 1950s church membership and population data found that the source of the so-called "religious revival" was an increase in the number of children and the number of family units (Marler 1995: 37–8; Nash and Berger 1962; Nash 1968). In fact, 1946 witnessed the highest number of marriages to date in the United States and the highest marriage rate ever recorded in the US (Gottlieb 1993: 23; US Bureau of the Census 1975: 64). By 1960, almost half of all American households consisted of families with children under the age of 18. This household homogeneity was compounded by the rise of the suburbs. Millions of nuclear families now lived in close proximity to one another and a suburban culture was a byproduct. All denominations in the US capitalized on and profited from a burgeoning family church culture. This included an increase in suburban church planting and an increase in family-oriented church programming (Hadaway and Marler 2006).

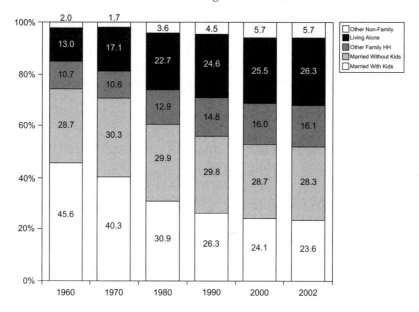

Figure 1.9   The changing structure of households in the United States

From a fifties peak the proportion of married persons with children in the US began to decline. Nevertheless, the American Protestant church continued as a 'nuclear family' and an 'ex-family' preserve (Marler 1995: 39–45). The next charts show the proportion of married couples with children and without children by age for the US population, a random sample of 72 Protestant congregations, and a United Church of Christ congregation in Massachusetts (see Fig. 1.10).

Compared to the general population, Protestant congregations and the Massachusetts church consisted of a higher proportion of middle-aged nuclear families. Married couples without children in the congregational sample and the Massachusetts church were predominantly older, empty-nested couples.

Despite several decades of household change and family disruption, the white Protestant church continued to attract and hold its market share of nuclear families. Because of relatively strong religious identities and years of social habit, the older 'ex-family' character of the church became increasingly prominent. The congregational constituency was older than the population and composed of persons in nuclear families and those who used to be.

Compared to older ex-family members, nuclear family members – primarily represented in church activities by the wife – took a decidedly consumer orientation. The church met a busy (working) mother's need for childcare and social support. This orientation to the church was in stark contrast to the traditional producer orientation of older women. They opined the decline of many church programs because of 'all these working mothers' (Marler 1995). Late twentieth-century grandmothers expressed a narrative of loss for the fifties family and the stay-at-home, work-at-church mother very reminiscent of the 'woman as moral guardian' rhetoric of mid-century Britain.[31]

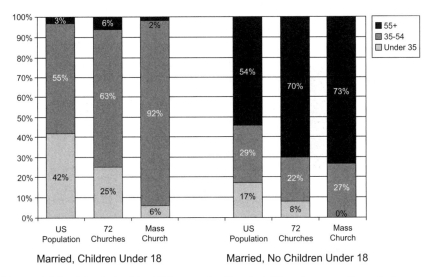

Figure 1.10   Married with children and without children by age of married person: US population and churches

The primary groups that were left out of the American Protestant church in the late eighties were precisely those gaining increasing shares of the household market, singles and non-traditional families. That this situation has in no way reversed is demonstrated by the recent findings of the U.S. Congregational Life Survey. Sixty-one per cent of church attendees are predominantly female, and the largest cohort is 45 to 64 years of age. Sixty-six per cent of church members are married, about half have children, and over half are in the labour force (Bruce and Wool ever 2002). The English Church Life Profile found that UK church attendees are also predominantly female (65 per cent) and older than the general population (Cameron and Escott, 2002).

The gravity of the situation for future religious trends in the US is illustrated in the next chart (see Fig. 1.11).

---

[31]   From this perspective, the US appears to be tracking a similar trajectory as the UK – albeit at a slower pace. The peak for institutionalized religion in the UK occurred in the mid-nineteenth century and the peak for the US in the mid-twentieth century. The ascendancy of the US, however, in terms of technology and global capitalistic development greatly contributed to the acceleration of its postindustrial phase as compared to Europe after World War II. Arguably, this process and the restructuring of the workplace (as described above) and therefore the family and women's roles in it, quickened deinstitutionalization in the religious sphere in the US in the post-sixties period. As suggested, all of this led to a situation where US mothers of the fifties sound very like UK women of the thirties and women of the seventies, like young women in the fifties in the UK.

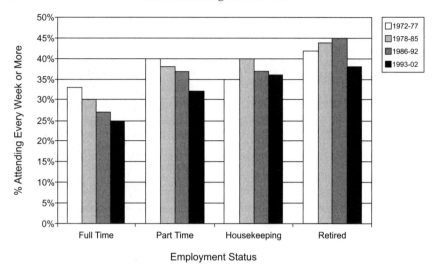

Figure 1.11   Weekly worship attendance for women in the US by employment status: 1972–2002

It shows worship attendance trends among US women by employment status. Except for the homemaker category, percentage weekly worship attendance declined for all groups, and retired persons show the highest attendance, followed by homemakers, and part-time workers. Women who work full-time, moreover, are significantly less likely to attend church frequently. Additionally, census data show that the percentage of women 16 and over in continuous full-time employment increased from 21 per cent in 1970 to 37 per cent in 2000. That women's work affects church attendance has been corroborated by a number of studies (Azzi and Ehrenberg 1975; Ehrenberg 1977; De Vaus and McAllister 1987).[32]

In summary, the proportion of the US household population composed of nuclear families is shrinking while religious denominations continue to program and compete for that demographic. Data show that churches – particularly liberal 'mainline' denominations – are finding it increasingly difficult to retain their young adults and attract younger families. Women have fewer children and are more likely to work outside the home than their own mothers did. Women who do continue to attend church do so as 'consumers' rather than 'producers' or volunteers.

---

[32]   In an analysis of the 1983 Australian Values Study, De Vaus and McAllister find that 'females in the full-time workforce are less religious than those out of it and have a broadly similar religious orientation to males' (1987: 480). They theorize three possibilities in relation to this finding: a) work replaces religion in terms of self-esteem for women; b) as workplace subordinates, women tend to assimilate the irreligious values of dominant males; and c) work, simply, affects the amount of time and attention available for involvement in religious activities.

American women (and men): belonging but not behaving

If religious trends are tied to changes in women's lives – to marital status, fertility, and work status – why have rates of religious participation in the United States remained relatively high? Puzzled by disparity between declining denominational statistics and poll-based measures of church attendance that stabilized at about 40 per cent from 1950 to 1990, Hadaway, Marler and Chaves (1993) conducted research whose conclusions raised substantial doubts about the extent of American religious 'exceptionalism'. In a poll versus church count-based test among Protestants in Ashtabula County, Ohio and Catholics in eighteen dioceses, they found that church-based attendance counts were approximately half of poll-based estimates.[33]

Concurrently, Hadaway and Marler (1993, 1997) began a national study of Protestant marginal church members, the large and growing segment of persons who identify and/or belong to local churches but who seldom if ever attend. Both correlation and cluster analyses demonstrated the presence of a generational cohort effect: current marginal Protestants were drawing from childhood religious participation reserves and not making similar behavioural investments in their children's religious socialization. This amounted, they argued, to a legacy effect that has serious implications for the second and third generations. As described above, problems with intergenerational transmission of religious belief and practice have been documented in the UK (Voas and Crockett 2005; Voas 2006; Crockett and Voas 2006).

Research among US Catholics reveals a linear decline from the oldest to the youngest cohorts on key indices of belief and practice (Fulton *et al.* 2000). Post-Vatican II Catholics are less orthodox and more influenced by Vatican II ideas of democracy and the changeability of church teachings than the Vatican II or pre-Vatican II cohorts, respectively (Davidson *et al.* 1997). Post-Vatican II children attend church less than their parents or grandparents, and analysis of national polls shows that this cohort reports much lower levels of attendance than either group at a comparable age (D'Antonio *et al.* 1989; Hoge 1981).

The only time series data dealing with age for actual church participants are from the United Church of Christ (UCC), a mainline Protestant denomination. The first study was conducted in mid-1970 and the second, in the spring of 2002. The results are striking: attendees age 15–34 declined from 24 per cent in the mid-1970s to only ten per cent in 2002 and attendees age 65 or older grew from 23 per cent in the mid-1970s to 43 per cent of all UCC attendees in 2002. The large disparity between UCC attendees age 15–34 and the U.S. population widened slightly from 21 to 25 percentage points between the mid-1970s and 2002. The disparity between UCC attendees age 65 and over and the US

---

[33] Using an alternative method made possible by two more recent congregation-based studies including Chaves' National Congregations Study (Chaves et al. 1999) and the United States Congregational Life Study (Bruce and Woolever 2002), Hadaway and Marler (2005) concluded that a) the best estimate for the total number of American congregations is 331,000, 25 per cent of which are mainline Protestants, 54 per cent conservative/evangelical Protestants, seven per cent Catholic/Orthodox, 11 per cent other Christian, and three per cent non-Christian; b) average worship attendance varies among denominational groups, ranging from 125 or less for mainline Protestants, evangelicals, and other Christian groups to over 850 participants for Roman Catholics; and c) therefore, 21 per cent of Americans attend worship during an average week.

population, on the other hand, grew enormously, increasing from nine percentage points to over 27 percentage points. There are, unfortunately, no similar studies of attendees in the 1950s or 1960s. However, from the mid-1960s to the mid-1970s the proportion of UCC members with children under 18 in the home dropped from 66 per cent to only 32 per cent (McKinney 1982; Hadaway 2002; Hadaway and Marler 2006).

Given the growing gap between religious belonging and behaving, especially evident in declines among younger cohorts, it is not surprising that poll-based measures of US church attendance dropped ten points in the past decade and that defection to 'no religion' doubled from eight to 16 per cent since 1980 (Hadaway and Marler 2005).[34] A cohort analysis conducted by Hout, Greeley and Wilde (2002) confirmed the 'demographic imperative' in religious change in the United States, linking growth and decline to the birthrate. Additionally, analysis of switching behaviour in American religion demonstrated the significance of differential fertility – especially among sectarian groups with strong childbearing orientations – immigration, and intermarriage for explaining affiliation trends (Sherkat 2001). As in the UK, the importance of a mother's religiosity for the development and maintenance of religious identity and practice has been documented (Nelson 1990; Hadaway and Marler 1996, Marler and Hadaway 1993; Smith 2005).

Late modern women's spirituality as 'default religion'

Accompanying deinstitutionalizing trends in American religion are perceived increases in spirituality. As Heelas and Woodhead (2005) found, this trend may be related to changes in women's lives. This chart shows the relationship between frequent worship attendance and 'closeness to God' by gender and work status (see Fig. 1.12).

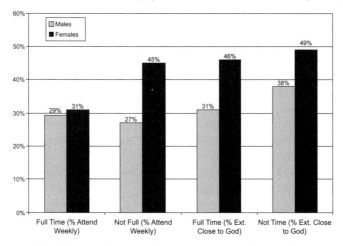

Figure 1.12   Worship attendance and closeness to God by gender and work status (US Protestants)

---

[34]   While not supplying comparisons over time, the most recent survey of American teenagers finds that 16 per cent consider themselves not to be religious and nearly half attend religious services once a month or less (Christian 2005: 37).

Interestingly, full-time work status affects women's church attendance but it does not affect self-reported 'closeness to God'. Might a continued 'closeness to God' represent a religious kind of 'lagged adaptation' to change in women's lives? Or, is 'closeness to God' or sensitivity to the supernatural essential to women as some physiological and psychological research suggests? And/or as women become disconnected from the traditional church, do they substitute 'spiritual' self-care for 'religious' other care, as Hochschild suggests?

In a review of research on the definition of and relationship between 'being religious' and 'being spiritual,' Marler and Hadaway (2001) found that the majority of persons who self-identify as 'spiritual' also claim to be 'religious' (see Table 1.1).

Table 1.1   'Being Religious' and 'Being Spiritual': Research among US respondents, 1991–2000

Category	Sample			
	Protestants (Marler/Hadaway) 1991	Boomers (Roof) 1995–6	National (Scott) 2000	Protestants (Scott) 2000
Religious and Spiritual	64%	59%	61%	67%
Spiritual only	18	14	20	18
Religious only	9	15	8	9
Neither	8	12	11	6
(N)	(1,884)	(409)	(487)	(270)

A recent interview study of American teenagers aged 13–17 explored the extent to which respondents considered themselves to be 'spiritual but not religious' (Christian 2005: 72–107). Only eight per cent responded that this was 'very true'. Forty-six per cent said that this was 'somewhat true' and 43 per cent responded 'not true at all' (2005: 78). Based on interview responses, the authors concluded that only a minority of American teens can be categorized as spiritual seekers: in fact, 'most teens literally did not understand what they were talking about' (2005: 78). Moreover, some of the 'spiritual but not religious' teens interviewed used the category 'not to disparage or distance themselves from organized religion per se, but to emphasize the importance of a personally meaningful faith that is practiced in the context of organized religion' (2005: 81). Marler and Hadaway found something similar among marginal Protestant church members (Hadaway and Marler 1992, Marler and Hadaway 1993, Marler and Hadaway 2001).

In 1991, Hadaway and Marler surveyed American Protestants and identified 736 marginal Protestants – persons who claimed a Protestant denominational identity but who attended church 'several times a year or less'. In 1992, 432 of these respondents completed a longer telephone interview. By definition, these respondents were 'less religious' based on institutional measures despite the fact that they continued to identify with a particular denomination: they 'belong' to a church but no longer 'behave' according to traditional churchgoing norms. Were these 'less religious'

Americans also 'more spiritual' as some sociologists predicted (Roof 2000, 1993; Cimino and Lattin 1998; Warner 1993; Hammond 1992)? Compared to the general population of Protestants, Marler and Hadaway (2001) found that marginal Protestants are much less likely to see themselves as 'religious and spiritual' (46 per cent), more likely to see themselves as 'spiritual only' (25 per cent), slightly more likely to see themselves as 'religious only' (10 per cent), and more likely to see themselves as 'neither' (18 per cent). The pattern of response was similar to that of the youngest cohort ('baby busters') in their general sample of American Protestants. Marginal Protestants were much less likely to see themselves as religious or spiritual – in any way – than more churched respondents. Larger proportions of the 'spiritual only' and 'religious only' were more than offset by lower numbers of the 'religious and spiritual' and higher numbers of the 'neither religious nor spiritual'.

Forty-nine face-to-face interviews with representative marginal Protestants from the original sample were conducted in 1993 and 1994. Marler and Hadaway (2001: 295) found that 63 per cent identified 'being religious' and 'being spiritual' as different but interdependent concepts, 28 per cent as the same concept, and 8 per cent as different and independent concepts. Generally, then, marginal US Protestants talked about the religious and spiritual as different but interdependent concepts. They recognized the possibility of both a 'naked' spirituality and an empty or 'soul-less' religion. Most of those who saw themselves as 'spiritual only' did so by default. They were less religious rather than more spiritual.

As in the Heelas and Woodhead (2005) study of Kendal, respondents who viewed themselves as 'spiritual only' were disproportionately female, middle-aged, and socially liberal. Many experimented with non-traditional religions, attended spirituality seminars and self-help groups, and read popularized books on numerology and Native American spirituality as well as more scholarly books on world religions. Nearly all were raised in a Protestant denomination which provided them the necessary language and norms for active contest and ultimate rejection of that tradition, renegotiation of religious practice within another Christian tradition, and/or experimentation with alternative spiritualities.

Two interviewees represent the personal biographies and religious rhetoric of 'spiritual' American Protestant women. One, a forty-something mother of three and married to her 'Sunday School sweetheart' who is a marginal Congregationalist, talks about her great grandmother as a kind of 'moral hero' a la Brown (2001) and herself as the primary – although less and less effective – 'moral guardian' to her religiously inactive family. She was raised in a very religious Congregational (United Church of Christ) family in New England with two generations of missionaries to China on her maternal side. Like other marginal Protestants, she ceased to attend church after marriage; returned briefly when her children were young because 'Children are supposed to be brought up in a church'; and now attends very infrequently because Sunday morning is a time 'when nobody has political meetings' (her husband is a city councilman) and 'the family can be together'. When she does go, she usually goes alone, and 'Every time I go, I say why don't I do this more?' At this point in the interview she cries and says, 'I don't feel guilty as if I'm being bad. I feel, I feel as if, as if it's something I am neglecting that's important to me'. For her, spirituality is more 'personal' – a way to look at life with a 'lower case "l"' rather than 'a capital

"L'" – and 'Religion can be the clothing for that'. She considers herself to be more spiritual than religious but she does not pay attention to 'crystals and stuff like that'. Instead, she admits that she still likes religious 'trappings' like 'having a dress on [on] Sunday' and 'singing the songs'.

Another, an affluent professional woman in her late fifties from Phoenix, Arizona was raised the daughter of a Midwestern Pentecostal minister. She has two grown daughters, has been married three times, and her religious journey reflects her own upward mobility: from the Assemblies of God to the Presbyterian and then the Anglican Church and finally, to experimentation with non-traditional spiritualities through occasional seminars, visiting non-traditional churches in San Francisco with her daughter, and reading popular books about spirituality. She equates church with religion and 'big business' and spirituality with 'the Spirit' that is 'pure and looks within'. Despite her rejection of fundamentalist doctrine and patriarchy in Pentecostalism, she appreciates the early gift of the 'Holy Spirit' experienced in that fellowship. That spiritual experience, she says, continues to be her 'joy'.

'Being religious' or 'being spiritual,' Marler and Hadaway concluded, is not a zero-sum proposition. The foregoing data demonstrate that these concepts are most often seen as distinct but interdependent. As such, their separation among younger Protestants and the religiously marginal suggests that being less religious is simply that, being less religious. This is why some marginal Protestants, including many women, readily admit they are 'less religious' but say they are 'spiritual' by default (2001: 289–299). It is what is left: a residual spirituality that is sometimes described as something less, something 'naked' or less 'powerful' and other times described as something more, something institutionally unfettered and 'pure'. From this perspective, women's late-modern spirituality in the West might be best understood as default religion

From religious 'homemaker' to spiritual 'self-maker'

Disproportionate interest and engagement in the holistic health and spirituality milieu is a trend discussed in Hochschild's recent work, *The Commercialization of Intimate Life* (2003). She theorizes that a care deficit among women who struggle to balance work and family life is created and exploited by the new 'religion of capitalism' through the self-care industry. Advanced capitalism, she argues, needs women's labour as tertiary workers and primary consumers. Therefore it creates an expansive market of care providers. As a result, the wife-mother role is 'hypersymbolized', condensing the burden of emotion and care once vested in communities, church, and the family to the mother alone (Hochschild 2003: 38–39).[35]

---

[35] Hochschild acknowledges that a 'commodity frontier' has been a part of Western domestic life for a long time. For example, in the eighteenth and nineteenth centuries, there was 'a greater cultural blur between service and server'. Whereas earlier one purchased a person (slave, indentured servant), now it is the 'services, classified and priced' that are bought and sold in the marketplace. Moreover, Hochschild adds, commercial substitutes today are billed as and/or imagined to be better than the 'real thing': cleaning services clean better;

As discussed above, most women in Europe and the US take primary responsibility for homemaking and working outside the home simultaneously or they are the principal employers and supervisors of 'professional' homemaker and/ or childcare providers. According to Hochschild, this 'pressured' – or in McGee's (2005) terms 'belabored' – role makes meaningful relationships with those women who have traditionally cared for such as children and the elderly more difficult. From Hochschild's perspective, families – and especially women who are responsible for their practical and emotional well-being – are 'shock absorbers' for a stalled gender revolution. Institutional arrangements, still governed by men, make it difficult if not impossible for women to meet the demands of the 'second shift' (2003: 26–28, 106–108).[36]

In the industrial era, the pious wife supported the domestic sphere making it possible for husbands to engage in the useful capitalistic fiction of the 'self-made' man (McGee 2005: 171–4). This 'self-making' was a rational and instrumental extension of Weber's concept of work as a 'calling' augmented by the expressive self-culture of Transcendentalism and the personal conversion narrative of Protestant revivalism in the nineteenth century. It was women who came to inhabit the 'softer' expressive and pietistic side of work (or rather, domestic labour) that was so necessary as a bolster and buffer for industrialization (McGee 2005: 25–36).

In the postindustrial situation, women's work is required and by default the ideology of 'self-making' is extended to include them. As a result, there is a dramatic shift from the home as the site of piety and the woman as its moral hero or guardian to the piety and industry of the woman herself. The woman's role moves from homemaking to self-making, a shift which legitimates her changed position in the labour market. Concurrently – especially among older and middle-aged generations – the ideal of women's piety and the necessity of their domesticity lingers. Much as spiritualism, mesmerism, and religious volunteerism answered the need for a 'calling' among homebound middle-class women in the nineteenth century, contemporary 'spirituality' responds to persistent desires for a 'calling' among belaboured twenty-first-century women (McGee 2005: 36).

In addition to care providers, capitalism in late modernity also produces an expressive-therapeutic and spirituality market to answer women's changing needs (Hochschild 2003: 13–29). This is especially required for the large demographic category dubbed 'adaptives' whose self-identity is an active negotiation between career and homemaker roles (Hakim 2001). As a reflection of this give and take, Heelas and Woodhead (2005) found both themes of subjectivization and relationality

---

therapists process feelings with greater skill; and childcare workers are more 'even-tempered' (2003: 37).

36   McGee's concept of 'belabored' focuses on contradictory cultural messages more than confounding structural arrangements: messages that devalue the labors of care providers while at the same time characterizing such labour as private and valuable; messages that encourage pursuit of self-invention and mastery while not recognizing that such work is dependent on those whose labour provides the 'necessities of daily life'; and messages to be flexible in the context of a volatile labour market while also striving to cultivate an 'authentic self' unaffected by economic change, or even, continued inequality (2005: 9).

in their exploration of the holistic milieu in Kendal.[37] One outcome is that women can find their fulfillment 'within', and the un/intended result is that issues of economic injustice in the labour market are avoided (McGee 2005: 172–174). As McGee suggests, self-care through spirituality without a political context works to 'keep women in their place' in a still-male oriented economy (2005: 180). Another possibility, which McGee admits is not as yet fully realized, is that women may infuse the late modern, western 'naked public square' with a new sense of public commitment that is grounded in communitarian or global 'homemaking' as well as individual 'self-making'.

Recently, Sarah Imhoff (2006) described renewal movements in American Judaism which are rich examples of subjectivization and relationality. The *havurah*, a small study group movement initiated as Havurat Shalom in 1967, became a haven for progressive women as participants and organizers. Imhoff emphasizes the similarity between feminist and *havurah* ideologies of 'personal development through community and human relationship with God' (2006: 73). When other movements of the sixties waned, the *havurah* continued as a model not only of personal religiosity but also of social justice with a universal vision. On the other side of the ideological spectrum, Orthodox women have formed prayer groups, or *teffilot*, where they openly experience and express their devotion to God in ways denied to them in Orthodox worship (Imhoff 2006: 75–76). As with the Christian women's groups studied by Winter, Lummis, and Stokes (1994), many women excluded from predominantly male power structures in conservative and liberal denominations in America essentially 'defect in place'. They continued to identify with their cradle denominations, while experimenting with alternative spirituality individually or in smaller groups of women. Such a move, many argue, provides spiritual renewal for individual women and increases the possibility of internal denominational reform.

Conclusion

In conclusion, it would not be a stretch to describe the institutional Christian church as a 'pink collar' piety industry that materially supported and religiously legitimated the industrial and capitalist and masculinist economies of the West. That religious trends, particularly over the last century, have been closely linked to the nuclear family is clear; that mothers, grandmothers, and younger children in their

---

[37] Notably, when asked about their reasons for involvement in the holistic milieu, more respondents said 'health and fitness' (23.2 per cent) , 'stress relief' (15.2 per cent), and 'bodily pain or illness' (13.9 per cent) rather than specifically 'looking for spiritual growth' (19.4 per cent) or more generally 'looking for personal growth' (13.5 per cent). Explicitly relational responses to this item were 'to meet like-minded people' (5.1 per cent) and 'emotional support or human contact' (3.8 per cent) (Heelas and Woodhead 2005: 91). On the other hand, Heelas and Woodhead (2005) noted that respondents' definitions of 'spirituality' which included 'being a decent and caring person' (21 per cent), 'love' (20 per cent), and 'healing oneself and others' (10 per cent) were 'strongly relational'. Practitioners in the holistic milieu, they said, were especially likely to view the consequences of involvement in terms of the integration of mind, body, and spirit and to emphasize the growth of self through relational interconnection (98).

care disproportionately constituted the active participants and volunteer workforce of the church is also clear; and that family change focused in the changed lives of women was an important force promoting institutional decline is also apparent. Despite the fact that women continue to be overrepresented among the churched in the West, empirical evidence points to the likelihood of their continued defection from traditional religious denominations.

There is still a strong neo-conservative 'family values' backlash in the West, and especially, in the United States, but the cultural tide is certainly turning on these factions. The majority of recent ethnographic studies of conservative evangelical (and particularly, Pentecostal) women show that even their constituencies are increasingly liberated from older feminine ideals through work, through dissatisfaction with husbands who do not 'keep their promises', and through networks of mutual support (Griffith 1997; Ingersoll 2002; Brasher 2001).[38] At the same time, many feminist women are attracted to the holistic health and spirituality milieu as an attempt to produce felt well-being and provide meaning. The religious and spiritual explorations of both camps are supported by and promote a burgeoning market of products.[39]

In the end, women's religious 'musicality' – whether physiologically female, psychologically feminine, socially learned or structurally imposed – becomes both the reason to stay connected to the church and the reason to experiment outside it. The late modern explosion in expressive-therapeutic media and consumer technology, combined with women's increasing independence and purchasing power, provide both the market and the means for such seeking. For understanding religious developments in the future, it will remain important to watch the women.

---

[38] The 'charismatisation of the global' through the exportation of advanced capitalism and a 'loosely associated' Pentecostalism poses new possibilities and problems. For all the friendly comparisons between the epistemology of charismatic forms of evangelicalism and the postmodern verve, there lurks a very modern and patriarchal orientation to family, work, and gender roles (for a discussion of the connections, see for example, Martin 2005 and Coleman 2000).

[39] As a side note on the state of feminist scholarly work in the United States, Donaldson (2001) critiques the feminist spirituality movement for appropriating ancient and indigenous religious rituals and artifacts in an ahistorical, decontextualized way. Such 'postmodern' movements, she argues, constitute a 'commodity fetishism,' a kind of (late) capitalism 'cloaked in mystic terminology' (2001: 237–253). On the more conservative side, Griffith (1997) describes the irony of a Pentecostal women's group that anchors spiritual fidelity to physical perfection and exploits the increasing independence and earning power of women through a vast array of target-marketed products. More recently, Griffith (2004) catalogues the history of American's obsession with the body and its relationship to nineteenth century evangelicalism, New Thought philosophy, Eastern religious practice, the women's movement, and the Christian fitness industry. She concludes that 'Christian body practices offer, in short, a model for tracking the ways that ordinary middle-class white bodies have bee tutored in the obligatory hungers and subtle yet stringent regulations of consumer capitalism' (2004: 249).

References

Ahlstrom, S., *A Religious History of the American People, Volume 2* (Garden City, NY: Doubleday/Image, 1975).

Anderson, M., 'British Population History, 1911–1991', in M. Anderson (ed.), *British Population History: From the Black Death to the Present Day* (Cambridge: Cambridge University Press, 1996).

Anderson, M., 'Population Change in North-Western Europe, 1750–1850', in M. Anderson (ed.), *British Population History: From the Black Death to the Present Day* (Cambridge: Cambridge University Press, 1996).

Artis, J. and Pavalko, E., 'Explaining the Decline in Women's Household Labor: Individual Change and Cohort Differences', *Journal of Marriage and the Family*, 65(3) (2003): 746–761.

Azzi, C. and Ehrenberg, R., 'Household Allocation of Time and Church Attendance', *The Journal of Political Economy*, 83(1) (1975): 27–56.

Barker, E., 'The Post-war Generation and Establishment Religion in England', in W.C. Roof, J.W. Carroll and D.A. Roozen (eds), *The Post-War Generation and Establishment Religion: Crosscultural Perspectives* (Boulder, CO: Westview, 1995).

Boeri, T., Del Boca, D. and Pissarides, C., *Women at Work: An Economic Perspective* (Oxford: Oxford University Press, 2005).

Bose, C., 'Dual Spheres', in B.B. Hess and M.M. Ferree (eds), *Analyzing Gender: A Handbook of Social Science Research* (Thousand Oaks, CA: Sage, 1987).

Brasher, B., *Godly Women: Fundamentalism and Female Power* (San Francisco, CA: Jossey-Bass, 2001).

Brown, C., *The Death of Christian Britain: Understanding Secularization, 1800–2000* (London: Routledge, 2001).

Brown, C., *Religion and Society in Twentieth-Century Britain* (Harlow: Pearson Education, 2006).

Bruce, D. and Woolever, C., *A Field Guide to U.S. Congregations: Who's Going Where and Why* (Louisville, KY: Westminster John Knox, 2002).

Bruce, S., *Religion in Modern Britain* (Oxford: Oxford University Press, 1995).

Bruce, S., *Choice and Religion: a Critique of Rational Choice Theory* (Oxford: Oxford University Press, 1999).

Bruegel, I., 'Whose Myths are They Anyway?', *The British Journal of Sociology*, 47(1) (1996): 167–174.

Cameron, H. and Escott, P., 'The Community Involvement of Church Attenders: Findings from the English 2001 Church Life Profile,' paper presented at the *ISTR Fifth International Conference*, Cape Town, South Africa, 2002.

Carroll, J., Hargrove, B. and Lummis, A., *Women of the Cloth: a New Opportunity for the Churches* (San Francisco, CA: Harper and Row, 1983).

Chaves, M., *Ordaining Women: Culture and Conflict in Religious Organizations* (Cambridge, MA: Harvard University Press, 1999).

Cimino, R. and Lattin, D., *Shopping for Faith: American Religion in the New Millennium* (San Francisco, CA: Jossey-Bass, 1998).

Cliquet, R., 'Major Trends Affecting Families in the New Millennium: Western Europe and North America', in *Major Trends Affecting Families: A Background Document*, report for the United Nations, Department of Economic and Social Affairs, Division for Social Policy and Development, Program on the Family, (2003): 1–40.

Coleman, S., *The Globalization of Charismatic Christianity: Spreading the Gospel of Prosperity* (Cambridge: Cambridge University Press, 2000).

Cornwall, M., 'The Influence of Three Agents of Religious Socialization: Family, Church, Peers', in D.L. Thomas (ed.), *The Religion and Family Connection: Social Science Perspectives* (Provo, UT: Brigham Young University, Religious Studies Center, 1988).

Crispell, D., 'Myths of the 1950s', *American Demographics*, 14(8) (1992): 43.

Crockett, A. and Voas, D., 'Generations of Decline: Religious Change in 20th-Century Britain', *Journal for the Scientific Study of Religion*, 45(4) (2006): 567–584.

Crompton, R. and Harris, F., 'A Reply to Hakim', *The British Journal of Sociology*, 49(1) (1998): 144–149.

Crompton, R. and Lyonette, C., 'The New Gender Essentialism – Domestic and Family 'Choices' and their Relation to Attitudes', *The British Journal of Sociology*, 56(4) (2005): 601–620.

D'Antonio, W.V., Davidson, J.D., Hoge, D. and Wallace, R., *American Catholic Laity in a Changing Church* (Kansas City, MO: Sheed & Ward, 1989).

Davidman, L., *Tradition in a Rootless World: Women Turn to Orthodox Judaism* (Berkeley, CA: University of California Press, 1991).

Davidson, J.D., Williams, A.S., Lamanna, R.A., Stenftenagel, J., Weigert, K.M., Whalen, W.J. and Wittberg, P., *The Search for Common Ground: What Unites and Divides American Catholics* (Huntington, IN: Our Sunday Visitor Press, 1997).

Davie, G., *Religion in Britain since 1945: Believing Without Belonging* (Oxford: Blackwell, 1994).

Davie, G., *Religion in Modern Europe: A Memory Mutates* (Oxford: Oxford University Press, 2000).

DeVaus, D. and McAllister, I., 'Gender Differences in Religion: A Test of the Structural Location Theory', *American Sociological Review*, 52(4) (1987): 472–481.

Dex, S., Walters, P. and Alden, D.M. *French and British Mothers at Work* (Hampshire: Macmillan, 1993).

Donaldson, L.E., 'On Medicine Women and White Shame-ans: New Age Native Americanism and Commodity Fetishism', in E. Castelli (ed.), *Women, Gender, Religion: A Reader* (New York: Palgrave, 2001).

Drew, E., 'Reconceptualising Families', in E. Drew, R. Emerek and E. Mahon (eds), *Women, Work and the Family in Europe* (New York: Routledge, 1998).

Drew, E., Emerek, R., and Mahon, E., *Women, Work and the Family in Europe* (New York: Routledge, 1998).

Ehrenberg, R., 'Household Allocation of Time and Religiosity: Replication and Extension', *The Journal of Political Economy*, 85(2) (1977): 415–423.

Festy, P., 'Looking for European Demography, Desperately?', paper presented at the *Expert Group Meeting on Policy Response to Population Ageing and Population*

Decline in New York, Population Division, Department of Economic and Social Affairs, United Nations, 16–18 October, 2000.

Francis, L.J. and Wilcox, C., 'Religiosity and Femininity: Do Women Really Hold a More Positive Attitude Toward Christianity?', *Journal for the Scientific Study of Religion*, 37(3) (1998): 462–469.

Francis, L.J., Jones, S.H., Jackson, C.J. and Robbins, M., 'The Feminine Personality Profile of Male Anglican Clergy in Britain and Ireland: a study employing the Eysenck Personality Profiler', *Review of Religious Research*, 43(1) (2001): 14–23.

Fulton, J., Abela, A., Borowik, I., Dowling, T., Marler, P.L. and Tomasi, L., *Young Catholics at the New Millennium: The Religion and Morality of Young Adults in Western Countries* (Dublin: University College Dublin Press, 2000)

General Assembly Missions Council, *Membership Trends in the United Presbyterian Church in the U.S.A.* (New York: United Presbyterian Church, USA, 1976).

Gershuny, J. and Robinson, J., 'Historical Changes in the Household Division of Labor', *Demography*, 25(4) (1998): 537–552.

Ginn, J., Arber, S., Brannen, J., Dale, A., Dex, S., Elias, P., Moss, P., Pahl, J., Roberts, C. and Rubery, J., 'Feminist Fallacies: A Reply to Hakim on Women's Employment', *The British Journal of Sociology*, 47(1) (1996): 175–177.

Gottleib, A., *Do You Believe in Magic?: The Second Coming of the Sixties Generation*, (New York: Times Books, 1993).

Griffith, R.M., *God's Daughters: Evangelical Women and the Power of Submission* (Berkeley, CA: University of California Press, 1997).

Griffith, R.M. *Born Again Bodies: Flesh and Spirit in American Christianity* (Berkeley, CA: University of California Press, 2004).

Hadaway, C.K., *A Report on Episcopal Churches in the United States* (New York: The Domestic and Foreign Missionary Society, 2002).

Hadaway, C.K. and Marler, P.L., 'The Problem with Father as Proxy: Denominational Switching and Religious Change, 1965–1988', *Journal for the Scientific Study of Religion*, 35(2) (1996): 156–164.

Hadaway, C.K. and Marler, P.L., 'Methodists on the Margins: The "Self-authoring" of Religious Identity', in D.M. Campbell and R.E. Richey (eds), *Connectionalism: Ecclesiology, Mission and Identity* (Nashville, TN: Abingdon, 1997).

Hadaway, C.K. and Marler, P.L., 'The Measurement and Meaning of Religious Involvement in Great Britain', paper presented at the *Annual Meeting of the International Society for the Sociology of Religion*, Toulouse, France, 1997.

Hadaway, C.K. and Marler, P.L., 'How many Americans Attend Worship each Week?: An Alternative Approach to Measurement', *Journal for the Scientific Study of Religion*, 44(3) (2005): 307–322.

Hadaway, C.K. and Marler, P.L., 'Growth and Decline in the Mainline', in C. Lippy (ed.), *Faith in America: Changes, Challenges, New Directions*, *Volume 1* (Westport, CT: Praeger, 2006).

Hadaway, C.K., Marler, P.L. and Chaves, M., 'What the Polls don't Show: A Closer Look at U.S. Church Attendance', *American Sociological Review*, 58(6) (1993): 741–752.

Hakim, C., *Work-Lifestyle Choices in the 21ˢᵗ Century: Preference Theory* (Oxford: Oxford University Press, 2000).

Hammond, P.E, *Religion and Personal Autonomy: The Third Disestablishment in America* (Columbia, SC: University of South Carolina Press, 1992).

Haraway, D., '"Gender" for a Marxist Dictionary: The Sexual Politics of a Word', in E. Castelli (ed.), *Women, Gender, Religion: A Reader* (New York: Palgrave, 2001).

Hattery, A., *Women, Work and Family: Balancing and Weaving* (Thousand Oaks, CA: Sage, 2001).

Heelas, P. and Woodhead, L., *The Spiritual Revolution: Why Religion is Giving Way to Spirituality* (Oxford: Blackwell, 2005).

Hochschild, A., *Working Parents and the Revolution at Home* (New York: Viking, 1989).

Hochschild, A., *The Time Bind: When Work Becomes Home and Home Becomes Work* (New York: Metropolitan, 1997).

Hochschild, A., *The Commercialization of Intimate Life: Notes from Home and Work* (Berkeley, CA: University of California Press, 2003).

Hoge, D., *Converts, Dropouts, Returnees: A Study of Religious Change among Catholics* (New York: Pilgrim, 1981).

Hoge, D., Johnson, B. and Luidens, D.A., *Vanishing Boundaries: The Religion of Mainline Protestant Baby Boomers* (Louisville, KY: Westminster John Knox, 1994).

Hout, M., Greeley, A., and Wilde, M., 'The Demographic Imperative in Religious Change in the United States', *American Journal of Sociology*, 107(2) (2002): 165–190.

Imhoff, S., 'The Spirit of the Law: Spirituality in American Judaism', in C. Lippy (ed.), *Faith in America: Changes, Challenges, New Directions, Volume 1* (Westport, CT: Praeger, 2006).

Ingersoll, J., *Evangelical Christian Women: War Stories in the Gender Battles* (New York: New York University Press, 2003).

Kaufman, D.R., *Rachel's Daughters: Newly Orthodox Jewish Women* (New Brunswick, NJ: Rutgers University Press, 1991).

Kosmin, B.A. and Lachman, S.P., *One Nation under God: Religion in Contemporary American Society* (New York: Harmony Books, 1993).

Kupinsky, S., 'The Fertility of Working Women in the United States: Historical Trends and Theoretical Perspectives', in S. Kupinsky (ed.), *The Fertility of Working Women: A Synthesis of International Research* (Westport, CT: Praeger, 1977).

Laslett, P., 'Characteristics of the Western Family Considered Over Time', *Journal of Family History*, 2(2) (1977): 89–114.

Lawless, E., *Handmaidens of the Lord: Pentecostal Women Preachers and Traditional Religion* (Philadelphia, PA: University of Pennsylvania, 1988).

Lehman, E., *Women Clergy: Breaking through Gender Barriers* (Somerset, NJ: Transaction Books, 1985).

Lehman, E., *Work and Gender: The Case of the Clergy* (Albany, NY: SUNY, 1993).

Marler, P.L., 'Lost in the Fifties: The Changing Family and the Nostalgic Church', in N. Ammerman and W.C. Roof (eds), *Work, Family and Faith: New Patterns among Old Institutions* (New Brunswick, NJ: Rutgers University Press, 1995).

Marler, P.L. and Hadaway, C.K., 'Toward a Typology of Protestant Marginal Members', *Review of Religious Research*, 35(1) (1993): 34–54.

Marler, P.L. and Hadaway, C.K., 'Being Religious or Being Spiritual in America: A Zero-Sum Proposition?', *Journal for the Scientific Study of Religion*, 41(2) (2001): 289–300.

Martin, D.A., A *General Theory of Secularization* (New York: Harper and Row, 1978).

Martin, D.A., *On Secularization: Towards a Revised General Theory* (Aldershot: Ashgate, 2005).

Martin, G. and Kats, V., 'Families and Work in Transition in 12 countries, 1980–2001', *Monthly Labor Review*, 126(9) (2003): 3–31.

McGee, M., *Self-help, Inc.: Makeover Culture in American Life* (Oxford: Oxford University Press, 2005).

McKinney, W., *Population Changes and the Growth and Decline of the United Church of Christ* (New York: United Church Board for Homeland Ministries, 1982).

Mensch, B., Susheela Singh, S. and Casterline, J.B., 'Trends in the Timing of First Marriage among Men and Women in the Developing World', in *Policy Research Division Working Paper*, No. 202 (New York, NY: Population Council, 2005).

Meyer, L., 'Economic Globalization and Women's Status in the Labor Market', *The Sociological Quarterly*, 4(3) (2003): 351–383.

Miller, A. and Hoffman, J., 'Risk and Religion: An Explanation of Gender Differences in Religiosity', *Journal for the Scientific Study of Religion*, 34(1) (1995): 63–75.

Nash, D., 'A Little Child shall Lead them: A Statistical Test of an Hypothesis that Children were the Sources of the American "Religious Revival"', *Journal for the Scientific Study of Religion*, 7(2) (1968) 238–240.

Nash, D. and Berger, P., 'The Child, the Family, and the "Religious Revival" in Suburbia', *Journal for the Scientific Study of Religion*, 2(1) (1962): 85–93.

Nelson, H., 'The Religious Identification of Children and Interfaith Marriages', *Review of Religious Research*, 32(2) (1990): 122–134.

Nesbitt, P., *Feminization of the Clergy in America: Occupational and Organizational Perspectives* (Oxford: Oxford University Press, 1997).

Population Reference Bureau Staff, 'Transitions in World Population', *Population Bulletin*, 59(1) (2004).

Proctor, I. and Padfield, M., 'Work Orientations and Women's Work: A Critique of Hakim's Theory of Heterogeneity of Women', *Gender, Work and Organization*, 6(3) (1999): 152–162.

Robbins, M., Francis, L.J., Haley, J.M. and Kay, W.K., 'The Personality Characteristic of Methodist Ministers: Feminine Men and Masculine Women?', *Journal for the Scientific Study of Religion*, 40(1) (2001): 123–128.

Roof, W.C., A *Generation of Seekers: The Spiritual Journeys of the Baby Boom Generation* (San Francisco, CA: Harper-Collins, 1993).

Roof, W.C., *Spiritual Marketplace: Baby Boomers and the Remaking of American Religion* (Princeton, NJ: Princeton University Press, 2000).

Roozen, D., *Church Attendance from a Social Indicators Perspective: An Explanation into the Development of Social Indicators of Religion from Existing Data*, unpublished dissertation (Atlanta, GA: Emory University, 1979).

Sherkat, D.E., 'Tracking the Restructuring of American Religion', *Social Forces*, 79(4) (2001): 1459–1493.

Smith, C., *Soul Searching: The Religious and Spiritual Lives of American Teenagers* (Oxford: Oxford University Press, 2005).

Smith, D.S., 'American Family and Demographic Patterns and the Northwest European model', *Continuity and Change*, 8(3) (1993): 389–415.

Stark, R., 'Physiology and Faith: Addressing the "Universal" Gender Difference in Religious Commitment', *Journal for the Scientific Study of Religion*, 41(3) (2002): 495–507.

Stolte-Heiskanen, V., 'Fertility and Women's Employment outside the Home in Western Europe', in S. Kupinsky (ed.), *The Fertility of Working Women: A Synthesis of International Research* (Westport, CT: Praeger, 1977).

Thompson, E. and Remmes, K., 'Does Masculinity thwart being Religious? An Examination of Older Men's Religiousness', *Journal for the Scientific Study of Religion*, 41(3) (2002): 521–532.

Tiano, S., 'Gender, Work, and World Capitalism: Third World Women's Role in Development', in B.B. Hess and M.M. Ferree (eds), *Analyzing Gender: A Handbook of Social Science Research*, (Thousand Oaks, CA: Sage, 1987).

Tilly, L. and Scott, J., *Women, Work and Family* (New York: Holt and Rinehart/ Times Books, 1987).

US Bureau of the Census, Historical Statistics of the United States, *Colonial Times to 1970, Bicentennial Edition, Part 2* (Washington, D.C.: U.S. Government Printing Office, 1975).

Voas, D., 'Religious Decline in Scotland: New Evidence in Timing and Spatial Patterns', *Journal for the Scientific Study of Religion*, 45(1) (2006): 107–118.

Voas, D. and Crockett, A., 'Religion in Britain: Neither Believing nor Belonging', *Sociology*, 39(1) (2005): 11–28.

Wallace, R., *They Call her Pastor: A New Role for Catholic Women* (Albany, NY: SUNY, 1992).

Warner, S., 'Work in Progress toward a New Paradigm for the Sociological Study of Religion in the United States', *American Journal of Sociology*, 98(5) (1993): 1044–1093.

Winter, M.T., Lummis, A. and Stokes, A., *Defecting in Place: Women Claiming Responsibility for their own Spiritual Lives* (New York: Crossroad, 1994).

Woods, R.I., 'The Population of Britain in the Nineteenth Century', in M. Anderson (ed.), *British Population History: From the Black Death to the Present Day* (Cambridge: Cambridge University Press, 1996).

Zikmund, B.B., Lummis, A. and Chang, P., *Clergy Women: An Uphill Calling* (Louisville, KY: Westminster John Knox, 1998).

Chapter 2

Singleness and Secularization: British Evangelical Women and Church (Dis)affiliation

Kristin Aune

Those studying religion have only recently begun to attend to differences that complicate gender (Aune 2004: 188–9). Factors including social class, ethnicity, marital status, sexuality and age interact with gender in complex ways, making it inadvisable to consider gender as the sole variable when studying religiosity. This chapter investigates the intersection of marital status, gender and church affiliation amongst single women. Specifically, it addresses the fact that, although women account for the majority of churchgoers (Brierley 2006: 12.3; Woolever *et al.* 2006), being unmarried negatively affects women's religiosity (and men's too). Single women are more likely to attend church because of their gender, but less likely because of their marital status. Contemporary Christian single women's religiosity is an area in which there is almost no existing literature,[1] which makes focusing on them rather than their married counterparts worthwhile. In this chapter 'single' is generally taken to mean 'unmarried'. This is not unproblematic: singleness is usually defined as not being married or in a relationship, but this is complex as what constitutes a 'relationship' is not clear-cut and self-definitions do not always match 'commonsense' categorizations.

Quantitative research on singleness and churchgoing

Unmarried people have lower church participation rates. The International Congregational Life Survey conducted among 1.2 million worshippers in Australia, New Zealand, England and the United States in 2001 found that one-third of worshippers were not married (Bruce *et al.* 2006). The US findings revealed a lower proportion of non-married people attending church than in the general population. While 49.5 per cent of US women were married, this increased to 61.3 per cent of female churchgoers. This disparity is even more apparent among men: married men constitute 52.9 per cent of the population but 72.5 per cent of churchgoers. Churches attract a smaller proportion of never-married, separated and divorced people but a higher proportion of widows (Woolever *et al.* 2006). George Barna's (2003)

---

[1] For an exception see Aune 2002.

telephone surveys across the US in 2000 and 2001 also demonstrate lower rates of private and public religiosity among never married and divorced people.

Canada shows a similarly low religiosity among singles. In 1998 Statistics Canada's General Social Survey interviewed 10,700 adults aged 15 and over living in private households and collected information about frequency of religious attendance. Church attendance is at its lowest for those between their mid teens and late twenties – ages at which marriage rates are lowest. Church attendance is considerably higher amongst the married than the unmarried. At all ages and in all categories women attend more than men. Amongst young married people (aged 15–24), 44 per cent attend religious services regularly (at least once a month) compared to 26 per cent of their non-married counterparts. Within all age groups except 65 and over (where singles actually attended more than married Canadians) married people were more likely to be regular religious attendees. Clark believes this higher attendance among married people is linked to the presence of pro-marriage and family values in religious communities (Clark 2000: 23–4). Results from the 1995 General Social Survey indicate that those who attend religious services weekly consider marriage and parenthood more important than those who never attend, and demonstrate somewhat more commitment to home life than their secular, more job-oriented peers (Clark 1998). He also suggests that those brought up in faith communities tend to marry and have children earlier and to be more likely to attend religious services throughout their lives. Indeed, those without children were less likely than couples with children to attend regularly (27 per cent as opposed to 33 per cent). Unlike Barna, Clark (2000: 23–34) classifies non-married cohabiters separately, demonstrating that cohabiters have the lowest of all rates of attendance, attending only half as often as single or divorced people and a third as often as married people (in the 25–44 age group the rates were 10 per cent for cohabiters, 22 per cent for singles and separated and divorced people and 33 per cent for marrieds); cohabitation may therefore be more significant than non-partnership in predicting non-attendance.

However, the lower religiosity among never marrieds is also a function of youth, which is associated with more liberal attitudes and reduced religious participation. The generational factor is very significant, and the higher rates of churchgoing amongst widowed people owe as much to their age as to their widowed status. Thus marital status should not be studied in isolation from variables like age (Chaves 1991; Stolzenberg *et al.* 1995).

But it is not simply that different marital states differ in religious practice, with married and widowed people more likely to attend church. It is also that there is a strong tie between the traditional family – if traditional is taken in the sense of older, belonging to modernity rather than late or post-modernity – and churchgoing. Quantitative and qualitative empirical research has established this, especially within Protestantism. Furthermore, this tie to the traditional family is not only evident in the greater proportion of traditional family members than non-traditionalists who attend church, but also in the kinds of ideas and ideals promoted by churches (Ammerman and Roof 1995; Marler 1995). US research shows that marrying and having children are factors that encourage adults to return to church. Cohabitation, conversely, decreases the likelihood of church attendance. But the relationship between marriage and churchgoing is not necessarily straightforward or shared by women and men. After divorce, women are more likely than men to return to church, while after a cohabiting relationship ends the reverse occurs (Chaves 1991; Wilson and Sherkat 1994; Stolzenberg *et al.* 1995; Clark 1998).

In the UK, David Voas' (personal communication, 2006) analysis of wards in England and Wales demonstrates an association at area level between marital status and the percentage of men describing themselves as having no religion. Given that this correlation applies to aggregate statistics rather than individuals it does not necessarily mean that the unmarried are more likely not to be religious; however, this is a likely conclusion to draw.

Voas' (2006) quantitative analysis of the Church Life Profile Survey, conducted in 2001 and incorporating responses from nearly 100,000 adults in 2,000 English churches, reveals that the majority of churchgoers are part of a couple. Almost all of these couples are married; cohabitation is rare among churchgoers, even in the younger age groups.[2] 'It is hardly an exaggeration to say that in England individuals do not go to church, couples do', Voas asserts. Of all adults aged 25 and over, 38 per cent of female churchgoers and 18 per cent of male churchgoers are single. This figure is below the proportion of single people in the general population: the 2001 Census found that in 2001 42 per cent of women and 36 per cent of men in that age group were single, taking single to include all those who are not legally married (ONS 2003: 27). When it comes to those attending church in the 35–64 age group, 86 per cent of male churchgoers and 80 per cent of female churchgoers have partners. Moreover, 93 per cent of the wives of these men and 70 per cent of the female churchgoers' husbands also go to church. And while in the older age groups women without partners outnumber those with partners, 'the overwhelming majority of elderly churchgoers now on their own were once married' (Voas 2006). So not only are single people under-represented in church attendance; single men are even more under-represented than single women, an issue deserving further research.

As the nuclear family is being squeezed out from its hegemonic position by diverse family and relational ties church attendance is also declining. The evidence points to a connection between marriage and churchgoing: if one declines, so does the other. As Penny Marler puts it, 'as the family goes, so go the churches' (cited in Ammerman and Roof 1995: 11); her essay in this volume also points to this. This makes this historic link between religion and marriage increasingly problematic for those committed to the future of traditional religion and traditional families. How to retain a focus on marriage and children while appearing inclusive and relevant to those who are not married? In the British context, which is the focus of this chapter, while most people will at some stage marry, marriage is barely now the majority experience.[3]

---

[2]   Cohabitation is highest among younger people. But even in the 25–34 age group, where 23 per cent of men and 21 per cent of women are cohabiting, the figures for churchgoers are much lower, at around eight per cent for both sexes.

[3]   Population estimates for mid 2003 put married men at 53.3 per cent and married women at 50.2 per cent of the UK male and female adult population (ONS 2006).

Singleness as non-normative: an evangelical case study

Several months into my fieldwork among members of an evangelical congregation I gave the pseudonym Westside, I discussed with Jenny, a middle-aged divorcee, her growing unhappiness with the church. Her disquiet appeared to relate to her marginal position within the congregation. She was a confident woman who was generous with her time and resources and participated enthusiastically in church events. But when it came to officially recognized leadership positions she believed she was passed over in favour of those who were younger, married and male. This appeared to be the case, and other members of the congregation sometimes made comments suggesting their preference for young, married men in the allocation of public tasks like leading meetings, running 'house groups'[4] and leading Bible studies. Jenny regularly expressed to me her frustration that Westside and NFI, the larger movement of which Westside was a part, prohibited women from being 'elders' (overall church leaders). Moreover, she considered single and middle-aged women particularly excluded. When I asked why she did not leave and attend a more egalitarian church she replied, 'Maybe I will.' Three years after fieldwork was complete, not only was Jenny no longer attending Westside; she had also lost her faith.

The main elements of Jenny's story recurred in the experiences of most of the single women at Westside. The experiences of the single women in this congregation are worthy of analysis because they are illustrative of core dynamics surrounding single women's lower participation in, and disaffiliation from, conservative Protestant churches. In this chapter I will argue that single women's lower church commitment is connected to, and probably issues from, evangelicalism's construction of women's singleness as a *non-normative* status. Thus unmarried people's lower rates of religiosity outlined in the early part of this chapter are arguably related to the way singleness is dealt with by the churches.

If something is normative it is considered the standard pattern of behaviour; the term carries with it an expectation that particular behaviour ought to occur (Gilbert 2003). But norms are not simply ideas; norms operate through social practices and are difficult to remove from their material context. Norms 'may or may not be explicit, and when they operate as the normalizing principle in social practice, they usually remain implicit' (Butler 2004: 41). Norms are materialized expectations; they are constructions that incorporate both attitudes and action. They are imbued with power: to define what is considered normal and abnormal, to provoke in individuals who fail to adequately embody them a sense of failure. Within evangelicalism, marriage is the norm, singleness the reverse: it is *non-normative*. To construct singleness as non-normative is to act as if it were non-standard, even deviant, behaviour and to generate within single people a sense of insignificance.

The data for this chapter come from fifteen months as a participant observer at the congregation (with twenty-four members by the time research ceased) I called Westside. Westside was part of the New Frontiers International movement (hereafter,

---

[4]   A weekly group consisting of approximately eight to twelve people meeting in someone's home during the evening for worship, prayer and Bible study.

NFI). Additionally, I conducted structured interviews with 20 congregational members and studied NFI's publications and audiotaped sermons from their yearly festival Stoneleigh Bible Week. With 28,000 members in approaching 250 churches in the UK, NFI is the largest surviving network of the House Church or Restorationist movement, now more often called New Churches (Walker 2002). New Churches began in the 1970s as small groups meeting in homes and grew rapidly through the 1980s. Their theological roots lie in the nineteenth-century Brethren movement and Catholic Apostolic Church, and in twentieth-century Classical Pentecostalism. They adhere to mainstream evangelicalism's four interlinked emphases of conversionism, activism, biblicism, and crucicentrism (Bebbington 1989). Like earlier Pentecostalists, NFI see being 'born again' as essential and practise believers' baptism in water and 'of the Holy Spirit' and spiritual gifts such as tongues-speaking, a feature they share with the charismatic movement.

Three features distinguish them from their Pentecostal forerunners. First, they believe denominations should not exist and should be replaced by the Church or 'kingdom'. Second, they aim to 'restore the church' to what they perceive as the New Testament pattern for church life. Men known as apostles, around whom house churches gathered, oversee networks of churches, which are led by elders. The third is the controversial doctrine of discipleship or 'shepherding', in which Christians submit themselves to leaders' guidance and authority (Walker 1998).

For Westside, singleness was highly significant. It was discussed casually on average once or twice per gathering I attended. The higher than average proportion of single women in the congregation probably precipitated this. When I joined Westside there were five single women (and one single man, three married women and three married men). When I departed 15 months later the congregation had doubled and the number of single women had grown to 14 (with four married men, four married women and two single men). Apart from the divorced middle-aged Jenny, none of the 14 had ever married and, to the best of my knowledge, only two were in dating relationships (with men). Although single women were in the majority they remained socially marginalized. Approximately four out of five discussions of, or allusions to, being single presented it mainly negatively, as a situation of waiting for a partner. Women's singleness was constructed as non-normative discursively and materially – if such a distinction may be drawn. This was evident through social interaction, opportunities for public ministry given to single women and interviews with congregational members. This positioning of single women as abnormal, I will suggest, ultimately led to their disengagement from the church. I will outline how this occurred by looking first at the way single women were encouraged, despite the lack of suitable men, to find a Christian husband. Discussion will subsequently move to data from interviews with Westside members about the relative merits of being single and married. Next, consideration will be given to how ministry opportunities are impacted by women's singleness. Finally, the relationship between single women's greater egalitarianism and lower religiosity will be discussed.

The 'problem' of singleness: constructing the need for a husband

Participants often discussed Westside's lack of men. The gender imbalance was judged problematic, and members regularly debated what could be done to increase male membership. It became clear that a key reason why they regretted the lack of men is that lack of men renders their women unable to marry. The following conversation at an evening house group about Westside's lack of men turned to single women's 'need' for partners:

> Chris: Lots of couples meet each other at Stoneleigh.
> Emma: I never have and I always hang round other people's tents.
> [Someone suggests a trip to 'Northside' (pseudonym), an NFI church in another city attended by friends of Chris, Sarah and Rachel, who spend several minutes considering which men in that church are still single.]
> Chris: So you want to pair Emma off with all the second class Northside men?...We should give an announcement "Come and join the Westside church plant – there are some single women there"...
> ?:   Emma, do you want an artist?[5]
> Emma: No. Definitely not. I want someone with money.
> Jenny: Emma, what were we saying about materialism earlier!
> Chris: What about Alec? He's loaded.
> Sarah: But he's not really on fire for God...
> Rachel: You'd better hurry up, Emma. All the best men from Northside are taken.
> Jenny: You shouldn't be so fussy, Emma, I told you
> ?:   In Northside everyone gets married really quickly.
> Chris: When you've been going out six months people start asking you if you're getting married.

Emma becomes the focus of group concern as she personalizes Chris's comment by admitting her desire, and failure, to meet a partner at Stoneleigh. Emma's openness is not unusual – during my time with them several of the single women talked publicly about wanting to marry. In this incident single and married people construct singleness as desire for marriage and something to escape. Marriage normally occurs at a young age and 'really quickly'. Although discernment is needed to ensure women marry men who are financially and spiritually successful, these concerns are secondary to the women's need to find husbands. While those around Emma exhibit benevolent concern for her undesired singleness, their sympathy turns to impatience; those who are married (in Jenny's case, divorced) chide: 'You'd better hurry up,' and 'you shouldn't be so fussy.'

The lack of suitable male marriage partners is rarely considered a structural factor beyond women's capacity to solve. Instead, the 'problem' is individualized (Beck and Beck-Gernsheim 2001); it is thrown back on the women, who are made to feel individually responsible for finding a husband and individual failures if they do not. Jenny often asked the younger women if they had 'met anyone yet'. Sometimes she and several married people considered aloud whether they knew any suitable men. Implicit within this is the assumption that single women want or need partners. This attitude was articulated at a service at the church some Westside members attended

---

5   Emma enjoys painting.

before Westside began Sunday services. Before the sermon, the preacher announced the weekly financial offering. He joked:

> While the offering's still going round, let me say there's also a special two-for-one offer for any couples. Everyone has to put five pounds in, and if you're a couple you only need to put in £2.50 each. And if you're single and are going to ask someone out this afternoon – do you hear that you singles at the back? – we'll give you £10. OK? [Congregation laughs].

While this congregation was somewhat more gender balanced than Westside, making 'coupling up' easier, single women still outnumbered single men. This statement positions single people as outside the main body of the congregation, perhaps infantilizing them as rebellious onlookers.

Lack of men in the church renders women unable to marry because of NFI's practice of homogamy (marriage within the faith). This evangelical requirement is particularly problematic in a context where women so significantly outnumber men. The gender imbalance within evangelical churches, prohibitions against pre-marital sex and the practice of homogamy have not only brought female singleness sharply into focus; they have also drastically reduced women's likelihood of finding partners they or NFI consider suitable. NFI's encouragement to marry cannot be fulfilled for many single women. By remaining in church, single women remain subject to this non-normative construction of their singleness. Single women must either leave or concede to their second-class status. The non-normative construction of singleness is, I suggest, a major factor in single women's lower church attendance and disaffiliation.

Interview responses – the relative merits of singleness and marriage

In my interviews with Westside members I asked the question 'Which (if either) do you think has greater advantages, being married or being single? What do you think these advantages are?' Seven out of the 20 considered marriage more advantageous, 11 did not state a preference and two favoured singleness. Chris, Westside's leader, began by answering that singleness was the theologically preferable state but moved on to demonstrate his perception of singleness as non-normative. His response is important because of his influence as leader; it also reveals some of the dynamics at work in interviews with other Westside members.

> I think, my understanding is that that's a biblical principle, you know, it is better, it's Paul isn't it, that says it's better to be single um so um, so I think it probably is. But then having said that I think it's really good, it's just fun – it's great to be married um, and I think it's a natural thing and I think, you know, you'd expect for most people to get married in the end. So I think my advice to people would be to really make use of their single years and really enjoy them, not spend the whole time hankering after a partner. And someone once said to me that if you get two people and they're looking up to Jesus, then one day they'll bump into each other, and I think that's quite a good principle. [...] I guess it gets to the point when you're in your thirties where to do some practical things to meet some some, er, people from the opposite sex is a good thing and I think sometimes in churches people,

um, people aren't practical enough in terms of meeting potential boyfriends or girlfriends and I think we could get a bit smarter in the church to introduce, you know, people to each other, if we believe that it's right for, for Christians to go out with Christians ... So my understanding is biblically it's better to be single but you know, great to be married and feel like it's a, I think it's a really natural thing for people to go on and be married and it's right and all that kind of thing, so, so er that's biblical, you know, that's my feeling.[6]

Chris' juxtaposition of the 'biblical principle' elevating singleness and his own preference or 'feeling' for marriage as 'really good', 'natural' and 'fun' is revealing. Singleness is constructed as a potential calling, but it is an unusual one ('you'd expect for most people to get married in the end'). His 'advice' that single people should 'really make use of their single years' positions singleness as a transitional period in one's twenties before a partner arrives. Chris does not envisage long-term singleness, for when people reach their thirties he advises that they 'do some practical things to meet some…people from the opposite sex' and says that churches should do more to facilitate this.

Singleness and ministry opportunities

Evangelical communities preach a theology of the giftedness of all Christians. Each Christian is part of the 'body of Christ' and has a distinctive contribution to make. These gifts are commonly formalized into roles such as 'house group leader', 'worship leader' (music leader) or 'elder' or tasks like preaching, prophesying or leading a meeting. These roles do not always seem to be allocated according to the principle of equal giftedness.

Westside use single women as worship leaders and house group leaders and to conduct teaching within group settings. Jenny was appointed the church's 'prayer director'. At the beginning of my fieldwork, the core leadership team comprised the three married couples and one single woman. Towards the end of the fieldwork period they appointed another single woman, Marion, to oversee the house groups. Being single appeared to present no absolute barriers to ministry, other than those present by virtue of femaleness (women are not allowed to preach formally to mixed groups or become elders). During one house group, Alison said that her former NFI church's restriction of lower-level female leadership roles to married women had initially put her off Christianity. Simon and Sarah immediately reassured her that 'that's not the case here'.

Although Westside claim no ideological barriers, some single women believe that certain of Westside's leaders' attitudes discourage them from fully employing single women's talents. While single women constitute the majority of Westside members, they are not proportionally represented in leadership roles. Several Westside

---

[6]   I transcribed each interview word-for-word, including hesitations and features such as laughter. In re-presenting their words, I did not 'tidy up' participants' speech. Mindful of stereotypical notions of evangelical Christians as dogmatists who confidently recite well-learned ideological scripts, making hesitations visibly refutes such stereotypes. Chris, surprisingly, given his public role as leader, spoke particularly hesitantly.

members questioned why Jenny was not on the mixed-gender wider leadership team that existed during my first year of research. She had come to the city shortly after Chris and Sarah to start the church. Until Harry and Ann arrived she was the oldest member of Westside by twenty years and had been a Christian for some time. Jenny told me she felt 'older single women are invisible' in the New Churches. Other NFI churches she had attended ignored her, and she felt 'marginalized'. A conversation with Jenny concerning the publication of my book on single women's place in evangelicalism (Aune 2002) exposed these concerns:

> Jenny: What's your main argument?
> KA: That single women aren't treated very well and aren't given equal roles to married women.
> Jenny: Middle-aged women are just used in supportive roles, although there's so many of them.
> KA: Like babysitting?
> Jenny: Babysitting and cooking.
> KA: But in this group you're prayer director. That's a role.
> Jenny: But it's patronizing. It was done to patronize me. I told Chris that. It's because they don't want me to lead a group.
> KA: Because you're single?
> Jenny: Because they only want couples and I'm a single middle-aged woman.

Jenny's ambiguous position provided the greatest evidence that single women were marginalized. Another time Jenny told me that Chris had said she could lead a house group if she recruited attendees from outside Westside.[7] One evening, Chris announced that Simon and Rachel, a married couple, would take over leading a house group. Endorsing them as sharing his values he added: 'when we've got some more strong Christian couples they can lead groups'. Objecting to Chris singling out married people as leaders, Simon said quietly, 'they don't have to be couples', to which Jenny added, 'and they don't have to be young'. Chris challenged neither interpolation.

Whether ministerial marginality leads to disaffiliation is not yet clear. Some have cited this as a precipitant of church leaving (Miles 1994; Wraight 2001: 63–67), but there is also evidence that women tolerate ministerial marginality in order to preserve their friendships within their congregations (Ozorak 1996; Francis *et al.* 2005: 68–69). Where social and ministerial marginality combine, single women are particularly likely to disaffiliate, as data collected for my (2002) questionnaire study of nearly 100 evangelical single women suggest. But if Westside is not anomalous, it is likely that singleness makes women more inclined than married women to disaffiliate. A further explanation for this relates to single women's greater egalitarianism and the connection between egalitarianism and non-religiosity.

---

[7]   This is not the usual method of starting house groups. Normally, following 'cell church' ideology, when a growing group reaches 14–16 members it splits into two groups and an extra leader is appointed.

Single women, egalitarianism and religiosity

Studies have noted the negative correlation between feminism or egalitarianism and religiosity (Feltey and Poloma 1991; Gesch 1995). Those with gender conservative views are more likely to be religious, while those with egalitarian views are less likely to be. Findings from Westside moreover suggest that it is single women who are most likely to hold feminist views. Of the four status groups (single women, single men, married women and married men), single women were the most likely to assert that there should be no difference between male and female roles in society, marriage, family or church. They were more likely to favour allocating church roles according to ability rather than gender. They were also less inclined to believe that there should be a definable difference between Christian ideals of masculinity and femininity.[8] While the responses of the other three status groups tended towards the gender-differentiated end of the spectrum, the egalitarian attitudes of single women were strikingly different. Single women were also more willing to challenge what they perceived as sexist attitudes and practices.

Whether this makes single women more secular than married women is a difficult question. Advocating equal rights does not necessarily make someone secular. In the US congregation Becker (1999: 127–130, 177–178) observed, the 'liberal' stance on gender equality espoused by some members derived not from societal norms but from evangelical feminist hermeneutics. Westside single women saw their egalitarian motivations as spiritual. They wanted to 'follow the Holy Spirit', as one put it, rather than depending on hierarchical methods derived from the secular marketplace.

Single women and disaffiliation

By the time I left Westside, Jenny had finally been given permission to lead a group when she recruited some local non-churchgoers who had expressed interest in a Bible study group. Because no men were interested in joining, this group consisted only of women, a situation Jane, a married woman who led a group with her husband Mark, described to me in her interview as 'not healthy' and 'not fun'. But a few months later, perhaps regarding Jenny as threatening, Westside's leaders gave leadership of her women-only group to the older married couple, Harry and Ann, and a younger single woman. Shortly after this Jenny left, initially to move to another part of the country, but ultimately to cease attending church. Several years later, Jenny had lost her faith. As my research was officially over I did not attempt to interview her about how or why this had occurred.

When I returned to Westside two and a half years after leaving it, my biggest surprise was discovering that only three of the 14 single women who had been members in the latter part of my fieldwork remained. Two of these, Ruth and Karen, were no longer single, having married men who now belonged to the church. Most of the other 11 had moved to other towns or churches (in two cases, other countries).

---

8   Because only two single men took part in the interviewing, it is not possible to generalize about single male attitudes. These two men were less egalitarian than single women, but slightly less conservative than married people.

Several had left to attend larger, non-NFI churches in search of eligible single men. Marion and Emma, long-term NFI members who as much as women were able had held valuable leadership roles, had considered finding a husband a greater priority than remaining at NFI. Several had married or formed relationships with men who were from other churches or were not Christians. Their departure, I believe, demonstrates the consequences of constructing singleness as a non-normative status. Single women are, it seems, voting with their feet, responding to their marginalization by departing.

Conclusion

The construction of singleness as non-normative has historical origin and contemporary resonance in nonreligious environments. Dominant conceptions of singlehood from at least the nineteenth century position it as marginal, threatening, subversive of 'correct' femininity and, consequently, as a state of waiting to be married (Chandler 1991; Gordon 1994; Vicinus 1985). Treatment of singleness as non-normative is by no means unique to evangelicalism – instead, it may be one that has been adopted from the wider society – though evangelical Protestantism's preference for marriage historically associated with Reformation Christianity (Ruether 2001) probably exacerbated it.

It may even be that the very ordinariness of what these religious believers are doing is what inclines them toward association of marriage with normativity. In one of the last conversations I had with Chris, he explained the congregation's desire to be 'normal people doing normal jobs and living normal lives but also being Christians'. Despite its numerical decline, marriage continues to hold sway as the normative status in contemporary Britain. Singleness (at least if equated with the growth of lone person households) may have increased in prevalence, but it has not necessarily increased in acceptability. The kinds of discussions that occur about singleness in evangelical circles may show greater preference for marriage than is found in non-religious environments, but it is a difference of degree rather than kind. In Christian and secular contexts the 'normal' life is rarely constructed as a single life.

Questions about disaffiliation remain. What precise dynamics occur when single women leave churches? Beyond the overarching factor of the non-normative positioning of female singleness, evidence from Westside and my 2002 research suggests a variety of reasons for departure. Are they, like Westside's Marion, leaving to find Christian partners in other churches? Are they, like Emma, leaving to find partners who do not share their faith? Or are they, like Annie, a single mother who had been at Westside only a short time, leaving to cohabit with male partners? Are they leaving, as Lara did, to marry their boyfriends and attend a different church? Do they leave to take up non-heterosexual relationships, or to stay single in environments that are more accepting of long-term singleness? Are they departing because of loss of faith when they fail to find the husband they desire? Or, like Alison, Dawn and Imogen, are they simply moving location because of a change of job and planning to join another evangelical community?

Within Westside and evangelicalism generally the paradox highlighted by essays within this book occurs: women are more numerous than men but are turning their backs on church. I have shown that marital or partnership status has a bearing on the kind of women who stay and the kind of women who leave: single women have greater secularizing tendencies than married women. Yet the diversity of single positions complicates this further, for different categories of single women (widowed, divorced, separated, never-married and cohabiting) have different relationships with the church. Moreover, the religiosity of single women is related to differences such as ethnicity, class, sexuality and age.

In a culture where feminist reform of religion has not been as significant as might be necessary to retain egalitarian women's commitment, it may be that feminist women are finding it harder to remain religiously orthodox. Single women are challenging their congregations on issues of equality and, if they dislike the outcome, may leave. And without churchgoing partners the decision to leave is easier to carry out; as Voas (2006) points out, most married people attending church attend the same church together, which means ceasing attending would probably become a decision to be made by both partners. Furthermore, with a lower level of practical responsibility for running church activities disentangling oneself from the church community could occur more easily and quickly for a single woman.

The non-affiliation or disaffiliation of singles with religion becomes more significant when future trends in family forms and personal relationships are considered. For it is the groups, such as the single, that show the least religiosity whose proportion amongst the UK population is increasing. Secularization is related to changes in the make-up of households, families and relationships. The family forms of the future look like being those who are the least religious. The religiosity of the single woman, therefore, is far more significant than many congregations realize.

Acknowledgements

I would like to thank David Voas for his helpful comments on a draft of this chapter.

References

Ammerman, Nancy Tatom and Roof, Wade Clark, 'Introduction: Old Patterns, New Trends, Fragile Experiments', in Nancy Tatom Ammerman and Wade Clark Roof (eds), *Work, Family, and Religion in Contemporary Society* (New York: Routledge, 1995).

Aune, Kristin, *Single Women: Challenge to the Church?* (Carlisle: Paternoster, 2002).

Aune, Kristin, 'The Significance of Gender for Congregational Studies', in Mathew Guest, Karin Tusting and Linda Woodhead (eds), *Congregational Studies in the UK: Christianity in a Post-Christian Context* (Aldershot: Ashgate, 2004).

Barna, George, *Single Focus: Understanding Single Adults* (Ventura, CA: Gospel Light, 2003).

Bebbington, D.W., *Evangelicalism in Modern Britain: A History from the 1730s to the 1980s* (London: Unwin Hyman, 1989).

Beck, Ulrich and Beck-Gernsheim, Elisabeth, *Individualization: Institutionalized Individualism and its Social and Political Consequences* (London: Sage, 2001).

Becker, Penny Edgell, *Congregations in Conflict: Cultural Models of Local Religious Life* (New York: Cambridge University Press, 1999).

Brierley, Peter, *UKCH Religious Trends No. 6 2006/7* (London: Christian Research, 2006).

Bruce, Deborah A., Sterland, Samuel J.R., Brookes, Norman E. and Escott, Phillip, 'An International Survey of Congregations and Worshipers: Methodology and Basic Comparisons', *Journal of Beliefs and Values*, 27(1) (2006): 3–12.

Butler, Judith, 'Gender Regulations', in *Undoing Gender* (New York: Routledge, 2004).

Chandler, Joan, *Women Without Husbands: An Exploration of the Margins of Marriage* (Basingstoke: Macmillan, 1991).

Chaves, Mark, 'Family Structure and Protestant Church Attendance: The Sociological Basis of Cohort and Age Effects', *Journal for the Scientific Study of Religion*, 30(4) (1991): 501–514.

Clark, Warren, 'Religious Observance, Marriage and Family', *Canadian Social Trends*, Autumn (1998): 2–7.

Clark, Warren, 'Patterns of Religious Attendance', *Canadian Social Trends*, Winter (2000): 23–27.

Feltey, Kathryn and Poloma, Margaret, 'From Sex differences to Gender Role Beliefs', *Sex Roles*, 25 (1991): 181–183.

Francis, Leslie, Robbins, Mandy and Astley, Jeff, *Fragmented Faith? Exposing the Fault-lines in the Church of England* (Milton Keynes: Paternoster, 2005).

Gesch, Lyn, 'Responses to Changing Lifestyles: "Feminists" and "Traditionalists" in Mainstream Religion', in Nancy Tatom Ammerman and Wade Clark Roof (eds), *Work, Family, and Religion in Contemporary Society* (New York: Routledge, 1995).

Gilbert, Margaret, 'Norms', in William Outhwaite, (ed.), *The Blackwell Dictionary of Modern Social Thought*, 2nd edn (Oxford: Blackwell, 2003).

Gordon, Tuula, *Single Women: On the Margins?* (Basingstoke: MacMillan, 1994).

Marler, Penny Long, 'Lost in the Fifties: The Changing Family and the Nostalgic Church', in Nancy Tatom Ammerman and Wade Clark Roof (eds), *Work, Family, and Religion in Contemporary Society* (New York: Routledge, 1995).

Office for National Statistics (ONS), *Census 2001 National Report for England and Wales* (London: The Stationery Office, 2003).

Office for National Statistics, 'Mid-2003 Marital Status Population Estimates: England and Wales; estimated resident population by single year of age and sex', 2006 www.statistics.gov.uk/STATBASE/ssdataset.asp?vlnk=8631 Accessed 14 February 2006.

Ozorak, Elizabeth Weiss, 'The Power but not the Glory: How Women Empower themselves through Religion', *Journal for the Scientific Study of Religion*, 35(1) (1996): 17–29.

Ruether, Rosemary Radford, *Christianity and the Making of the Modern Family* (London: SCM, 2001).

Stolzenberg, Ross M., Blair-Loy, Mary and Waite, Linda J., 'Religious Participation in Early Adulthood: Age and Family Life Cycle Effects on Church Membership', *American Sociological Review*, 60(1) (1995): 84–103.

Vicinus, Martha, *Independent Women: Work and Community for Single Women 1850–1920* (London: Virago, 1985).

Voas, David, 'The Inter-generational Transmission of Churchgoing', unpublished working paper, 2006.

Walker, Andrew, *Restoring the Kingdom: The Radical Christianity of the House Church Movement*, 4th edn (Guildford: Eagle, 1998).

Walker, Andrew, 'Crossing the Restorationist Rubicon: From House Church to New Church', in Martyn Percy and Ian Jones (eds), *Fundamentalism, Church and Society* (London: SPCK, 2002).

Wilson, John and Sherkat, Darren E., 'Returning to the Fold', *Journal for the Scientific Study of Religion*, 33(2) (1994): 148–161.

Woolever, Cynthia, Bruce, Deborah, Wulff, Keith and Smith-Williams, Ida, 'The Gender Ratio in the Pews: Consequences for Congregational Vitality', *Journal of Beliefs and Values*, 27(1) (2006): 25–38.

Wraight, Heather, *Eve's Glue: The Role Women Play in Holding the Church Together* (Carlisle: Paternoster, 2001).

Chapter 3

When Young Women Say 'Yes': Exploring the Sexual Selves of Young Canadian Women in Protestant Churches

Sonya Sharma

Introduction

> I cannot say that the 'good girl' died the moment I had sex… Being a good Christian girl was so entrenched in my sexual experiences that I could not surrender to the sexual experiences I was having. To express the love that I felt for one guy, it was squashed because of the sins that I was afraid to commit… when I eventually decided to have sex I was embarrassed that I had not… (Anita age 28, Baptist, left the church)[1]

What happens when a young woman's identities as a Christian and as an embodied sexual woman collide? This chapter considers the impact of the membership of Protestant church communities on young women's sexual selves. It argues that a conflict between Christian and sexual identities contributes to women leaving the church and moving towards other forms of spiritual practice that resonate with their evolvement as women and with their sense of themselves as sexual beings.

Growing up in Canada, I attended church every Sunday with my family, but not until adolescence did my Christian faith take shape. It did so amongst a group of Christian female friends with whom I went to youth group and spent summers at an evangelical Christian camp. Amongst my friends at church the message about sex was clear: our youth leaders, both men and women, preached and taught that sex is only for heterosexual marriage. Throughout the years and into our early twenties conversations about sex remained shrouded, even though we knew some of us had done 'it'. It was evident, however, that the social and cultural contexts, including the church, affected how we dealt with matters related to sex. Some Christian female friends expressed satisfaction with being sexual whilst a Christian. Others expressed conflict and misgivings. Many believed that 'traditional marriage converts bodily sex into something spiritual' and anything outside of this was perceived as sinful or ungodly (Moon 2004: 156). This investigation into the sexual selves of young women who have been members of Protestant church communities focuses on the powerful message Protestant church culture gives about sex and sexuality; the shame and guilt embodied in young women's experiences of sex because of

---

[1]   All participants' names are pseudonyms. (Name, age, church affiliation between 18–25, and current church status).

concepts like sin; and young women's negotiations of sexual experiences, given that they live in cultures that simultaneously normalize and encourage sexual exploration and permissiveness.

The women in this research

This research focuses primarily on the age period of 18–25 with participants who are both within this age group and who are reflecting back on this time. I gathered women beyond the 18–25 year-old period because I wanted to know if their church involvement during these ages church affected their later sexual experiences. I focus on this particular age period because it is around the ages of 18 to 25 that young women are developing themselves in a variety of ways. This time often involves a transition into independent adulthood: completing high school, moving away from home, entering higher education, travelling, obtaining employment, developing and assessing their voices in new situations and relationships and discovering their sexual self (Clark 2000: 23). By 'sexual self', I also mean sexual identity and sexual behaviour, experiences and desires. In the research discussed here, I examine how the culture of a Conservative or Mainline Protestant church impacts the sexual selves of young women not only during their transition into adulthood and independence, but also beyond.[2] I utilize the term 'culture' in my description of Conservative and Mainline Protestant churches because the context of church communities not only includes Sunday services, but also Bible study groups, youth groups, ministry organizations and Christian educational settings along with traditional and contemporary forms of Christian-focused literature, popular magazines, music, and television and radio programmes.

This investigation is based on 36 qualitative interviews. Participants in this research are from mainly middle-class backgrounds, white, heterosexual and British. Not all participants identify as heterosexual or white and not all participants are of British origin. Throughout this chapter, the focus will be on the small sample of Canadian participants (six) who took part in this study. These women are mostly from Conservative Protestant backgrounds, meaning they have spent all or a large portion of their time during the age periods of 18–25 in a Baptist or Alliance church (four out of six). The others attended Mainline Protestant churches such as Anglican or the United Church of Canada during this time (two out of six). Interviews with the women were semi-structured and conversational in style. Questions were open-ended, and divided into four sections: level of church involvement; the church's impact while growing up; the church communities' impact on issues of sex, and how church involvement impacted their voice as a young woman. The categories 'attends church', 'left the church', and 'in between finding a church' indicate their current church status. From here I look at how these young women's church status coincides with the process of secularization in Canada.

---

[2]   By Conservative and Mainline Protestant, I follow Canadian sociologist Reginald Bibby's (2002: 37) groupings. Bibby includes amongst Conservative Protestants: Baptists, Pentecostals, Mennonites, Alliance and Nazarenes and amongst Mainline Protestants: United Church of Canada, Anglicans, Lutherans and Presbyterians.

Canada and secularization

The notion that Canada is a secular society is a debatable issue. Although it is often placed in between the religious trajectories of the USA and Europe/UK (Brown 2001; Martin 2005), Reginald Bibby argues that his statistical findings 'point to a religious and spiritual renaissance in Canada – new life being added to old life, sometimes within religious groups but often outside them' (2002: 4). The process of secularization may have significantly reduced the influence of Catholic and Protestant groups in Canada (Bibby 2000: 239), but 'Canadians continue to be deeply spiritual. In [Bibby's] latest survey, '81 per cent of respondents attested to a belief in God, including 55 per cent of those who never attend religious services' (Bibby 2000 in Bergman 2002: 2).

Furthermore, the declining interest in traditional church communities that my Canadian participants demonstrate from the age of 18 mirrors the findings of Bibby and Statistics Canada's General Social Survey. According to the Canada's General Social Survey (GSS) in 1988, 34 per cent of people aged 15 to 24 were regular church attendees. By 1998, the attendance rate – for the group of people whom had now reached the ages between 25 and 34 – had dropped to 24 per cent (Clark 2000: 23). Amongst my own Canadian participants, four out of six participants attended church regularly in 1988 with the degree of attendance remaining the same in 1998. However by 2001, only two interviewees attended church regularly, confirming the GSS findings that 'those aged 25–34 have the lowest church attendance in Canada' (Clark 2003: 3). Participants' church attendance remained the same in 2004, when the interviews took place. Significantly, those who no longer take part in traditional church communities continue to have spiritual needs (Bibby 2002: 200). Participants who no longer attend church have gone on to find and express their spirituality in Buddhism and/or holistic spiritualities including therapeutic and social activism communities, confirming Bibby's (2002) findings that Canadians are spiritual but not necessarily practicing their spirituality within traditional religious groups.

The questions that introduce this edited volume, if women undergird the foundations of traditional religious groups, what causes them to leave? What do they end up doing? Where do they have their spiritual needs met and why? These are illuminated by Bibby's research that asserts that although Canadians leave the churches, they remain affiliated with church communities through identification [to Protestant and Catholic denominations] because of tradition (2000: 239) and eventually become non-attendees because churches are not aware of individual needs nor of the array of relational issues people are confronting (2002: 238). The success of the churches in retaining their membership boils down to a question succinctly articulated by Bibby: 'Beyond platitudes and ideals, what do churches *really* have to offer?' (2002: 238). What church attendance offers to young women amid their growing identities as Christians and sexual women is the question I turn to next.

Sex is only for marriage

Although each denomination is unique in how they carry out the Christian faith, one commonality amongst Conservative and Mainline Protestant denominations is the ideal that sex should take place only within the context of marriage and between a man and a woman.[3] The General Social Survey's finding that there is a positive association between religious participation and traditional attitudes about family formation may be one reason why this ideal is sustained in church culture (Clark 2000: 23). Church attendance is significantly higher for those who are married and have children (Clark 2000: 23) and 'men and women who attend church regularly placed greater importance on lasting relationships, being married, and having at least one child than those who did not attend' (Clark 1998: 4). These men and women were also more supportive of women's traditional feminine roles (Clark 1998: 4). A culture that strongly supports marital and family values and traditional gender roles can lead to the message that sex is only for marriage being given greater weight; women's sexuality is confined to marriage and thus in effect the 'sex is for marriage' message of the churches can be seen to enforce and enable patriarchal control over women's selves and bodies. Marriage in church culture is usually accorded greater status, and sex within this context is deemed sanctified compared to non-marital sex. Yet for Canadian women marriage is something that they are committing to later in life, which means that church culture's message for sex is not always relevant or easy to uphold. For instance, 52 per cent of women between the ages of 20–24 in Canada live at home with their parents, while the proportion of women in this age group getting married has dropped from 46 per cent in 1996 to 26 per cent in 2001 (Canadian Census 2001). Confining sexuality to heterosexual marriage is not an ideal that many people easily live out especially during a time of personal development and life change amidst mainstream cultures that offer a multitude of conflicting ideas around sex and sexuality.

Shame and guilt, and being 'a good Christian girl'

All of the interviewees discussed being taught that sex is only for marriage in youth and young adult groups during adolescence and their early twenties. Despite this message, all participants had sexual experiences, some including sexual intercourse. Only one woman waited until marriage to have sexual intercourse.[4] A main theme that emerged for five out of the six Canadian women interviewed were the feelings of shame and guilt in relation to their early sexual experiences. It is important to

---

[3]   In recent years marriage as that which only takes place between a man and a woman has been debated amongst Mainline Protestant Church denominations specifically the Anglican Church of Canada, which has experienced conflict amongst its dioceses on the issue of blessing same-sex unions.

[4]   In this chapter, I am referring to participants' definition of sexual intercourse as the penetration of a woman by a man. Refraining from this act along with other genital and non-genital sexual activity is what I mean by remaining chaste. While there is much written on the theology of celibacy this is not the focus here.

understand these feelings as shaped by social and cultural norms and values, by social conventions, and the expectations of others.[5] What makes this theme interesting in terms of the women interviewed in this research is the way in which the close relationships and sense of belonging forged through church communities can *also* perpetuate and enforce feelings of guilt and shame in relation to one's identity as a young, sexual being living simultaneously in secular cultures that normalize sex and sexuality as integral to youth. The messages that young women receive are conflictual to say the least. Like the young woman quoted in the beginning of this chapter, they are torn between the imperative of remaining sexually abstinent, and non-church peer pressure that often encourages sexual experimentation. Not only this but the aspects frequently most valued about church membership – friendship and belonging – can induce the most painful feelings of guilt and shame in relation to sex and sexuality.

Interviewees who discussed shame and guilt while involved in a church community made no distinction between these feelings even though shame and guilt can be seen to have different meanings. Shame emerges from the negative evaluation of the self, while guilt is associated with the evaluation of wrongful behaviour (Lewis 1971; Bradshaw 1988; Crawford *et al.* 1992; Dryden 1994).[6] Shame and guilt expressed by participants in this chapter are also gendered in that they relate to not living up to conventional femininity, particularly a Christian femininity that emphasizes remaining chaste until marriage. Women experienced shame and guilt when they did not experience themselves as being a 'good Christian girl', someone who follows the 'rules', who remains sexually 'abstinent' (Beth age 34, Baptist, left the church). Conforming to gendered ideals is another theme that runs through the stories of these women especially for those who went against their church's morals for sex. Here, 'good' or 'bad' act as powerful normative values that deeply impact young women's growing identities. 'Good' and 'bad' are categories that discipline sexuality, especially women's sexuality, keeping it under patriarchal control.

In the dark: teachings about sex in church communities

To begin to understand the young women's experiences of sex while in church community, I asked them what their church had taught them about sex. The main teaching participants received about sex from their churches was that sex should be confined to a heterosexual marriage. All participants said that they had received teaching on matters of sex during youth and young adult groups, but it was rare that they heard a sermon on sex preached at a Sunday morning service. I asked women

---

[5]   The emotions my participants experience in church community are socially shaped. 'Emotion is viewed as an intersubjective rather than an individual phenomenon, constituted in the relations between people (Lupton 1998: 16). Emotions also communicate commitment to one another and to one's cultural values (Crawford et al. 1992: 36).

[6]   Helen B. Lewis, researcher on shame and guilt, helps to clearly differentiate shame from guilt: 'The experience of shame is directly about the self, which is the focus of evaluation. In guilt, the self is not the central object of negative evaluation, but rather the thing done or undone is in focus' (Lewis 1971 in Helm Jr., Berecz and Nelson 2001: 27).

to reflect on what they had been taught about sex whilst attending church during the age period of 18–25. These are some of their responses:

> Beth: That it is okay at the right time, in the right context…
> Interviewer: That being marriage?
> Beth: Yeah, and other than that: No! No! No! (Beth age 34, Baptist, left the church)

> My Christian identity dictates how I act as a woman or as a person, like I won't have sex before marriage. (Mina age 24, Alliance, attends church)

Participants from both Baptist and Alliance church denominations demonstrated similarities in their views on sex, while a participant from the United Church of Canada discussed a youth group experience that was more open to talking about issues on sexuality:

> When I was growing up… not much about sex, nothing about lesbians at all…but when I was around 18, I was part of the youth group there and there was a discussion about sexuality and the guy that was leading that group was really progressive and he brought books about sexuality and wanted us to talk about it, I thought it was an openness… (Simone age 38, United Church, left the church)

This difference between participants' church contexts and between community attitudes to sex and sexuality raises an important point that feminist theorist Stevi Jackson identifies:

> How we make sense of sexual experience depends on the discourses, narratives, scripts available to us, and it is through these interpretative processes that we link our experience and practice. The way we narratively construct our experience will depend on our location within our society and culture. (1996: 33)

The discourses presented to interviewees as a result of their location within church communities contributes to how they interpreted and experienced sexual activity during the age period of 18–25. For example for Kimberly:

> Sex was just mixed with so much shame and guilt that it meant that I was a bad Christian… I think because my early sexual learning was so shrouded with shame my sexual self didn't get to grow. It was kind of like a plant that was put in a closet and kept in the dark. (Age 34, Baptist, attends church)

Emotions like shame and guilt contribute to how young women in church communities conduct their sexual selves. Departure from religious scripts that contain the standards of holiness and righteous behaviour including how to dress, walk and behave can cause feelings of great shame and guilt (Bradshaw 1988: 66). While most of the young women in this chapter have not lived out the ideal their church has had for sex, they have lived with this ideal in mind due to their guilt and shame about sexual events. The grip of the values around 'good' and 'bad' femininity reaches deep into the embodied identities of the women interviewed in this research.[7]

Embodiment of shame and guilt

For young women in this chapter, shame and guilt are embodied emotions; these feelings are internalized and lived out in young women's bodies, especially when they behave contrary to the notions of a Christian femininity that are inscribed on the bodies of young women in church community. A well-managed body in church community is in control of sexual desires and experiences and presents itself as feminine, through, for example, appropriate dress. Shame and guilt combine to function as the internal compass for how young women present themselves and live out sexual experiences whilst involved in church culture. Beth shares her account of sexual events at the time she was involved in a Conservative Protestant church:

> At church it was 'no sex before marriage' and you know… I was having sex at that time. I was in a relationship, but there was this guilt, you didn't talk about it, you didn't really talk about it with your closest friends because you weren't supposed to do it. So, where is the joy in that, it was like living a secret! …I never really thought that I'm going to go to hell for doing this. I just thought, I am not a good Christian girl, but in the back of my mind this is ridiculous, who's imposing these rules? Who? You're taught abstinence, you just don't do that and then you think, well, is oral sex okay? Where do you draw the line? But definitely that sense of, 'bad dog, what have you done?!' Sometimes a sense of shame, but never a sense of true peace with it…and I hurt myself over that. I remember with my boyfriend, we were having sex and knowing that we shouldn't be having sex and I physically hurt myself over that. I became a cutter. I cut my own skin with knives, slashed a few places. I think that says a lot…the cutting didn't last for long, you know, a few isolated incidents, but…I was failure, I had failed God in His eyes, you know, bad girl, I was a failure, no will power, not strong enough faith, God wasn't enough in my life. I had to repent. All those big words; sin, repent, you know. It was horrible… I remember going through turmoil, horrible turmoil and praying for forgiveness. I felt I had to do that, to pray and repent to save my soul. It's oppressive. I don't think I had anyone to talk to…somehow I think that my friends knew, but we never really talked about it. (Age 34, Baptist, left the church)

Two ways Beth lives out her embodiment of shame and guilt is keeping sexual activity a secret and cutting herself. Secrecy lived out in church community is one way Beth manages her reputation: 'a girl's reputation is always under threat, not merely if she is known to have had sex…but for a whole range of other behaviour that has little to do with actual sex' (Lees 1989: 20). Beth maintains her reputation as a 'good Christian girl' by keeping her sexual experiences secret and separate from her Christian identity,

---

7   Embodiment also means 'the experiential sense of living in and through our bodies. It is premised on the ability to feel our bodily sensations' such as, sexual desire and experiences (Tolman 2002: 50). Further, sexuality cannot be separated from gendered relations or one's perspectives on and investment in, the norms of femininity found within one's social contexts (Tolman 2002). Social and cultural expectations, arrangements and contexts are lived through the body. The social ways of being in the world, including emotions, are embodied.

which in the end helps her to maintain the connections that are important to her in her church community. Her self-monitoring behaviour that emerges from feelings of shame and guilt is tied to the ways in which patriarchal societies reward the performance of conventional femininity whereas going against conventional norms and the confines of feminine sexualities is penalized. 'Shame involves a recognition of the judgements of others and awareness of social norms: one measures oneself against the standards established by others' (Skeggs 1997: 123). Beth punishes herself for going against the conventional feminine standard her church has for sex by self-harming after sexual events. By cutting herself, Beth disciplines her unruly body and soul. This act helps her to negotiate her conflicting emotions, the belief that she is being a 'bad girl', and the powerful feelings of failure before God. Secrecy is how Beth manages her shame and guilt amongst her church peers, while cutting is a way through which she manages her shame and guilt before God.

Disembodied sexuality

While physical self-harm, such as cutting, may have provided Beth a means of negotiating experiences of guilt and shame, others' strategy for dealing with the conflict between Christian and sexual identities involved disengaging oneself from sexual acts that were taking place. Kimberly employed this strategy in order to deal with her identities as a sexual being and a Christian:

> At that time, I had quite a serious relationship. We went out from the time I graduated highschool to the age of 23. He was involved in the church and so was I. I think the church was the one good thing, the one consistent thing, although just considering that we were sexually active, that was kind of hard to be involved in church knowing that I wasn't making a wise choice in terms of being sexually active…I think about it and have to unlearn some of that shame and some of that kind of disappearing in sex because that might have been some odd attempt on my part to act as if it wasn't happening or I wasn't actually having sex when I darn well was, but if I allow this to happen to me [and] I am much more passive in the process [then] I am not as much of a bad girl. (Age 34, Baptist, attends church)

Kimberly's embodiment of shame and guilt meant she 'disappeared' when she was having sex. She shut her sexual experiences off because she believed that she was being bad. Kimberly became 'passive', meaning she was not fully engaged in receiving and giving sexual pleasure. For Kimberly, disappearing meant that she was detached and disconnected from her sexual desire and experiences, and therefore not fully participating in what church culture deems only appropriate for marriage. She was not giving her entire sexual self to the encounter, but rather reserving what she could for her husband for when she married. Kimberly's physical disconnection from her body speaks of the power of an ideal sexual self that many young women are to aim for while in church, and for Kimberly disappearing helps her to remain a good girl or 'not as much of a bad girl'. Her passivity keeps in place conventional modes of femininity. At the same time she gives enough sexually to hold her male partner, but always with the concern for her reputation (Holland *et al.* 1998: 109).

Kimberly's experience – outlined above – can be described through the concept of 'disembodied sexuality' (Holland *et al*. 1998: 108–109). Disembodied sexuality in the experiences of young women involves the 'sense of detachment from their sensuality and alienation from their material bodies... that produces a passive body and therefore a modest femininity' (Holland *et al*. 1998: 109). Kimberly's disembodied sexuality – 'disappearing in sex', and reasoning that 'if I allow this to happen to me [and] I am much more passive in the process [then] I am not as much of a bad girl' – enables her to negotiate her conflicting Christian and sexual identities.

The embodiment of shame and guilt that is a result of the inscribed Christian femininity on young women's sexual identities can result in young women experiencing disembodied sexuality while involved in church. Holland *et al*. indicate in their research that many non-Christian women also live out this experience of disembodied sexuality (1994, 1998, 2000). As such, the sense of disembodied sexuality is tied to the pressures of a socially constructed femininity that both allures and remains in control in order to be seen as decent (Holland *et al*. 1998: 109). Likewise, the women in this chapter also live these dynamics out, but with the added pressure of their church communities' ideal for sex.

I turn to Anita's experiences of sex while involved in church community to explain further the interaction between one's Christian identity and sexual experiences. Like Kimberly, she also describes a disembodied sexuality during sexual events, something that helped her to negotiate her conflicting identities as a Christian and growing sexual woman. From Anita's interview, I highlight three statements that summarize her struggle. Anita's first statement describes sexual disembodiment when she says, 'Well for instance a guy I dated [when I was 23 and attending church], he touched me and I didn't know what to do' (Age 28, Baptist, left the church). Here, she is not inside the sexual experience or sensations of her material body, but rather detached because of the internalization of her church community's expectations for sex. She demonstrates the conflict of desiring to be sexual, but is not able to because her Christian identity overshadows her sexual self. The power that Anita's Christian identity has over her sexual self is emphasized in her second statement: 'Being a single Christian woman and a sexual being, I think they were separate...being sexual is this thing you have to shut off and shut down' (Age 28, Baptist, left the church). In order to be an acceptable Christian woman she cuts her sexual self off, and subsequently experiences alienation from her body when her male partner attempts to give her sexual pleasure. Her experience of detachment from her body when with her boyfriend is one way that she monitors her reputation as a Christian woman.

The concession Anita makes for her identity as a Christian woman results in her 'not knowing what to do' sexually and her emerging feelings of shame. In the following statement she describes the opportunity to have sex but instead remains 'un-sexual' because of her Christian identity. This ongoing conflict causes her to feel ashamed in two ways. Her shame is felt within the church community because she is neither married nor sexual, and outside of it because she is not sexual in the way that secular cultures promote and normalize. She states:

The boundaries that Christianity puts on sex, I felt very un-sexual and ashamed for not being sexual, in and outside of church… in one opportunity to have sex I didn't because all I could think about was what is [the minister] going to think if I told him? …And this whole idea that if I am not a virgin what will my husband think? (Age 28, Baptist, left the church)

Here, Anita conveys the conflict she faces when wanting to say 'yes' to sexual experiences that the church deems sinful. On the one hand, she desires to have sex in order to be acceptable as mainstream cultures encourage, but on the other how can she be a good Christian girl and have sex? Furthermore, Anita's shame for feeling 'un-sexual' and not having sex is determined by the imagined views of male others that she has internalized. She lives out what feminist philosopher Sandra Bartky explains as 'the panoptical male connoisseur that resides within the consciousness of most women, standing perpetually before his gaze and under his judgement' (1990: 72). Anita embodies how men will view and evaluate her. She projects onto herself and her sexuality how they will appraise her if she is not a virgin. Anita monitors and disciplines her sexual behaviour resulting in the inability to achieve sexual embodiment.

Conclusion

The guilt and shame expressed by young women who have said 'yes' to sexual experiences provide important information about the impact Protestant church communities' ideal for sex can have on young women's sexual selves. In this chapter I have explored participants' feelings of shame and guilt that they experienced and embodied during sexual events and that resulted in them keeping sexual activity a secret. However, the impact of guilt and shame went even further, resulting in self-harming, as well as in disembodied sexuality where women disconnect themselves from sexual events by disappearing in sex or not knowing what to do sexually. By negotiating their conflicting identities as sexual women and as Christians, young women live out the gendered ideal of the 'good Christian girl' in their church communities, an act that enforces the power of Protestant church culture's historical patriarchal construct for sex.

Given the emotions and sexual experiences that have been discussed, for some young women the pressures created by the values perpetuated by their church communities have meant that they have left the church. As one participant said, the inability to fully explore her sexual self without feeling a sense of shame 'is rolled up into the same ball of wax' (Beth age 34, Baptist, left the church) with her decision to leave the community. Other reasons why these women left the church include disappointment about their church community's conservative views on homosexuality: 'When I became a lesbian, I had heard people from my own church saying that homosexuality was bad and I was personally hurt to hear things like that so that made me take a distance from the church' (Simone age 38, United Church, left the church). Although her former church in current times has progressively made steps to include gays and lesbians and bless same-sex unions in Canada, at the age of 18 she felt she could not 'act on her desire' while remaining in her church community. For other women the desire to have sex without feeling 'unworthy' has also been a reason for leaving: 'What is it about church that makes us feel bad and awful, unimportant, not valuable, the emphasis on sin all the time? We are okay. We are worthy!' (Veronica age 48, Anglican, left the church).

Rosie Miles's UK study of why women leave the church found that women leave because they were no longer comfortable trying to live within what they saw as constraints placed on them by the church (Miles 1994 in Wraight 2001: 66). The shame and guilt produced in relation to transgressing a marital-confined sexuality constrains both the sexual embodiment and the ability to discuss sexual experiences with other Christian women for the women interviewed in this research. For some women leaving church meant finally growing into their body that they had felt disengaged from: 'I began to feel more comfortable in my own body after leaving the church' (Anita age 28, Baptist, left the church).

Finally, returning to Bibby's research on Canada and secularization, he demonstrates that Canadians would find it worthwhile to be involved in a religious group if its organizational factors emphasized equality of sexuality and gender, 'recognizing that women are significant' (2002: 224). However, Bibby's data does not offer more on gender-related issues – a factor that could shed more light on Canadians' increasing absence from traditional religious groups. Out of my six Canadian participants, two women remain attending church, while the rest practice other forms of spirituality. Only one woman no longer believes in God. As such, leaving the church cannot be seen to result from the women no longer having a faith or not being spiritual. Rather the reason for leaving lies in what Canadian churches *do not* offer. This is a significant finding of Bibby's that highlights the need to examine more closely how issues of gender and sexuality in traditional church settings affect female attendees and their choice to stay or leave. Women in this chapter who have remained in the church are content to stay. However, those women who have left the church have moved towards other forms of spiritual practice that resonate with their evolvement as women and with their sense of themselves as sexual beings.

Acknowledgments

I would like to thank Eeva Sointu for her valuable feedback whilst writing this chapter.

References

Bartky, Sandra L., *Femininity and Domination: Studies in the Phenomenology of Oppression* (London: Routledge, 1990).

Bergman, Brian, 'Returning to Religion', *MacLean's*, 115(13) (2002): 48.

Bibby, Reginald, *Fragmented Gods* (Toronto: Stoddart, 1990).

Bibby, Reginald, 'Canada's Mythical Religious Mosaic: Some Census Findings', *Journal for the Scientific Study of Religion*, 39(2) (2000): 235–239.

Bibby, Reginald, *Restless Gods: The Renaissance of Religion in Canada* (Toronto: Stoddart, 2002).

Bradshaw, John, *Healing the Shame that Binds You* (Florida: Health Communications, 1988).

Brown, Callum, *The Death of Christian Britain* (London: Routledge, 2001).

Canadian Census (Ottawa: Statistics Canada, 2001).

Clark, Warren, 'Religious Observance: Marriage and Family', *Canadian Social Trends*, Autumn (1998): 2–7.

Clark, Warren, 'Patterns of Religious Attendance', *Canadian Social Trends*, Winter (2000): 23–27.

Clark, Warren, 'Pockets of Belief: Religious Attendance in Canada', *Canadian Social Trends*, Spring (2003): 2–5.

Cline, Sally, *Women, Celibacy and Passion* (London: Optima, 1994).

Crawford, June, Kippax, Susan, Onyx, Jenny, Gault, Una, and Benton, Pam, *Emotion and Gender: Constructing Meaning from Memory* (London: Sage, 1992).

Dryden, Windy, *Overcoming Guilt* (London: Sheldon, 1994).

Helm, Herbert W., Berecz, John M. and Nelson, Emily A., 'Religious Fundamentalism and Gender Differences: Religious Fundamentalism and its Relationship to Guilt and Shame', *Pastoral Psychology*, 5(1) (2001): 27.

Holland, Janet, Ramazanoglu, Caroline, Sharpe, Sue and Thomson, Rachel, 'Power and Desire: The Embodiment of Female Sexuality', *Feminist Review*, 46 Spring (1994): 21–38.

Holland, Janet, Ramazanoglu, Caroline, Sharpe, Sue and Thomson, Rachel, *The Male in the Head: Young People, Heterosexuality and Power* (London: Tufnell, 1998).

Holland, Janet, Ramazanoglu, Caroline, Sharpe, Sue and Thomson, Rachel, 'Deconstructing Virginity – Young People's Accounts of First Sex', *Sexual and Relationship Therapy*, 15(3) (2000): 222–232.

Jackson, Stevi, 'Heterosexuality and Feminist Theory', in Diane Richardson (ed.), *Theorising Heterosexuality* (Buckingham: Open University, 1996).

Lees, Sue, 'Learning to Love: Sexual Reputation, Morality and the Social Control of Girls', in Maureen Cain (ed.), *Growing Up Good: Policing the Behaviour of Girls in Europe* (London: Sage, 1989).

Lewis, Helen B., *Shame and Guilt in Neurosis* (New York: International Universities Press, 1971).

Lupton, Deborah, *The Emotional Self* (London: Sage, 1998).

Martin, David, 'Secularisation and the Future of Christianity', *Journal of Contemporary Religion*, 20(2) (2005): 145–160.

Moon, Dawne, *God, Sex and Politics: Homosexuality and Everyday Theologies* (Chicago: University of Chicago Press, 2004).

Skeggs, Beverley, *Formations of Class and Gender: Becoming Respectable* (London: Sage, 1997).

Tolman, Deborah, *Dilemmas of Desire: Teenage Girls Talk about Sexuality* (Cambridge, MA: Harvard University Press, 2002).

Walter, Tony and Davie, Grace, 'The Religiosity of Women in the Modern West', *British Journal of Sociology*, 49(4) (1998): 640–660.

Wraight, Heather, *Eve's Glue: The Role Women Play in Holding the Church Together* (Carlisle: Paternoster, 2001).

Chapter 4

Vocational Habit(u)s
Catholic Nuns in Contemporary Poland

Marta Trzebiatowska

Introduction

This chapter reveals a number of paradoxes. On the one hand the material demonstrates an overall decline in the number of women's 'vocations' in Poland over the past ten to twelve years. Nevertheless, the numbers remain high compared with other European countries and the United States. The public's attitudes towards nuns range from friendliness to outright verbal hostility. All of the sisters interviewed by the author in 2004 recounted one or more incidents of unpleasant treatment or verbal abuse from the general public and most nuns experienced considerable emotional turmoil when they revealed to their families their intention to join a convent. Their decision was often deemed 'abnormal' and they were accused of throwing their lives (and more importantly their femininity) away. Hence the paradox present in the Polish version of Catholicism in which piety and high church attendance coexist with aggressive criticism of the Catholic Church and its representatives: priests and nuns. The latter regularly encounter prejudice and rejection from strangers and even close family as a result of their choice of life. I do not intend to outline possible reasons for such attitudes here; however some are implicit in the course of this chapter. My aim is to attempt an answer to the question of who exactly are the young women in Poland who decide to become religious sisters despite the number of adversities they face. I base my arguments on data from 35 interviews with Polish nuns in five (habit and habitless) apostolic communities.

This chapter is divided into three main sections. The first briefly outlines the current situation of the Polish convents by combining a variety of historical and statistical data. The second describes the interviewees in terms of age, origins and qualifications. The third section unpacks the data by offering a portrait of the women who join religious communities in contemporary Poland. Three themes are discussed here. Firstly, family background and social circles have a significant impact on women's decisions. This argument is constructed around Pierre Bourdieu's notion of the 'habitus' (1977). Secondly, only women who have developed an appreciation of spiritual goods and are equipped with the appropriate spiritual capital choose a convent. Thirdly, the data is placed within the debate on women's religiosity demonstrating that Polish nuns see it as their duty as women to support the Catholic Church. In their own words, nuns are the 'light cavalry' of the Church (KAI 2005).

Nuns in Poland

The number of women who join religious communities in Poland has remained relatively high over the past decade–despite drastic shifts in the political, economic and cultural spheres, which have occurred since the fall of communism in 1989. Polish orders began in the nineteenth century – before then they had been adopted from other countries. Subsequently, numbers fluctuated due to the volatile political situation and the constant occupation and partitioning of Poland by the neighbouring countries.

However, new religious orders were being set up despite the oppressive conditions and by 1939 there were twenty times more Catholic nuns than in 1860. The Second World War caused serious disintegration and organizational problems for many communities due to the geographical alterations of the borders, lack of resources and mass repatriation. After the war, the relationship between the new communist government and the Church deteriorated. The Catholic Church was identified as the archenemy of the state and the new system put firmly in place. This meant serious restrictions of civic liberties for consecrated persons. In 1949 sisters began to be excluded from public life and the charity organizations run by them were taken over by the state and the social services. Religion as a subject was banned from schools and sisters had to obtain consent from the state in order to start any new projects, accept donations, or purchase property. Consecrated people were being made redundant across the public sector, thus they engaged in work in their local parishes. The state's targeting of religious communities resulted in growing solidarity amongst consecrated people and religious orders, and a certain degree of unification of their mission. After the collapse of the communist rule in 1989, religious communities welcomed back their primary missions (*charisms*).

Between the late 1960s and 2001 the number of consecrated women fell from 27,000 to 25,000. This has been attributed to the high mortality rates amongst sisters who joined before WW II (Łoziński 2002: 18). Vocations also decreased steadily from 1990 after the brief post-1989 surge. According to the vice-president of the Consulate of Major Religious Superiors of Women, this decline is caused by: stagnation in the population growth, the continuing process of secularization, a crisis in family values, and the changing role of women in Polish society (KAI 2005).[1] A statistical report released to the press by the Conference of the Polish Episcopate[2] in 2005 confirms this steady decline in the number of female vocations between 1993 and 2003.

Despite the numbers slowly decreasing, Poland continues to be a relatively fertile land for female vocations in Central Europe. The quantitative sources cited above, although helpful in creating a general overview of the situation in Polish convents, fail to tell us more about these women. Who are they? Where do they come from? What was their motivation to join? These questions can be partly answered by adopting a qualitative approach to the topic and mapping the themes appearing in nuns' own narratives.

---

[1]   For more details see www.zakony.katolik.pl/zz/stat.

Sisters

In the course of my field work I visited five religious communities and spoke to 35 nuns between the ages of 18 and 82. Over half of the interviewees were raised in the countryside, usually in small villages; seven came from small towns (between ten and thirty thousand inhabitants); and nine spent their whole lives in big cities where their religious community was located. All sisters were brought up as Catholic and socialized into the values and norms of the Church community. Those born in the country come from farmer families characterized by a high level of traditional religiosity and involvement in the life of their local parish.

A distinction needs to be made between the women who joined immediately after the war, those under the Stalinist regime (group I), those who joined in the 1980s when the communist system slowly began to crumble (group II), and finally those who became religious sisters after 1989 (group III). Predictably, generational differences between my informants were reflected in the manner in which they recounted their life. The most senior nuns delivered their life stories as a stream of consciousness where religious vocation was taken for granted in the sense that it was not presented as an extraordinary or unexpected element in their lives. They encountered historically, politically, and culturally specific difficulties and potential deterrents such as post-war poverty, their young age (below 15), an obligation towards their siblings and aging parents, or the precarious position of religious communities. These elements were absent from the stories of other nuns (groups II and III, aged between 18 and 45 at the time of the interviews). Instead, vocation was discussed in more indefinite and less absolute terms – as a reflexive process that never truly finishes. The implied social 'abnormality' of their choice constituted more of an obstacle for this group, and was accompanied by a fear of parental rejection. The *youngest* generation of nuns (current postulants and novices) was summed up by Sister Amata (71) as a product of the key problems in contemporary Polish society: moral relativism, chaos and permissiveness. According to her, such candidates required more effort and help than her own age group due to the lack of clear goals and motives before joining:-'In the old days the postulants were so decisive but those ones…you need to work on them because they are like the society they come from.'

Despite the cultural differences between various generations, a number of common themes emerge out of the nuns' life narratives. Discovery of one's calling is not an isolated solipsistic act of the self but is embedded within networks of social interaction. Family background constitutes one crucial example of such a network and its role in the formation of religious calling manifested itself very strongly in all interviews. Pierre Bourdieu's concept of habitus (1977) aids in developing an interactionist analysis of the relationship between family background and the elusive phenomenon of convent vocation.

Vocational habi(tu)s

Habitus

Bourdieu defines habitus as an open system of embodied dispositions affected by the experiences of agents and either reinforced, or altered as a result (Bourdieu and Wacquant 1992: 133). Such alterations can only be understood through alluding to 'complex processes of investment and negotiation' rather than the dichotomy of domination and resistance (McNay 2000: 58). Hence, dispositions come in the form of what Bourdieu refers to as 'regulated liberties' (1991: 102). These dispositions become inscribed in individuals from a very early age and they subsequently constitute the categories through which experiences are perceived. The process of internalization is not conscious or discursive, yet neither is it mechanical (Bourdieu 1977: 87–88) as the habitus acts as a generative rather than a determinist framework (McNay 2000).

Habitus operates 'from restructuring to restructuring' as it becomes slightly modified every time an individual enters a new social context in the course of her life (Bourdieu 1977: 87). According to Bourdieu daily participation in rituals and games, exposure to proverbs, sayings, or riddles familiarizes a social agent with the rationale for a certain course of action in her social context (1977: 88). Habitus is simultaneously a structured structure and a structuring structure because the conditions for action are also the predispositions for making sense of this action. In other words, experiences are made sense of through categories of perceptions already formed by previous experiences. Habitus organizes practices as well as the categories of perception of these practices.

Habitus enables social agents to deal with unforeseen circumstances because it equips them with strategies which are 'sedimentary', yet subject to manipulation and ad hoc application depending on the field in which the particular habitus is played out. By 'field' Bourdieu means a 'socially structured space in which agents struggle [...] either to change or to preserve its boundaries and form' (Bourdieu and Wacquant 1992: 17). The habitus of nuns will initially be acquired in a nominally secular field and subsequently modified/re-structured when they become consecrated persons and enter the religious realm. The institution of the Catholic Church constitutes a 'universe of practice' (Bourdieu 1990: 87) where spiritual capital brought in by nuns is valued more highly than in the outside world.

Religious calling

Sisters frequently recalled having heard a voice or experiencing a strong inner feeling of vocation at some point in their lives. Usually, the feeling intensified towards the end of high school and decisions were made after completing exit exams, although in a few cases sisters joined in their late twenties, having gained a degree or having been in full-time employment. The voice or conviction, that one should join a religious community does not arise in a vacuum however, and it is rarely triggered purely by the individual's private thought processes. A calling does not grow out of some sort of a seed or pre-existing essence (Bourdieu 1990: 55). Rather, it is the effect of the interaction between the habitus and accidental events in sisters' lives, which are then 'snatched' and made meaningful by the habitus. Spiritual leanings and tastes are likely to be positively sanctioned because they accord with the field in which they happen to be interpreted.

Sister Ruth (23), for example, had often contemplated vocation but never took her thoughts seriously. Shortly before deciding to join, she went on a week long pilgrimage to see a famous painting of the Virgin Mary in the sanctuary in Częstochowa. When she arrived, after a long and tiresome journey, the chapel was full of people taller than her and she could not see the painting. She said: 'I was angry with God because I had walked for eight days and for what? Then I smelled flowers. It was this very strong smell. It was as if He was giving me a sign. Maybe it was my imagination but it was very powerful.'

Bourdieu describes this as an instance of a virtuoso finding 'in his [sic] discourse the triggers for his discourse' (1990: 57). This is not to say that vocation should be regarded in structuralist terms but rather as a phenomenon that is subjective, yet non-individual. In other words, there are dominant characteristics in the discourse of vocation that are shared by nuns, however they are diverse in their homogeneity (Bourdieu 1990). The personal story of discovering one's calling is simultaneously the collectively created account. The habitus regulates the actions of which it is an outcome – nuns recount their past experiences in accordance with their present patterns of perception, which are themselves a product of the past. As Bourdieu states: '[habitus] adjusts itself to a probable future which it anticipates and helps to bring about because it reads it directly in the present of the presumed world, the only one it can know' (1990: 64).

In all cases, the decision to join was preceded by events of intense religious involvement and some nuns joined as a result of an epiphany they experienced as regards their human relationships. In one extreme instance, a single conversation with a male friend, who was training to be a priest, led a young woman to reconsider her sceptical views of religion and join a community.

Female role models

It is vital to point out that all of the nuns were raised in a strongly Catholic environment, and religious involvement was taken for granted in most families, especially for those living in rural places and small towns. My interviewees were constantly exposed to the Catholic ideology and lifestyle. A Catholic youth organization, 'Oasis'[2] was frequently mentioned in the interviews as a foundation for deepening sisters' faith prior to entering the convent. Many spoke of their desire to become a nun as a childhood dream resulting from early encounters with consecrated persons, be it priests or nuns, in their parish. Usually, even if the parents themselves did not express active interest in religious life, other (female) relatives and acquaintances did. Overall, mothers, grandmothers, aunts, female religion teachers and nuns in the local parish constituted crucial religious socialization agents and role models. None of the sisters described her father as more, or equally, religious as her mother.

---

[2]　A Catholic renewal movement.

Moreover, no male role models featured as instrumental to the process of vocation development. Even Catholic clergy seemed to exert a minimal amount of influence on the deepening of the future sisters' faith. In fact, most nuns recalled absorbing knowledge about Catholicism through repeated practices in the private sphere, or simply through being exposed to symbols, prayers and rituals performed by other women. Although men in the family usually took part in the obligatory Sunday prayer or mass, their piety was referred to as more 'understated' and separated from the secular life, whereas the women literally saturated everyday activities with elements of the Catholic faith such as prayers, songs, Catholic paraphernalia, Christian life philosophy and work ethic. For instance, this sister quotes her mother as a Catholic role model and she attributes her skilful application of religion to life to her gender by contrasting her with her father. Such contrasts were commonly employed by the informants.

> Dad also believes but this is a different kind of religiosity. Maybe it's because I am a girl that I was attracted more to the way my mum expressed her faith in her everyday life... to my mum's methods and authenticity (S. Little Black Number, 36)

Additionally, women's practical expression of their religious beliefs extended far beyond worship, or church-affiliated activities. The mothers' manifestation of religious faith through attitudes and activities in everyday life, although initially perceived as extreme or awkward, proved to act as the most motivating factor in the women's path to the convent. Charity, altruism and general interest in other human beings featured in most sisters' memories of their mothers and grandmothers.

> Granny's] religiosity was more about helping people than the Church or prayer.[...] she gave them things, like clothes and food...She was like a saint to me because she[practiced her faith in real life. [...] mum was the same... (S. Joanna, 45)

Polish sisters built on this discourse of lay sainthood in the world in that they opted for fulfilling their female role as the official representatives of the Catholic Church. Whilst their female relatives served God through living out their 'feminine' potential in the world, the nuns choose to follow the path especially extolled by Pope John Paul II in *Vita Consecrata* (1996): the consecrated life.

Apart from providing a largely conducive religious ground, most sisters' families fostered values of modesty, hard work, humility and respect towards God and the Church's teachings, as well as traditional views of gender roles. Thus, it is not surprising that all of them found the shift from the family home to the fairly austere and regimented convent life largely unproblematic. Their habitus could perhaps be argued to have equipped them with the means for adopting a convent lifestyle (Lovell 2000). Moreover, their 'feel for the game' is not facilitated merely by their spiritual capital but it extends to purely practical aspects of their background. Family homes were not described as destitute but still far from financially comfortable. They were 'poor but pious', as one sister put it. Living out the vow of poverty, therefore, does not imply difficulty because a virtue is made out of necessity, 'which continuously transforms necessity into virtue by inducing 'choices' which correspond to the condition of which it is the product' (Bourdieu 1977: 175). Obviously, there were one or two exceptions whereby the sisters claimed to have gravitated towards a deeper interest in the Catholic faith on their own, without being actively encouraged by anyone. However, none of them came from atheist families and religion always played an important role in their upbringing, regardless of their personal attitude towards God and the Church. Some parents appeared extremely pious and rigorous about sisters' involvement in the spiritual life, whereas many others embraced what can be referred to as the essence of Polish Catholicism, i.e. belonging without believing (Porter 2001).[3]

Thus, if we consider the fact that a great majority of my interviewees shared a very similar background, discourses of vocation and justifications of their decision to join, it would be tempting to adopt a rather fatalistic and deterministic view that their shared habitus guided their choices to a certain extent and that they display a typical *amor fati* (love of destiny) that Bourdieu refers to in his writings (1984). However, clearly not all women brought up in Catholic families progress to become nuns, and not all of the nuns I interviewed were actively encouraged by their environment to join. In fact, many were discouraged, regardless of the degree of their family and friends' spiritual involvement. In a society where the range of life possibilities and choices for women has increased rapidly over the past decade, joining a convent does not constitute a preferred career path and it is widely considered as an unfortunate turn of events in a young girl's life. Nowadays a voluntary choice of consecrated life strikes many as unreasonable or cowardly and thus sisters are suspected of joining by default: because of lack of other life opportunities, or as an eschewal from the demands of the complex socio-economic reality.

A note on joining and social sanctions

It is important to grasp the range of problems Polish nuns encounter both prior to entering the convent and *postfactum*. Before joining, the judgment comes from closest family, whereas once they become visible in their habits, strangers may subject them to criticism and ridicule. During the period of discovering their vocation the sisters would often be faced with negative attitudes on the part of their parents who, as a rule, did not conceive of joining a convent as a desirable 'career path' or 'lifestyle' for their daughters. In a surprisingly high number of cases, the life choice was deemed socially inadequate and embarrassing for the family. We could draw a continuum of responses ranging from sadness and disappointment to overt anger, desperate threats and emotional blackmail. These reactions stemmed from the apparent incongruence between the social expectations of a 'normal' life path and the choice these women made. The nuns themselves volunteered a justification for other people's unsympathetic evaluations by referring to the dominant, culturally specific discourses of 'normal' femininity. As Sister Karolina (36) summed up:

---

[3] To some, this could indicate the progressing secularization of the Polish society. In Poland, Catholicism tightly intertwined with the national identity and its various forms undoubtedly historically pervade all layers of society on political and cultural levels. Nevertheless, the majority of Polish respondents predict a steady decrease in the levels of the actual 'religiosity' during the first decade of the twenty first century (Mariański 2004).

'getting married is normal. Come on girl! You are so many years old, do something with your life – get married!'

In this case, personal concern for children rules over devotion to God's will, which to a certain extent demonstrates the power of the social context and the latent hold a local community may have over its members. Most parents eventually accept their daughter's choice, yet the public scrutiny commences once a sister puts on a habit and a veil and thus becomes visible as a consecrated member of the Catholic Church. Nuns are often greeted with respect and friendliness, however they also report an unexpectedly high number of instances in which outright hostility and contempt constitute the dominant reaction. The habit may provoke verbal abuse partly because it is a symbol associated with prevailing stereotypes of easy and 'socially useless' convent life and the Catholic Church as an institution exploiting ordinary, hard-working citizens. It could be argued that priests and nuns in certain regions of Poland receive the same treatment as Goffman's 'stigmatised individuals' (1968: 19). Thus, despite the fact that in 2001 98.3 per cent of Polish people declared their membership in the Catholic Church, and 53.4 per cent describe their relationship with the Church as 'close' (Borowik and Doktór 2001: 68–69) my informants reported a significant presence of anti-Church sentiments in Polish society. A third of Polish Catholics have been classed as "unwitting heretics" (Piwowarski 1983), meaning that they are selective in their adoption of the Church doctrines and morality. This brings me to the concept of spiritual capital – a type of unstable currency indispensable to *discovering* one's calling (Verter 2003).

Vocation and spiritual capital

In the course of internalizing their habitus, the future sisters also amass what can be referred to as spiritual (Verter 2003) or religious capital (Iannaccone 1990) to paraphrase Bourdieu's notion of 'symbolic capital' (1977: 173–183). Bourdieu draws attention to symbolic activities which are largely perceived as 'lacking concrete or material effect, in short gratuitous, i.e. disinterested but also useless' (1977: 177). Bourdieu points out that symbolic or spiritual interests are thought of as in direct opposition to material interests because of the strictly capitalist definition of economic interest. Moreover, symbolic interest, when recognized, tends to be perceived as the 'irrationality of feeling or passion' (Bourdieu 1977: 177). This point resonates strongly with the general perception of spiritual capital in the lay section of Polish society where it may often be judged as not serious, useless and impractical for young women who are only just starting their adult lives. Daily family prayer, church attendance, membership in youth religious groups and frequent interaction with consecrated persons all contribute to the gradual acquisition of symbolic/ spiritual capital which subsequently enables the sisters to enter and sustain their convent identity successfully and without major hindrances. The ones who lack such capital and who decide to join under the false impression of what convent life entails, ('strumming the guitar and singing' as Sister Joanna (45) remarked wryly), may leave or find it extremely hard to sustain their 'vocation'. In other words, a clash between reality and a romantic ideal of nuns' everyday life affects one's initial perception of their calling. Similarly, young girls who become postulants as a result of their disenchantment with the outside world were often described by older nuns as lacking the spiritual stamina to develop their vocation. According to a Mistress of Formation[4] the most promising type of calling stems from religious dedication and strong inner conviction rather than practical reasons, hence genuine piety and commitment are considered as essential prerequisites to entering a convent. Consequently, calling can be adequately recognized as valid only if the person experiencing it possesses the knowledge necessary to make sense of it. Spiritual capital thus lies at the heart of 'true' vocation.

According to Bourdieu, symbolic capital is convertible into economic capital which is what makes it valuable because

> practice never ceases to conform to economic calculation even when it gives every appearance of disinterestedness by departing from the logic of interested calculation [...] and playing for stakes that are non-material and not easily quantified. (1977: 177)

Others, such as Coleman (1988) and Putnam (2000) view symbolic/social capital as communally created and more easily transformed into other forms of capital (Leonard 2005). The spiritual capital of nuns predisposes them for their religious career; hence, it is translated into their membership in the community and sensitizes them to appreciating the symbols and spiritually significant collective acts that permeate convent life. Some elderly nuns claimed that certain sisters, who leave the convent before professing their final vows, do so having exploited the community to receive 'free' education and training for adult life. As S.Emanuela (71) said:-'Some of them go to university [during their time in the convent] or they do a teaching course or nursing courses and then they decide to leave! So we prepare them for adult life…and that's how they repay us…'. In this case, in fact, spiritual capital may also serve as a means to an end (albeit somewhat accidentally), the end being a secular career, which economically benefits an individual ex-sister. Conversely, habit sisters reported instances where their consecrated status gained them a discount, a free bus ticket, or free medical treatment. These were occurrences where the habit was recognized as a symbol representing the divine by lay individuals who presumably possessed a certain amount of spiritual capital themselves.

Bourdieu, in fact, discusses 'religious capital' and he outlines its two forms: 'religious symbolic systems (myths and ideologies)'and 'religious competences (mastery of practices and bodies of knowledge)' (Bourdieu 1991 quoted in Verter 2003: 157). However, whereas he perceives religious capital as a weapon applied in the course of 'symbolic violence', I prefer understanding it as the social cement that binds members of the community together and constitutes a foundation on which shared understandings and values are built. It is crucial for the new members to be equipped with spiritual capital prior to joining, yet they would not perhaps consider doing it in the first place, had they not acquired this type of capital before. In other words, 'subcultural identity shapes religious tastes' (Verter 2003: 169). This is not to mean that vocation is misrecognized as a natural attribute when it is clearly a

---

[4]   A senior nun who introduces novices to the rules of convent life and prepares them for taking their first vows.

socially structured one, as that would be questioning the adequacy of my informants' judgement of their experience. Nevertheless, I would like to emphasize the need to analyze vocation as arising out of social interaction and relations rather than it being a subjective feeling experienced independently of others or the social context the person finds herself in. Because if spiritual, or any symbolic, capital is not universally recognized (Verter 2003) its value will differ depending on the social field it is used in. The spiritual capital of sisters obtained in lay circles is only officially acclaimed when they join a community. Thus, paradoxically, the site of capital production is not necessarily the optimal one for its usage, although it may be the case on rare occasions.[5]

Developing and increasing this capital grants nuns a special status within the religious field; they occupy a somewhat problematic position between the clergy and the laity. Yet, their membership in an order seems to give them a sense of belonging and contextualizes their spiritual capital as well as legitimizes it. The habit acts as a totemic mark of their allegiance to Catholicism and their own vocation.

Women's piety

An alternative framework for making sense of the relatively large numbers of Polish women joining religious orders can be found in the debate on the relationship between religion and gender. Numerous studies reveal that on average women are more religious than men (e.g. Lenski 1953; Alston and McIntosh 1979; de Vaus and McAllister 1987; Cornwall 1989; McSheffrey 1995; Stark and Bainbridge 1985, 1997). The fact that females display a much greater degree of piety than males has also been demonstrated across cultures, and indeed in the survey of the Christian countries (World Values Survey 1991–1992, 1995–1997 quoted in Stark 2002).[6] Consequently, a number of possible explanations have been outlined and criticized by scholars (Luckmann 1967; Roof 1978; Suziedelis and Potvin 1981; Thompson 1991; Walter and Davie 1998; Francis 1991; Francis and Wilcox 1996, Francis *et al.* 2001). For the purposes of my analysis I do not need to engage in this debate. More important are the consequences of women's greater religiosity for women themselves. One of the outcomes could be turning their faith into a profession.

My respondents felt empowered by donning the habit. They saw habit communities as 'proper' or 'genuine' and many concluded that you 'might as well go all the way if you decide to take this step' (meaning you should choose a habit order as opposed to a habitless one). Thus, for many nuns the act of entering a convent consolidated and formalized their deep commitment to God and the Catholic Church – it made it

---

[5]   For instance, one of my interviewees came from the South-East of Poland referred to as a 'land of vocations'. In her village, over two-thirds of young men her age entered seminaries to become priests thus fulfilling the role expected of them by their community. The long-standing tradition of extreme religious piety and an implied obligation to replenish priestly ranks produced a setting in which spiritual capital is acquired, reinforced, and used as an asset. Contrary to the rest of Poland , in this village (and to a certain extent the whole region) priestly vocations are celebrated with pride by families of the clerics.

[6]   Incidentally, Poland scores the highest on both men's and women's religiosity.

'serious' and 'official'. Joining a religious order entails being granted a certain status and although sisters are often exposed to hostility and misunderstanding on the part of lay people, they also encounter respect and admiration from those who share their belief system.[7] In fact, sisters' experiences resemble those of religious converts if we agree to define 'conversion' as characterized not by transitions between religions but 'transitions within components of a religion, movements from low participation of commitment to an intensified involvement' (Robbins 1988: 64).

Thus, contrary to the assertion that men's irreligiosity could be seen as a variation of risky behaviour (Stark 2002), nuns could be argued to take a risk by plunging themselves into what is considered an extreme religious lifestyle, in a socio-cultural rather than theological sense. By drawing a complex analogy between studies of religion, and crime, Rodney Stark concludes that some men's physiology, and in particular high levels of testosterone, the deficiency in 'prefrontal grey matter' and in the fear- induced hormone (cortisol), explains their propensity for criminal (hence risky) behaviour (2002: 504). Because many criminal acts are also sins, and men commit more crimes than women; and women are on average more religious than men, there exists a correlation between criminal acts and irreligiosity.

Risk preference is commonly understood as the 'degree to which individuals are willing to accept [...] behaviors that could have negative consequences' (Sherkat 2002: 316). In the light of the negative reactions to their decisions, I would like to argue that sisters could be perceived as engaging in risky behaviour, i.e. going against the grain by choosing to enter a religious order, instead of following the commonly accepted route of (heterosexual) marriage and motherhood. In suggesting this I am turning Stark's argument around by emphasizing the contingent and contextual nature of risky behaviour. The risk here is differently positioned because the negative sanctions come from the immediate social environment, rather than the judicial system, or the divine judgment. On the contrary, nuns' 'crime' against the expected gender norm brings them closer to God and further away from the lay world. They find themselves in the field (religious institution) where their spiritual capital is positively sanctioned and it wins them benefits (spiritual and practical). The same could be argued to happen for criminals who find encouragement for their actions in their circles. Therefore, risky behaviour may be treated as a contingent concept depending on the group understanding. Prospective nuns move into a sympathetic social circle, which enables them to cultivate an identity scorned upon by the mainstream society.

Conclusion

Only certain Polish women claim to have been directly called by God and become nuns. They recognize God's voice because they are equipped with the appropriate spiritual capital acquired as a result of the interaction between their gender, social position and cultural background. In their interpretation of vocation they draw on the

---

[7]   Nuns referred to such people as 'real believers'.

specific cultural and spiritual resources in the absence of which the persistent 'inner voice' may normally be ignored.

Throughout this chapter I have demonstrated a combination of social factors instrumental in illuminating the phenomenon of female religious vocation in Poland. Nuns invest their spiritual capital in order to pursue their mission as both Catholic women and professionally religious women. In doing so, they balance between two 'life-worlds' (Schutz and Luckmann 1974): the lay realm and the Catholic Church. In the former they risk sanctions because of their radical departure from the ideal of 'female destiny'. Their membership in the latter is only valid if they succeed in developing 'spiritual femininity' – an identity positioned somewhere between the sacred and the profane. The vexatious, if fascinating, question of whether women who become nuns defy or consolidate dominant social values in contemporary Poland remains to be answered.

Acknowledgments

I would like to thank Grace Davie and Anthony King for their valuable feedback on earlier drafts of this chapter.

References

Alston, John P. and William A. McIntosh, 'An Assessment of the Determinants of Religious Participation', *Sociological Quarterly*, 20 (1979): 49–62.

Borowik, Irena and Tadeusz Doktór, *Pluralizm Religijny i Moralny w Polsce* (Kraków: NOMOS, 2001).

Bourdieu, Pierre, *Outline of a Theory of Practice* (Cambridge University Press, 1977).

Bourdieu, Pierre, *Distinction: a Social Critique of the Judgment of Taste* (London: Routledge, 1984).

Bourdieu, Pierre, *The Logic of Practice* (Cambridge: Polity, 1990).

Bourdieu, Pierre, *Language and Symbolic Power* (Cambridge: Polity, 1991).

Bourdieu, Pierre and Wacquant, Loïc J.D., *An Invitation to Reflexive Sociology* (Cambridge: Polity, 1992).

Carr, C. Lynn, 'Tomboyism or Lesbianism? Beyond Sex/Gender/Sexual Conflation', *Sex Roles*, 53(1–2) (2005): 119–131.

Coleman, James S., 'Social Capital in the Creation of Human Capital', *American Journal of Sociology*, 94 (1998) (Supplement): S95–S120.

Cornwall, Marie, 'Faith Development of Men and Women over the Life Span', in Steven J. Bahr, Peterson and Evan T. Peterson (eds), *Aging and the Family* (Lexington, MA: Lexington Books, 1989).

D'Aquili, Eugene G. and Newberg, Andrew B., *The Mystical Mind: Probing the Biology of Religious Experience* (Minneapolis: Fortress, 1999).

DeVaus, David and McAllister, Ian, 'Gender Differences in Religion: A Test of the Structural Location Theory', *American Sociological Review*, 52(4) (1987): 472–81.

Francis, Leslie J., 'The Personality Characteristics of Anglican Ordinands: Feminine Men and Masculine Women'? *Personality and Individual Differences*, 12(11) (1991): 1133–1140.

Francis, Leslie.J. and Wilcox, Carolyn, 'Religion and Gender Orientation', *Personality and Individual Differences*, 20(1) (1996): 119–121.

Francis, Leslie J., Jones, Susan H., Jackson, Chris J. and Robbins, Mandy, 'The Feminine Personality Profile of Male Anglican Clergy in Britain and Ireland: A Study Employing the Eysenck Personality Profiler', *Review of Religious Research*, 43(1) (2001): 14–23.

Goffman, Erving, *Stigma: Notes on the Management of Spoilt Identity* (Harmondsworth: Penguin, 1968).

Iannaccone, Laurence R., 'Religious Practice: A human Capital Approach', *Journal for the Scientific Study of Religion,* 29(3) (1990): 297–314.

Katolicka Agencja Informacyjna (KAI), *Lekka Kawaleria Kościoła – Międzynarodowe Spotkanie Sióstr w Warszawie*, Warsaw, 2005.

Kłoczkowski, Jerzy, *Dzieje Chrześcijaństwa Polskiego*, 2 (Paris: Editions du Dialogue, 1991).

Lenski, Gerhard E., 'Social Correlates of Religious Interest', *American Sociological Review*, 18(5) (1953): 533–544.

Leonard, Madeleine, 'Children, Childhood and Social Capital: Exploring the Links', *Sociology*, 39(4) (2005): 605–623.

Lovell, Terri, 'Thinking Feminism with and against Bourdieu', *Feminist Theory*, 1(1) (2000): 11–32.

Łoziński, Bogdan, *Leksykon Zakonów w Polsce* (Warsaw: KAI, 2002)

Luckmann, Thomas, *The Invisible Religion* (New York: Macmillan, 1967).

McNay, Lois, *Gender and Agency: Reconfiguring the Subject in Feminist and Social Theory* (Cambridge: Polity, 2000).

McRobbie, Angela, 'More! New Sexualities in Girls' and Women's Magazines', in James Curran, David Morley, and Valerie Walkerdine (eds), *Cultural Studies and Communications* (London: Arnold, 1996).

McSheffrey, Shannon, *Gender and Heresy: Women and Men in Lollard Communities, 1420–1530* (Philadelphia, PA: University of Pennsylvania Press, 1995).

Michałowicz, Tomasz, 'Kościołowi Ubywa Sióstr', *Gazeta Wyborcza*, 21 March, 2005.

Miller, Alan S. and Hoffman, John P., 'Risk and Religion: An Explanation of Gender Differences in Religiosity', *Journal for the Scientific Study of Religion*, 34(1) (1995): 63–75.

Piwowarski, Wacław (ed.), *Religijność Ludowa* (Wrocław: Wydawnictwo Wrocławskie, 1983).

Porter, Brian, 'The Catholic Nation: Religion, Identity, and the Narratives of Polish History', *The Slavic and East European Journal*, 45(2) (2001): 289–299.

Putnam, Robert, *Bowling Alone: The Collapse and Revival of American Community* (New York: Simon and Schuster, 2000).

Robbins, Thomas, *Cults, Converts and Charisma* (London: Sage, 1988).

Roof, Wade D., *Community and Commitment* (New York: Elsevier, 1978).

Sherkat, David E., 'Sexuality and Religious Commitment in the United States: An Empirical Examination', *Journal for the Scientific Study of Religion*, 41(2) (2003): 2, 313–323.

Schutz, Alfred and Luckmann, Thomas, *The Structures of the Life-World* (London: Heinemann Educational, 1974).

Stark, Rodney, 'Physiology and Faith: Addressing the 'Universal' Gender Difference in Religiousness', *Journal for the Scientific Study of Religion*, 41(3) (2002): 495–507.

Stark, Rodney and Bainbridge, William S., 1985, *The Future of Religions* (Berkley: University of California Press, 1985).

Suziedelis, Antanas and Potvin, Raymond H., 'Sex Differences in Factors Affecting Religiousness Among Catholic Adolescents', *Journal for the Scientific Study of Religion*, 20(1) (1981): 38–51.

Thompson, Edward H. Jr., 'Beneath the Status Characteristic: Gender Variations in Religiousness', *Journal for the Scientific Study of Religion*, 30(4) (1991): 381–394.

Verter, Bradford, 'Spiritual Capital: Theorizing Religion with Bourdieu against Bourdieu', *Sociological Theory*, 21(2) (2003): 150–174.

Vita Consecrata (1996).

Walter, Tony and Davie, Grace, 'The Religiosity of Women in the Modern West', *British Journal of Sociology*, 49(4) (1998): 640–660.

www.zakony.katolik.pl/zz/stat.

PART 2
Alternative Spiritualities

Chapter 5

The Spiritual Revolution and the New Age Gender Puzzle
The Sacralization of the Self in Late Modernity (1980–2000)

Dick Houtman and Stef Aupers[1]

Introduction

Secularization theory, once sociology of religion's proud theoretical flagship, has run into stormy weather since the 1980s. Once considered an empirically sound theory by the social-scientific community, many now feel that it has been exposed as a mere ideology or wish dream, intimately tied to the rationalist discourse of modernity (e.g., Hadden 1987; Stark and Finke 2000; Meyer and Pels 2003). It is hardly contested, to be sure, that church membership, adherence to traditional Christian doctrines and values, and participation in church rituals relating to birth, marriage, and death, have all declined considerably in western European countries. But precisely because of the one-sided attention to those prominent processes of religious decline, it is still quite unclear whether 'new' or 'alternative' types of religion have come to blossom outside the traditional Christian realm (e.g., Luckmann 2003; Knoblauch 2003; Stark *et al.* 2005).

Some observers have recently argued that such is indeed the case. What we are witnessing today, they argue, is not simply a process of secularization, but rather a decline of traditional Christian religion that goes along with a slowly unfolding spiritual revolution (Houtman and Mascini 2002; Heelas *et al.* 2005).[2] Contemporary

---

[1]   Delivered as a keynote lecture by the first author at the conference *Religion and Gender*, BSA Sociology of Religion Study Group, Lancaster University, 11–13 April 2005, this chapter has benefited greatly from research conducted during his visiting professorship at the Ecole des Hautes Etudes en Sciences Sociales, Marseille, France (November 2003). The authors further thank Sabine Lauderbach, Peter Mascini and Peter Achterberg for their useful comments on an earlier draft – especially Peter Achterberg's statistical advice was as useful as ever. Finally, they wish to acknowledge Linda Scheelbeek, because it was her Master's thesis (2003) that put the first author (who acted as her supervisor) on the track of the solution to the gender puzzle proposed here.

[2]   Heelas *et al.* only wish to speak of a 'spiritual revolution' when more people participate in the spiritual milieu than in the Christian congregational domain. Because in Kendal, United Kingdom, where they conducted their 'body count', five times as many people are involved in

spirituality is held to be an outgrowth of what emerged as the 'New Age' movement in the 1960s' counter culture as an offshoot of the tradition of western esotericism (Roszak 1969; Zijderveld 1970; Hanegraaff 1996).[3] With its gradual disembedding from this countercultural fringe, New Age has since expanded into the very centre of late-modern culture (Van Otterloo 1999). Sutcliffe and Bowman do not even seem to exaggerate when they observe that 'contrary to predictions that New Age would go mainstream, now it's as if the mainstream is going New Age' (2000: 11). The once typical belief in a dawning 'New Age of Aquarius' has waned in the process and the 'New Age' label has increasingly been replaced by that of 'spirituality'.

Unfortunately, there is hardly any hard evidence that spirituality has indeed become more widespread. Houtman and Mascini (2002), for instance, rely on one-shot-survey data, interpreting differences between age categories as processes of historical change. Heelas *et al.* (2005) offer convincing evidence, but assume that the bulk of spirituality can be found in the spiritual milieu – an assumption that seems unduly restrictive.[4] Judging from its virtual omnipresence on the internet and its prominence in contemporary business life, for instance, spirituality has by now moved well beyond the boundaries of the spiritual milieu (Aupers and Houtman 2005; Aupers and Houtman, 2006; Aupers *et al.*, 2008). A first aim of the present chapter, then, is to provide evidence for the spread of spirituality during the last few decades by studying spiritual beliefs and self-designations among the general populations of western countries.

---

the latter as compared to the former, they conclude that 'it is thus perfectly clear that a spiritual revolution has not taken place' (2004: 45). In the current chapter, we use the notion of a 'spiritual revolution' differently. Following Inglehart's (1977) conceptualization of the 'silent revolution', we do not consider the achievement of a majority position decisive, but rather the occurrence of a process of historical expansion that operates by way of cohort replacement and is caused by a medium-long term process of change that is unlikely to reverse.

[3]   There is an ongoing discussion about whether the neo-pagan movement (most notably Wicca) is a movement in its own right or part of the New Age movement. Although some argue that the two should be treated as different (cf. Adler 1979; Harvey 1997; Pearson 1998) and are obviously not identical (York 1995), the most common position seems to be that neo-paganism is a distinguishable subculture within the broader New Age movement (cf. Hanegraaff 1996; Heelas 1996). Because even specialists in neo-paganism such as Berger (1999: 5) and Luhrmann (1989: 30–31) take this position, we regard spirituality as affiliated with 'New Age', because New Age includes neo-paganism.

[4]   This is of course not to suggest that survey research enables one to estimate how many people are involved in spirituality (or traditionalism, racism, or whatever). This is impossible, because the per centage found depends on two more or less arbitrary decisions: 1) What particular items from a principally unlimited universe are to be used to measure it? and 2) How much agreement with the selected set of items is necessary to be able to speak of a 'real' New Ager (traditionalist, racist, or whatever)? Depending on decisions regarding those two questions (with especially the first one supplying the researcher with enormous degrees of freedom), one can in principle produce any per centage between 0 and 100. What survey research does permit, however, is studying whether – given the way one has decided to measure affinity with spirituality – the average score on this scale or index increases or decreases across time. This is precisely what we will do in this chapter.

This chapter's more important second aim is to refine Houtman and Mascini's (2002) theory that the spread of spirituality is caused by a process of detraditionalization. This refinement is called for, because in its original form it cannot explain the high levels of affinity with spirituality among women (although it does a good job in explaining those among the younger age cohorts and the well educated). With men and women being identical when it comes to levels of post-traditionalism, the question why women nevertheless display more affinity with spirituality than men remains 'an intriguing and theoretically important puzzle to be solved' (Houtman and Mascini 2002: 468). Solving this 'gender puzzle' (Heelas *et al.* 2005) requires gendering the theory of detraditionalization (see also Woodhead 2005, 2007). The second aim of the present chapter, in short, is to develop and test a gendered version of the theory of detraditionalization.

Conceptualising contemporary spirituality

Writings about contemporary spirituality typically invoke an image of a veritable implosion of religion and consumer choice, speaking of 'do-it-yourself-religion' (Baerveldt 1996), 'pick-and-mix religion' (Hamilton 2000), 'religious consumption à la carte' (Possamai 2003) or a 'spiritual supermarket' (Lyon 2000). This type of discourse is even used by defenders of secularization theory and New Agers, two otherwise radically different groups. The former use it to construct spirituality's widespread contemporary presence as confirming rather than contradicting secularization theory: 'The New Age is eclectic to an unprecedented degree and ... is ... dominated by the principle that the sovereign consumer will decide what to believe ... I cannot see how a shared faith can be created from a low-salience world of pick-and-mix religion' (Bruce 2002: 105).[5] New Age apologetics use this type of discourse to highlight the enormous variety within the spiritual milieu, so as to emphasize its openness to diversity and seemingly unprecedented opportunities for individual choice and liberty, characterizing the Christian churches as dogmatic and authoritarian in the process. The following explanation of a spiritual trainer of a Dutch New Age centre provides a good illustration:[6]

> New Age is like a religious supermarket. All aspects of religion ... are put together on a big pile and people can choose what is best for them at that moment in time. And that's the good thing about the New Age world – that nobody claims to have a monopoly on wisdom. Whereas the old religions argue "We possess the absolute truth and this is the only way to God", we say "There are ten thousand ways" and "There are as many ways as there are people".

Although, to be sure, those positions are not completely mistaken, they overestimate the individualistic character of spirituality. True, the well-packed shelves of the

---

[5] In a similar vein, the late Bryan Wilson argued already thirty years ago that the post-Christian cults 'represent, in the American phrase, "the religion of your choice", the highly privatized preference that reduces religion to the significance of pushpin, poetry, or popcorn' (1976: 96; see for another example: Becker *et al.* 1997).

[6] Interviewed in the context of a previous study (Aupers and Houtman 2003).

spiritual supermarket enable one to sample one's personal spiritual diet, but underneath the resulting diversity lies a shared belief that has been neglected all too often: 'The great refrain, running throughout the New Age, is that we malfunction because we have been indoctrinated ... by mainstream society and culture' (Heelas 1996: 18). The latter are thus conceived of as basically alienating forces, held to estrange one from one's 'authentic', 'natural' or 'real' self – from who one 'really' or 'at deepest' is:

> Perfection can be found only by moving beyond the socialized self – widely known as the 'ego' but also as the 'lower self', 'intellect' or the 'mind' – thereby encountering a new realm of being. It is what we are *by nature*. Indeed, the most pervasive and significant aspect of the *lingua franca* of the New Age is that the person is, in essence, spiritual. To experience the 'Self' itself is to experience ... 'inner spirituality'. ... The inner realm, and the inner realm alone, is held to serve as the source of authentic vitality, creativity, love, tranquillity, wisdom, power, authority and all those other qualities which are held to comprise the perfect life. (Heelas 1996: 19, his emphasis, DH/SA)

This, then, is the key tenet of spirituality: the belief that in the deepest layers of the self the 'divine spark' – to borrow a term from ancient Gnosticism – is still smouldering, waiting to be stirred up and succeed the socialized self. This constitutes a basically romanticist conception of the self that 'lays central stress on unseen, even sacred forces that dwell within the person, forces that give life and relationships their significance' (Gergen 1991: 19). Re-establishing contact with such a 'true', 'deeper' or 'divine' self is held to enable one to reconnect to a sacred realm that holistically connects 'everything' and to overcome one's present state of alienation. No wonder, then, that spirituality is deeply influenced by humanistic psychology and that '... "personal growth" can be understood as the shape "religious salvation" takes in the New Age Movement: it is affirmed that deliverance from human suffering and weakness will be reached by developing our human potential, which results in our increasingly getting in touch with our inner divinity' (Hanegraaff 1996: 46).

This 'sacralization of the self' encourages people to 'follow their personal paths', rather than conform to authoritative role models. Those concerned do not pursue meaning and identity from 'pre-given' sources located outside the self (e.g., the institutionalized answers offered by the Christian churches), but want to rely on an 'internal' source, located in the self's deeper layers. As such, spirituality conceives of itself as an epistemological third way of 'gnosis', rejecting both religious faith and scientific reason as vehicles of truth. Rather, it is held that one should be faithful to one's 'inner voice' and trust one's 'intuition':

> According to (gnosis) truth can only be found by personal, inner revelation, insight or 'enlightenment'. Truth can only be personally experienced: in contrast with the knowledge of *reason* or *faith*, it is in principle not generally accessible. This 'inner knowing' cannot be transmitted by discursive language (this would reduce it to rational knowledge). Nor can it be the subject of *faith* ... because there is in the last resort no other authority than personal, inner experience. (Hanegraaff 1996: 519, his emphasis, DH/SA)

Although the emergence of a pluralistic spiritual supermarket confirms Luckmann's (1967) classical predictions, it has simultaneously blinded many observers to the shared tenet of self-spirituality – the belief that the self itself is sacred. It is precisely this idea that not only accounts for the diversity at the surface of the spiritual milieu – an inevitable outcome when people feel that they need to follow their personal paths and explore what works for them personally – ,but that also provides it with unity at a deeper level. Spirituality is certainly individualistic, in short, but it is so neither because a shared worldview is absent, nor because those concerned are as authentic as they typically believe they are. It is individualistic because of its shared idea that personal authenticity needs to be attained by expressing a 'real' self, basically 'unpolluted' by culture, history and society.

Mapping the spiritual revolution

The World Values Survey (1981–2000)

Studies about spirituality are typically based on qualitative research, employing semi-structured interviews, ethnography, case studies, content analysis, etcetera. Those studies do not permit a systematic comparison of countries and periods, so as to find out whether spirituality has indeed become more widespread within a particular country, whether the same applies to other countries, and in which countries it has expanded most. These types of questions, addressed in the current chapter, require survey data and quantitative research methods.

Although good scales for the measurement of spirituality have become available during the last few years (e.g. Granqvist and Hagekull 2001; Houtman and Mascini 2002), such scales are unfortunately absent from the large international survey programs that enable comparisons between countries and across time. The *World Values Survey* (WVS) is no exception to this general rule and hence precludes a theoretically sophisticated measurement of the extent to which one identifies with spirituality. We nevertheless feel that it can be used to measure it in a satisfactory, albeit crude, way by strategically combining answers to some of its questions. And whereas no better data sources are available to satisfy our research needs, we feel that some pragmatism is justified – especially so, because the data of the *World Values Survey* are otherwise perfectly suited for our purposes. This is so for three reasons.

Firstly, the three available waves of the WVS (1981, 1990 and 2000) cover a range of twenty years. Of course, one would prefer to also have comparable data for 1970, or even earlier. But then again, twenty years is quite an impressive time span, especially if we realise that the large surveys fielded today hardly include better measures for spirituality. Moreover, it is often argued that the expansion of spirituality has particularly taken place during the 1980s (e.g. Hanegraaff 1996; York 1995), after its first emergence in the 1960s and 1970s counter culture (e.g. Roszak 1969; Zijderveld 1970). Secondly, the WVS covers a substantial number of countries. Obviously, not all of those have been included in all three rounds of data collection, not all of those are western countries with a Christian heritage and the crucial questions have not always been asked. We nevertheless have sufficient data to map and explain the spiritual revolution in fourteen western countries: France, Great Britain, West Germany, Italy, Netherlands, Denmark, Belgium, Spain, Ireland,

United States, Canada, Norway, Sweden and Iceland.[7] A third reason why the WVS perfectly meets our needs is that it strongly emphasizes the measurement of adherence to traditional moral values. This makes it highly useful for testing our theory on why a spiritual revolution has occurred in the first place, as we will explain below.

Measuring spirituality

The questionnaire of the *World Values Survey* contains one very simple question that explicitly and unambiguously taps spirituality as distinguished from traditional Christian religion. Respondents have been asked which of the following four statements comes closest to their personal beliefs: 'There is a personal God', 'There is some sort of spirit or life force', 'I don't really know what to think' and 'I don't really think there is any sort of spirit, God, or life force'. The second answer, belief in some sort of spirit or life force, implies belief in the immanence of the sacred – in stark contrast to traditional Christianity's belief that 'The truth is "out there" rather than within; ... transcendent rather than immanent' (Heelas *et al.* 2005: 22). Indeed, those who answer that they believe in 'some sort of spirit or life force' prove to score substantially higher on a valid and reliable scale for New Age affinity than those who give any of the three other answers (Houtman and Mascini 2002: 462–463).

Although the questionnaire contains no other questions that explicitly and unambiguously tap affinity with spirituality, we feel that four additional dichotomous indicators can be constructed by capitalising on the circumstance that spirituality sets itself apart from both the Christian churches and secularist rationalism (e.g. Hanegraaff 1996). Consequently, answers that may crudely indicate spirituality, but may also tap less orthodox Christian affinities, can further be polished by combining them with answers that unambiguously reveal that one critically distances oneself from the Christian church. Likewise, answers indicating such a critical distance can be polished by combining them with answers that indicate a rejection of secularist rationalism. The former strategy enables us to demarcate spirituality from Christianity; the latter to demarcate a rejection of the Christian churches from secularist rationalism.

The first additional indicator arrived at in this way robs the belief of a life after death from its traditional Christian associations by combining it with the feeling that the churches do not give adequate answers to people's spiritual needs. We take the combination of belief in a life after death and this criticism of the churches to indicate spirituality and the three remaining combinations to indicate its absence. The second additional indicator combines a belief in reincarnation (a principal tenet of New Age, closely related to the belief in an immortal self) with an absence of belief in God (compare Heelas 1996: 112). Those first two additional indicators solve the awkward problem of demarcating the boundary between spirituality and secular-humanist conceptions of 'expressive individualism' (e.g. Bellah *et al.* 1985; see on this boundary problem: Heelas 1996: 115–117). Both indicators are precisely convincing, because they do not simply tap arguably secular self-expression as a

---

[7]   For re-unified Germany in the data collection of 2000, we have included only the *Länder* that used to be part of West-Germany in our data analysis.

key value, but indeed express belief in the existence of a self that is essentially immortal.

The circumstance that spirituality presents itself as an alternative for both Christian religion ('faith') and secularist rationalism ('reason') is used to construct two further additional indicators. Both capture the idea of spirituality as a third way beyond faith and reason. The first has been constructed by cross-tabulating whether or not one considers oneself a convinced atheist (reason) and whether or not one belongs to a religious denomination (faith). We take a rejection of both of those identities, not belonging to a religious denomination, but not considering oneself a convinced atheist either, to indicate spirituality, coding the three remaining categories as its absence. Likewise, we conceive of having no or not very much confidence in the churches, although not considering oneself a convinced atheist, as a final indicator for spirituality. Table 5.1 displays the five resulting indicators.

Table 5.1   Five indicators for affinity with spirituality (N=61,352).

Indicators for affinity with spirituality	% no affinity	% affinity	% valid
Believes in the existence of a spirit or life force.	68.0	32.0	90.3
Believes in a life after death, but thinks that the churches do not give adequate answers to people's spiritual needs.	83.7	16.3	69.9
Believes in re-incarnation, but does not believe in God.	97.0	3.0	69.9
Does not belong to a religious denomination, but does not consider oneself a convinced atheist either.	85.0	15.0	92.3
Does not consider oneself a convinced atheist, but has not very much or no confidence in the churches.	58.9	41.1	89.7

More than 40 per cent consider themselves neither convinced atheists, nor have confidence in the churches. As such, this indicator generates the highest level of spirituality. At the other end, a mere three per cent believe in re-incarnation but do not believe in God. The three remaining indicators take up positions between those two extremes. We do not claim that a combination of those five dichotomous indicators constitutes a theoretically sophisticated measurement of spirituality. What we do claim is that an index based on those indicators can serve as a crude measure that can meaningfully be used for our purposes: mapping and explaining the spiritual revolution in fourteen western countries since 1981.[8]

---

[8]   With a mere five crude dichotomous indicators, it is hardly surprising that Cronbach's alpha is not higher than 0.42. Nevertheless, all zero-order correlations between the indicators are positive and significant ($p<0.001$) and item-total correlations range from 0.17 through 0.30. A principal component analyses yields a first factor that explains 30 per cent of the common variance. The two lowest factor loadings are 0.44 (for belief in a spirit or life force and for belief in a life after death, while feeling that the churches do not give adequate answers to people's spiritual needs) and all others are higher than 0.50. We feel that those findings justify our decision to combine those five indicators into a crude index for spirituality.

All five dichotomous indicators (1: spirituality; 0: no spirituality) have first been standardized and next combined into an index ranging 0 through 10. Correcting for the number of valid scores, scores have been assigned to all respondents with a valid score on at least three of those five indicators. For one of the 42 year-country combinations – Norway, 2000 – scores could not be assigned due to missing values. This produces measurements of affinity with spirituality for 92 per cent of the 61 352 respondents.

Results

Table 5.2 displays the distribution of spirituality across the fourteen countries and three years. Italy, Canada and Iceland prove exceptions to the general pattern of change that emerges in that spirituality has declined in those three countries since 1981.[9] With the exception of those three countries, however, the general pattern of change is clear enough. In the eleven remaining countries spirituality has become more widespread since 1981. The overall trend confirms the idea that a spiritual revolution has been going on during the last two decades.

Table 5.2   Mean affinity with spirituality in 14 western countries in 1981, 1990, and 2000 (N=56,513).

Country	1981	1990	2000	Total	Change (Pearson's r)[1]
France	1.61	1.97	2.07	1.90	0.11***
Great Britain	1.83	2.33	1.97	2.07	0.04**
West Germany	1.57	1.87	1.70	1.74	0.03**
Italy	1.74	1.46	1.37	1.50	-0.10***
Netherlands	2.26	2.76	3.03	2.67	0.16***
Denmark	1.43	1.71	1.62	1.58	0.05**
Belgium	1.35	1.69	2.10	1.76	0.17***
Spain	1.51	1.67	1.86	1.67	0.09***
Ireland	1.02	1.27	1.53	1.26	0.18***
United States	1.04	1.44	1.57	1.29	0.17***
Canada	1.89	1.89	1.71	1.82	-0.04**
Norway	1.53	1.77	-	1.65	0.09***
Sweden	1.78	1.84	2.29	1.97	0.14***
Iceland	1.88	1.53	1.65	1.70	-0.06***
Total	1.55	1.77	1.86	1.72	0.08***

[1] One-sided test
* p < 0.05; ** p < 0.01; *** p < 0.001

Spirituality has expanded most in the Netherlands, Belgium, Ireland and the United States. In the latter two countries, despite this substantial growth, it was least widespread in 1981 and those two countries still lag behind today (only for Italy, in which spirituality has declined since 1981, lower levels of affinity are found in 2000). The countries that lead the way with highest levels of affinity with spirituality

---

9   Probably due to a different operationalization, this finding for Canada is inconsistent with Bibby's (2002) observation that more Canadians say they're spiritual today than 30 years ago.

are France, Great Britain, the Netherlands and Sweden. It is clear from those findings that spirituality has become more widespread since 1981, confirming the occurrence of a spiritual revolution in late modernity.

But are we really dealing with a process of historical change here? Are differences across this twenty-year period really caused by an intergenerational replacement of older age cohorts with typically Christian affinities by younger age cohorts with spiritual ones? Because our data cover a time range of twenty years and because of the large number of respondents, we can distinguish age from birth year and, hence, disentangle 'age effects' and 'cohort effects'.[10] This enables us to test whether the higher levels of affinity with spirituality in the most recent period are caused by cohort replacement.

We have done so by means of multilevel analysis with Maximum Likelihood estimation. This method of analysis is used to analyse so-called 'nested' data, i.e., data in which cases defined at a lower level (typically, and also in this case, respondents) are embedded in contexts defined at a higher level (in this case: combinations of countries and years). Multilevel analysis enables one to assess the importance of both levels for explaining a variable defined at the individual level, to find out which contextual and individual variables are (most) consequential and to analyse whether the effects of variables defined at the individual level vary across contexts.

Table 5.3   The spiritual revolution as a historical change process (multilevel analysis, betas).

Predictors	(1)	(2)	(3)	(4)
Intercept	0.020	0.024	0.025	0.027
Contextual level				
1981 (reference category)				
1990		0.063		0.032
2000		0.085*		0.016
Individual level (fixed effects)				
Year of birth			0.222*	0.189***
Age			0.031	
-2 Log Likelihood	157230.3	157226.3	154168.7	154168.3
Variance contextual level	0.063	0.058	0.059	0.058
Variance explained contextual level (%)	0.0	7.9	6.3	7.9
Variance individual level	0.943	0.943	0.912	0.912
Variance explained individual level (%)	0.0	0.0	3.3	3.3

* $p < 0.05$; ** $p < 0.01$; *** $p < 0.001$

All variables have been standardized so as to produce standardized regression coefficients (betas) that enable a straightforward comparison of the strengths of the effects found. In this case, aimed at the explanation of individual-level spirituality,

---

[10]   Disentangling 'age effects' and 'cohort effects' is impossible, of course, when 'one-shot-survey data' are analysed. The correlation between age and birth year is then exactly -1.00. Because even with a twenty-year period we face a strong negative correlation between both variables, the extremely large sample is helpful in preventing problems of multicollinearity.

the explanatory role of the contextual level proves limited. Only about six per cent of the differences at the individual level can be attributed to differences between the years and countries, whereas the remaining 94 per cent is caused by individual characteristics (Table 5.3). Table 5.3 demonstrates that the higher level of spirituality in the more recent period emerges from the circumstance that respondents who most typically embrace spirituality have been born more recently (model 4 as compared to model 2). This means that the spiritual revolution is driven by cohort replacement: younger age cohorts with stronger affinities with spirituality have replaced older age cohorts with more typically Christian affinities.

Explaining the spiritual revolution

Detraditionalization and the sacralization of the self

Despite its shortcomings, to be discussed below, conventional secularization theory offers a fruitful point of departure for explaining the spiritual revolution. It is hardly contested, after all, that a process of rationalization has undermined religion's grip on social life (e.g., Wilson 1982; Luckmann 1967, 2003). This is so, because rationalization entails institutional differentiation: social functions are increasingly dealt with by specialized institutions. With increased specialization and institutional separation of the economy, the family, the state, science, art, etcetera, those increasingly come to be governed by their own particular institutional logic (compare Bell 1976). This causes a value pluralism that erodes the unquestioned legitimacy of the traditional moral values bound up with the Christian tradition that once morally overarched all of society as a sort of 'sacred canopy' (Berger 1967).

The ensuing process of 'detraditionalisation' (Heelas 1995) or 'individualisation' (Beck and Beck-Gernsheim 2002) is not simply the aggregated result of individual choice or desire, in short, but a more or less inevitable outcome – 'Individualization is a fate, not a choice', as Bauman (2002: xvi) aptly remarks. As the grip of external and authoritative sources of meaning and identity declines, the range of biographical and lifestyle options nevertheless widens considerably: 'It is ... (the) level of pre-conscious "collective habitualizations", of matters taken for granted, that is breaking down into a cloud of possibilities to be thought about and negotiated. The deep layer of foreclosed decisions is being forced up into the level of decision making' (Beck and Beck-Gernsheim 2002: 6).

Although all of the foregoing is by and large agreed upon, two radically different theoretical positions can be distinguished as far as the consequences for individual religiosity are concerned. The first, secularization theory, assumes that Christian religiosity and traditional moral values give way to a sort of rationalist worldview: 'People increasingly think that they can control and manipulate "their" world. They act more in terms of insight, knowledge, controllability, planning and technique and less in terms of faith (Dobbelaere 1993: 15, our translation from Dutch, DH/SA). In a similar vein, the late Bryan Wilson claims that '(i)n contemporary society, the young come to regard morality – any system of ethical norms – as somewhat old-fashioned. For many young people, problems of any kind have technical and rational solutions' (1982: 136). Conceiving of rationalism as the 'other' of religion, in short, this logic of secularization extends the process of rationalization to the level of individual consciousness. Given this theory's prominence in the recent past, there is embarrassingly little evidence that supports this assumption, however. More than that, '... a diminishing faith in rationality and a diminishing confidence that science and technology will help solve humanity's problems ... has advanced farthest in the economically and technologically most advanced societies' (Inglehart 1997: 79).

Although the assumption that rationalism replaces religion as a worldview may thus simply be mistaken, our ambition here is to explain a spiritual rather than a rationalist revolution. This is where a second theoretical logic comes in, that argues that the declining grip of external and authoritative sources of meaning and identity robs late-modern individuals of the protective cloak of 'pre-given' meaning and identity and throws them back upon themselves in dealing with their 'precarious freedoms' (Beck and Beck-Gernsheim 1992: 16). Under those circumstances, nagging questions haunt those who crave for the solidly founded answers that the late-modern condition precludes: 'What is it that I really want?', 'Is this really the sort of life I want to live?', 'What sort of person am I, really?'. Because it is ultimately only one's feelings and intuitions that remain as sources of answers to those questions, 'a shift of authority: from "without" to "within"' (Heelas 1995: 2) easily takes place, driving a voyage of discovery to the deeper layers of the self. And as we have seen above, this is precisely the key tenet of spirituality: the belief that 'real' meaning and 'real' identity can only be derived from such an 'internal' source.

Detraditionalization and the gender puzzle

The well-established research finding that spirituality is more typical of the young and the well educated than of the elderly and the poorly educated (e.g. Becker *et al.* 1997; Stark and Bainbridge 1985; Houtman and Mascini 2002) can easily be reconciled with the hypothesis that increasing levels of post-traditionalism drive the spiritual revolution. As it happens, the young and the well educated stand out as two of the most post-traditional demographic categories. To cite the most influential example only, Inglehart (1977, 1990, 1997) demonstrates that 'postmaterialism' is especially found among the younger age cohorts and the well educated and that it is strongly related to post-traditionalism, conceived of as a rejection of traditional values pertaining to gender roles, sexuality, child-rearing and so forth (1997: 47). Studies into the propensity to obey authorities have always arrived at precisely the same conclusion: the young and the well educated are least likely to do so (see Houtman 2003, for a review of the relevant studies). The spiritual affinities of the young and the well educated seem attributable to their high levels of post-traditionalism, in short.

Besides the young and the well educated, however, women of course also stand out with high levels of affinity with spirituality. This constitutes a difficult problem of explanation, because men and women do not differ with regard to post-traditionalism (e.g. Houtman 2003; Houtman and Mascini 2002). As a consequence, unlike those of the young and the well educated, women's affinities with spirituality cannot simply be attributed to a high level of post-traditionalism. Instead, gendering the theory of detraditionalization is called for, so as to give due to the circumstance that detraditionalization means different things to men and women.

And indeed, detraditionalization is likely to engender gender-specific burdens and anxieties (see also Woodhead 2005, 2007). Whereas traditional male gender roles virtually coincide with the role of the breadwinner, traditional female gender roles, organized around the provision of care for others, are defined precisely in contrast to this work role. Although due to the more general process of detraditionalization discussed above, normative acceptance of those traditional gender roles has declined, this does not mean that traditional gender arrangements and role expectations have dissolved altogether. As a consequence, many women who reject traditional gender roles still find themselves confronted with the corresponding role expectations and face a 'second shift' when returning home after a day's work (Hochschild 1989; see also Hochschild 1997).

Even apart from the double weight on their shoulders this produces, women's work experiences acquire radically different meanings from those of men, because they are also measured against traditional female gender roles that situate women in the domain of the household and the family: 'In the space of a few generations, women have made a leap between ... two frames of reference which men have never experienced in the same way' (Beck and Beck-Gernsheim 1992: 75). Detraditionalization produces burdens and anxieties for working post-traditional women, in short, to which working post-traditional men remain by and large immune.

Although the domain of work, increasingly invaded by women during the last few decades, is likely to be of overriding importance, other life spheres also add to post-traditional women's burdens and anxieties. The erosion of traditional female sexual prohibitions, for instance, engenders a new experience of the sexual domain: 'Without a strict "no" imposed from the outside, (women) must increasingly find their own rules and behaviour' (Beck and Beck-Gernsheim 1992: 69). Contraception by means of 'the pill', for instance, requires rational and conscious planning in advance, that easily contradicts with a desire for romanticism – to 'simply let it happen' when romance strikes like lightning.

Even though the loss of the protective cloak of 'pre-given' meaning and identity creates tensions and anxieties for men and women alike, women are substantially more likely to become caught up in new webs of contradiction and ambiguity, in short (see also Bobel 2002). Post-traditional women are therefore more likely than post-traditional men to be haunted by the questions of meaning and identity that are evoked by detraditionalization and that stimulate late-modern individuals to explore the depths of their souls – 'What is it that I really want?', 'Is this really the sort of life I want to live?', 'What sort of person am I, really?'. Post-traditional women are more likely than post-traditional men to embark on a spiritual quest and sacralize their selves, in short.

Testing the gendered theory of detraditionalization

We test the gendered theory of detraditionalization by means of a second series of multilevel analyses. Following Houtman (2003: 83–102) and Houtman and Mascini

(2002), post-traditionalism is operationalized by combining three measures that tap acceptance or rejection of traditional moral values (i.e., acceptance or rejection of the traditional hierarchical relationship between parents and children, of traditional values pertaining to sexuality and of traditional male and female gender roles) with Inglehart's index for postmaterialism.

First, self-direction or conformity as a parental value is measured by means of respondents' selection of a maximum of five from a list of qualities that may be encouraged in children. Their evaluation of six of those qualities is used here: 'determination/perseverance,' 'imagination' and 'independence' (indicating 'self-direction') and 'obedience,' 'religious faith' and 'good manners' (indicating 'conformity'). With all of those qualities coded either 0 ('not chosen') or 1 ('chosen'), the more goals one selects from the former three and the less from the latter three, the higher one's level of post-traditionalism.[11]

Second, sexual permissiveness is measured as judgements about the acceptability of five activities: married men/women having an affair, sex under the legal age of consent, homosexuality, prostitution and abortion. Scores range from 'never justified' (1) to 'always justified' (10) and high scores are taken to indicate high levels of post-traditionalism.[12]

Third, three questions are used to measure the degree to which traditional gender roles are accepted or rejected. The first two are statements that 'a woman has to have children to be fulfilled' and that 'a single woman should have the right to have a child' and the third is a question about whether or not one feels that marriage is an out-of-date institution.[13]

Fourth and finally, Inglehart's index for postmaterialism is constructed on the basis of the prioritization of four political goals by the respondents. Those who select 'Giving the people more say in important government decisions' and 'Protecting free speech' as the two most important goals are coded 'postmaterialists' and those

---

[11]   An overall factor analysis produces a single factor with an eigenvalue higher than one, explaining 28 per cent of the common variance. All six factor loadings are higher than 0.40 and the signs of the loadings for the indicators for self-direction are positive, whereas those for conformity are negative. If a factor loading for a particular indicator was below 0.30 for a country-year combination, it has been coded missing for that particular country-year combination. After reversing the scores on the indicators tapping conformity, scores have been assigned as mean standardised scores to all respondents with at most two missing values. This produces valid scores for more than 99 per cent of the respondents.

[12]   An overall factor analysis produces a single factor with an eigenvalue higher than one, explaining no less than 54 per cent of the common variance. All factor loadings are higher than 0.65 and scores have been assigned as mean scores to all respondents with no more than two missing values, yielding valid scores for 96.9 per cent of the respondents.

[13]   Response categories for those three questions are, respectively, yes/no, yes/depends/ no (recoded into yes versus depends/no) and yes/no. An overall factor analysis produces a single factor with an eigenvalue higher than one that explains 40 per cent of the common variance with factor loadings of 0.41, 0.73 and 0.71, respectively. Scores have been assigned to 97.6 per cent of the respondents with at most one missing value.

who choose 'Maintaining order in the nation' and 'Fighting rising prices' are coded 'materialists'. Remaining respondents are coded as a mixed category in between.[14]

As expected, those four measures are strongly related among themselves. A second-order factor analysis produces a first factor that explains 46 per cent of the common variance with factor loadings of 0.65 (rejection of traditional gender roles), 0.59 (postmaterialism), 0.68 (emphasis on self-direction rather than conformity as a parental value) and 0.77 (sexual permissiveness). Scores for post-traditionalism are therefore assigned as mean standardised scores to 98.7 per cent of the respondents with valid scores on at least three of those four measures. In effect, those who are postmaterialists, critical of traditional gender roles, critical of conformity as a parental value and sexually permissive receive highest scores on post-traditionalism.

Table 5.4   Explaining the spiritual revolution from detraditionalization (multilevel analysis, betas).

Predictors	(1)	(2)	(3)	(4)
Intercept	0.020	0.025	0.021	0.026
Contextual level				
1981 (reference category)				
1990		0.022	-0.000	0.005
2000		-0.010	-0.064	-0.038
Mean post-traditionalism		0.151***	0.135**	0.055
Individual level (fixed effects)				
Year of birth			0.170***	0.102***
Education			0.068***	-0.006
Female				-0.015
Post-traditionalism				0.276***
Post-traditionalism*female				0.036***
Individual level (random effects)				
Year of birth			0.004***	0.004***
Education			0.002*	0.001*
Female				0.002**
Post-traditionalism				0.008***
Post-traditionalism*female				0.000
-2 Log Likelihood	157230.3	157213.9	148670.9	143236.0
Variance contextual level	0.063	0.042	0.043	0.036
Variance explained contextual level (%)	0.0	33.3	31.7	42.9
Variance individual level	0.943	0.943	0.901	0.837
Variance explained individual level (%)	0.0	0.0	4.5	11.2

* $p < 0.05$; ** $p < 0.01$; *** $p < 0.001$

Our second series of multilevel analyses confirms the gendered version of the theory of detraditionalization. As expected, the higher levels of spirituality in the most recent period are caused by a process of detraditionalization (model 2 in Table 5.4) and precisely those who stand out as most post-traditional embrace spirituality

---

[14]   Valid scores are available for 89.9 per cent of the respondents.

(model 4 as compared to model 2). Moreover, all affinity with spirituality of the well educated and a substantial part of that of the younger birth cohorts is caused by post-traditionalism (model 4 as compared to model 2). Whereas traditional men and traditional women are equally unlikely to embrace spirituality, post-traditional women are more likely to do so than post-traditional men (i.e., the significant interaction effect of post-traditionalism and female gender in model 4). Hence, the female drift toward spirituality applies to post-traditional women only. This confirms our theory, based on the assumption that detraditionalization produces stronger tensions and anxieties in post-traditional women, making them more likely to sacralize their selves than post-traditional men.[15]

Table 5.5   Zero-order and partial correlations of post-traditionalism and affinity with spirituality by gender and country.

Country	Pearson's r[1]			Partial r[2]		
	Men	Women	N	Men	Women	N
France	0.25	0.28	3,614	0.18	0.22	3,506
Great Britain	0.21	0.28	3,454	0.19	0.23	3,294
West Germany	0.31	0.39	4,065	0.27	0.31	4,018
Italy	0.32	0.44	5,172	0.30	0.40	5,105
Netherlands	0.34	0.41	3,086	0.27	0.33	3,041
Denmark	0.16	0.27	2,948	0.11	0.20	2,913
Belgium	0.26	0.35	5,390	0.22	0.27	5,108
Spain	0.21	0.31	8,015	0.19	0.21	7,447
Ireland	0.40	0.45	3,159	0.30	0.37	3,056
United States	0.27	0.31	5,075	0.24	0.27	4,742
Canada	0.31	0.32	4,158	0.27	0.28	4,055
Norway	0.29	0.42	2,392	0.25	0.34	2,326
Sweden	0.15	0.21	2,824	0.13	0.13	2,663
Iceland	0.20	0.24	2,549	0.17	0.18	2,466
Total	0.27	0.35	55,901	0.23	0.29	53,736

[1]   All zero-order correlations significant at $p < 0.001$ (one-sided test).
[2]   All partial correlations, controlling for year of birth and education, significant at $p < 0.001$ (one-sided test).

Correlations between post-traditionalism and spirituality have been computed for men and women separately to be able to inspect the statistical relationships that underlie the interaction effect of gender and post-traditionalism in more detail (Table 5.5). Post-traditionalism is positively related to spirituality in each of the fourteen countries studied. Although this applies to men and women alike, the relationship is stronger for women than men in all of those countries, with the single exception of

---

[15]   Finally, the strengths of the effects of birth year, gender and post-traditionalism vary between contexts (model 4, random effects): they are stronger in some years and countries and weaker in others. Additional analyses, not shown in Table 5.4, point out that those differences cannot be attributed to the circumstance that some years and countries are more post-traditional than others.

Sweden (in which there is no difference). It is evident that those findings confirm our gendered version of the theory of detraditionalization: spirituality is more typically embraced by post-traditional women than by post-traditional men.

Conclusion and debate

Traditionally considered as inevitably incompatible, many today conceive of modernity and religion as mutually accommodating. Woodhead and Heelas' anthology *Religion in Modern Times* (2000), for instance, juxtaposes theories of secularization and theories of sacralization, rejecting the idea that those are necessarily incompatible. Indeed, our findings indicate that the decline of the Christian churches in most western countries has gone along with an increasing sacralization of the self. What we are witnessing today, then, is not so much a disappearance of the sacred, but rather its dramatic relocation from Christian heaven to the deeper layers of the self.

And yet, theoretical controversy persists. Heelas *et al.* (2005) predict a future in which spirituality supersedes religion, we ourselves envisage one in which religion does not only give way to spirituality, but to secularism, too (Houtman and Mascini 2002), and Bruce (2002) forecasts a by and large secular future.[16] Two issues seem vitally important for pushing the frontiers of knowledge further forward and clarifying the futures of spirituality and secularism: processes of socialization through which people come to adopt a spiritual discourse about the self and the role played by problems of meaning and identity in making people amenable to such a discourse.

Processes of socialization into a spiritual discourse about the self have been seriously neglected in empirical research, probably due to sociology of religion's orthodoxy – originating from Luckmann (1967) – that spirituality is 'not institutionalised', 'purely privatised', and 'strictly individualistic', so that socialization into spirituality 'is unnecessary and it is impossible' (Bruce 2002: 99). As we have emphasised above, however, the ethic of self-spirituality constitutes a remarkably coherent doctrine of being and wellbeing, and it would therefore be sociologically naive to assume that no processes of socialization are taking place. This is not to suggest that this type of socialization remains necessarily confined to the spiritual milieu, of course. With spirituality's strongly increased significance in the public domain of work, for instance, even management courses may today stimulate one to embark on a spiritual journey to the deeper layers of the self (Aupers and Houtman 2006). Be this as it may, predictions about the future of spirituality cannot be made without insight into the social mechanisms through which it spreads,

---

[16]   The exact nature of secularism is a seriously neglected issue in the research literature, however. Due to the strong focus on the decline of the Christian churches in the west, 'few attempts have been made to look at the other side of the equation, at what has been called the "left-over", if one may say so' (Knoblauch 2003: 268). Whereas secularization theory assumes that religious worldviews are increasingly being replaced by rationalist ones, there are also indications that rationalist conceptions of the self increasingly give way to postmodern ones (e.g. Gergen 1991).

but precisely this is a badly neglected research area (see however: Luhrmann 1989; Hammer 2001, 2004; Hanegraaff 2001).

The role played by problems of meaning and identity constitutes a second important issue for future research. Post-traditionalists may after all either embrace spirituality or adopt a secularist posture (Houtman and Mascini 2002) and we have argued that the experience of problems of meaning and identity decides which of each occurs. Our finding that, as predicted, post-traditional women more typically embrace spirituality than post-traditional men is consistent with this argument, but does not necessarily prove it. It is vital, therefore, to study in future research whether this difference is really caused by post-traditional women being haunted more severely by problems of meaning and identity, as our gendered version of the theory of detraditionalization suggests. Such a study promises not only highly relevant insights into what causes post-traditionalists to convert to either secularism or spirituality, but above all constitutes the definitive test of the proposed solution to the New Age gender puzzle.

References

Adler, Margot, *Drawing Down the Moon: Witches, Druids, Goddess-Worshippers, and Other Pagans in America Today* (Boston: Beacon, 1979).

Aupers, Stef, and Houtman, Dick, 'Oriental Religion in the Secular West: Globalization, New Age and the Reenchantment of the World', *Journal of National Development*, 16(1&2) (2003): 67–86.

Aupers, Stef, and Houtman, Dick, '"Reality Sucks": On Alienation and Cybergnosis', in Erik Borgman, Stephan van Erp, and Hille Haker (eds), *Cyber Space – Cyber Ethics – Cyber Theology*, special issue *Concilium: International Journal of Theology*, 2005(1) (2005): 81–89.

Aupers, Stef, and Houtman, Dick, 'Beyond the Spiritual Supermarket: The Social and Public Significance of New Age Spirituality', *Journal of Contemporary Religion*, 21(2) (2006): 201–222.

Aupers, Stef, Houtman, Dick and Pels, Peter, 'Cybergnosis: Technology, Religion and the Secular', in Hent de Vries (ed.), *Religion: Beyond a Concept* (New York: Fordham University Press, 2008): pp. 687–703.

Baerveldt, Cor, 'New Age-religiositeit als individueel constructieproces' [New Age-Religiosity as a Process of Individual Construction], in Miranda Moerland (ed.), *De kool en de geit in de nieuwe tijd: Wetenschappelijke reflecties op New Age* [The Fence, the Hare, and the Hounds in the New Age: Scientific Reflections on New Age] (Utrecht: Jan van Arkel, 1996).

Bauman, Zygmunt, 'Foreword: Individually, Together', in Ulrich Beck and Elisabeth Beck-Gernsheim, *Individualization: Institutionalized Individualism and Its Social and Political Consequences* (London: Sage, 2002).

Beck, Ulrich, and Beck-Gernsheim, Elizabeth, *Individualization: Institutionalized Individualism and Its Social and Political Consequences* (London: Sage, 2002).

Becker, J.W., De Hart, J., and Mens, J., *Secularisatie en alternatieve zingeving in Nederland* [Secularization and Alternative Religion in the Netherlands] (Rijswijk: SCP, 1997).

Bell, Daniel, *The Cultural Contradictions of Capitalism* (New York: Basic Books, 1976).

Bellah, Robert N., Madsen, Richard, Sullivan, William M., Swidler, Ann and Tipton, Steven M., *Habits of the Heart: Individualism and Commitment in American Life* (Berkeley, CA: University of California Press, 1985).

Berger, Helen A., *A Community of Witches: Contemporary Neo-Paganism and Witchcraft in the United States* (Columbia: University of South Carolina Press, 1999).

Berger, Peter L., *The Sacred Canopy: Elements of a Sociology of Religion* (New York: Doubleday, 1967).

Bibby, Reginald, *Restless Gods: The Renaissance of Religion in Canada* (Toronto: Stoddart, 2002).

Bobel, Chris, *The Paradox of Natural Mothering* (Philadelphia, PA: Temple University Press, 2002).

Bruce, Steve, *God is Dead: Secularization in the West* (Oxford: Blackwell, 2002).

Dobbelaere, Karel, 'Individuele godsdienstigheid in een geseculariseerde samenleving' [Individual Religiosity in a Secularized Society], *Tijdschrift voor Sociologie* 14(1) (1993): 5–29.

European Values Study Group and World Values Survey Association, *European and World Values Surveys Integrated Data File, 1999–2002, Release I* (computer file) (Netherlands: Netherlands Institute for Scientific Information Services (NIWI)/ Ann Arbor, MI: Inter-university Consortium for Political and Social Research (distributors), 2004).

Gergen, Kenneth J., *The Saturated Self: Dilemmas of Identity in Contemporary Life* (New York: Basic Books, 1991).

Granqvist, Pehr, and Hagekull, Berit, 'Seeking Security in the New Age: On Attachment and Emotional Compensation', *Journal for the Scientific Study of Religion*, 40(3) (2001): 527–545.

Hadden, Jeffrey, 'Towards Desacralizing Secularization Theory', *Social Forces*, 65(3) (1987): 587–610.

Hamilton, Malcolm, 'An Analysis of the Festival for Mind-Body-Spirit, London', in Steven Sutcliffe and Marion Bowman (eds), *Beyond New Age: Exploring Alternative Spirituality* (Edinburgh: Edinburgh University Press, 2000).

Hammer, Olav, *Claiming Knowledge: Strategies of Epistemology from Theosophy to the New Age* (Leiden: Brill, 2001).

Hammer, Olav, 'Contradictions of the New Age', in James Lewis (ed.), *The Encyclopedic Sourcebook of New Age Religions* (Buffalo, NY: Prometheus, 2004).

Hanegraaff, Wouter J., *New Age Religion and Western Culture: Esotericism in the Mirror of Secular Thought* (Leiden: Brill, 1996).

Hanegraaff, Wouter J., 'Prospects for the Globalization of New Age: Spiritual Imperialism versus Cultural Diversity', in Mikael Rothstein (ed.), *New Age Religion and Globalization* (Aarhus: Aarhus University Press, 2001).

Harvey, Graham, *Listening People, Speaking Earth: Contemporary Paganism* (London: Hurst & Company, 1997).

Heelas, Paul, 'Introduction: Detraditionalization and its Rivals', in: Paul Heelas, Scott Lash, and Paul Morris (eds), *Detraditionalization: Critical Reflections on Authority and Identity* (Oxford: Blackwell, 1995).

Heelas, Paul, *The New Age Movement: The Celebration of the Self and the Sacralization of Modernity* (Oxford: Blackwell, 1996).

Heelas, Paul, Woodhead, Linda, Seel, Benjamin, Szerszynski, Bronislaw, and Tusting, Karin, *The Spiritual Revolution: Why Religion is Giving Way to Spirituality* (Oxford: Blackwell, 2005).

Hochschild, Arlie, *The Second Shift: Working Parents and the Revolution at Home* (New York: Viking, 1989).

Hochschild, Arlie Russell, *The Time Bind: When Work Becomes Home and Home Becomes Work* (New York: Metropolitan, 1997)

Houtman, Dick, *Class and Politics in Contemporary Social Science: 'Marxism Lite' and Its Blind Spot for Culture* (New York: Aldine de Gruyter, 2003).

Houtman, Dick, and Mascini, Peter, 'Why Do Churches Become Empty, While New Age Grows? Secularization and Religious Change in the Netherlands', *Journal for the Scientific Study of Religion*, 41(3) (2002): 455–473.

Inglehart, Ronald, *The Silent Revolution: Changing Values and Political Styles among Western Publics* (Princeton, NJ: Princeton University Press, 1977).

Inglehart, Ronald, *Culture Shift in Advanced Industrial Society* (Princeton, NJ: Princeton University Press, 1990).

Inglehart, Ronald, *Modernization and Postmodernization: Cultural, Economic, and Political Change in 43 Countries* (Princeton, NJ: Princeton University Press, 1997).

Knoblauch, Hubert, 'Europe and Invisible Religion', *Social Compass*, 50(3) (2003): 267–274.

Luckmann, Thomas, *The Invisible Religion: The Problem of Religion in Modern Society* (London: MacMillan, 1967).

Luckmann, Thomas, 'Transformations of Religion and Morality in Modern Europe', *Social Compass*, 50(3) (2003): 275–285.

Luhrmann, Tanya M., *Persuasions of the Witch's Craft: Ritual Magic in Contemporary England* (Cambridge, MA: Harvard University Press, 1989).

Lyon, David, *Jesus in Disneyland: Religion in Postmodern Times* (Oxford: Polity, 2000).

Meyer, Birgit, and Pels, Peter (eds), *Magic and Modernity: Interfaces of Revelation and Concealment* (Stanford, CA: Stanford University Press, 2003).

Pearson, Jo, 'Assumed Affinities: Wicca and the New Age', in Jo Pearson, Richard H. Roberts, and Geoffrey Samuel (eds), *Nature Religion Today* (Edinburgh: Edinburgh University Press, 1998): pp. 45–56.

Possamai, Adam, 'Alternative Spiritualities and the Cultural Logic of Late Capitalism', *Culture and Religion*, 4(1) (2003): 31–45.

Roszak, Theodore, *The Making of a Counter Culture: Reflections on the Technocratic Society and Its Youthful Opposition* (New York: Doubleday, 1969).

Scheelbeek, Linda, *'Ik ben een God in 't diepst van mijn gedachten'* [I am a God in the Depths of my Thoughts], MA thesis sociology (Rotterdam: Erasmus University, 2003).

Stark, Rodney, and Bainbridge, William Sims, *The Future of Religion: Secularization, Revival and Cult Formation* (Berkeley: University of California Press, 1985).

Stark, Rodney, and Finke, Roger, *Acts of Faith: Explaining the Human Side of Religion* (Berkeley: University of California Press, 2000).

Stark, Rodney, Hamberg, Eva, and Miller, Alan S., 'Exploring Spirituality and Unchurched Religions in America, Sweden, and Japan', *Journal of Contemporary Religion*, 20(1) (2005): 3–23.

Sutcliffe, Steven J., and Bowman, Marion (eds), *Beyond New Age: Exploring Alternative Spirituality* (Edinburgh: Edinburgh University Press, 2000).

Van Otterloo, Anneke H., 'Selfspirituality and the Body: New Age Centres in The Netherlands since the 1960s', *Social Compass*, 46(2) (1999): 191–202.

Wilson, Bryan, *Contemporary Transformations of Religion* (Oxford: Oxford University Press, 1976).

Wilson, Bryan, *Religion in Sociological Perspective* (Oxford: Oxford University Press, 1982).

Woodhead, Linda, 'Gendering Secularisation Theory', *Kvinder, Køn og Forskning*, 14(1&2) (2005): 24–35.

Woodhead, Linda, 'Why So Many Women in Holistic Spirituality? A Puzzle Revisited', in: Kieran Flanagan and Peter Jupp (eds), *A Sociology of Spirituality* (Aldershot: Ashgate, 2007).

Woodhead, Linda, and Heelas, Paul (eds), *Religion in Modern Times: An Interpretive Anthology* (Oxford: Blackwell, 2000).

World Values Study Group, *World Values Survey, 1981–1984 and 1990–1993* (computer file) (Netherlands: Netherlands Institute for Scientific Information Services (NIWI)/Ann Arbor, MI: Inter-university Consortium for Political and Social Research (distributors), 1994).

York, Michael, *The Emerging Network: A Sociology of the New Age and Neo-Pagan Movements* (Lanham, MD: Rowman and Littlefield, 1995).

Zijderveld, Anton. C., *The Abstract Society: A Cultural Analysis of Our Time* (Garden City, NY: Doubleday, 1970).

Chapter 6

The Soul of Soulless Conditions: Paganism, Goddess Religion and Witchcraft in Canada

Síân Reid

Religion is the sigh of the oppressed creature, the heart of a heartless world, just as it is the soul of soulless conditions. It is the opium of the people.

Karl Marx, *Contribution to the Critique of Hegel's Philosophy of Law.*[1]

In 1843, Karl Marx denounced religion as a tool of the bourgeois establishment, an ideology through which the proletariat could be reconciled to their miserable lot with the promise of eternal happiness as the reward for a life lived in submission and acquiescence to inhumane labour conditions. The high offices of religion, populated by the elite, could not help but devise an institution that served their own narrow interests and not the broader interests of all humanity. Religion was one of the many persuasive channels of false consciousness – the distortion of one's perception of what is truly in one's own best interest. When the revolution came, and the proletariat realized that religion's beauty and comfort existed only to make palatable inequality and injustice, religion would be exposed for the traitor it was, and the newly liberated proletariat would shun and starve it until it faded into nothingness. The proletarian revolution, sadly, never came, but declines in the centrality of religious ideologies have been visible throughout the developed world through the nineteenth and twentieth centuries.

One of the key debates in the sociology of religion during the past fifty years is whether or not 'religion' is in 'decline' or if 'religion', like many traditional institutions carried forward into modernity, is merely adapting and changing form (Wilson 1966; Berger 1967; Luckmann 1967; Stark and Bainbridge 1985, 1987). Steve Bruce, a firm contemporary proponent of the secularization thesis, asserts '… the basic elements of "modernisation" fundamentally altered the place and nature of religious beliefs, practices and organisations so as to reduce their relevance to the lives of nation-states, social groups and individuals, in roughly that order' (1996:1). Evidence of secularization, he states, can be found through three main trends '… the decline of popular involvement in the churches; the decline in the scope and influence of religious institutions; and the decline in the popularity and impact of

---

[1]   http://www.Marxists.org/archive/marx/works/1843/critique-hpr/intro.htm.

religious beliefs' (1996: 26). Secularization, he believes, is the most significant story to tell about religion in the modern world.

While I do not disagree with his historical observations, or even with the analysis he makes of them, I do disagree that this is the most interesting feature of modern day religion. The world, as Max Weber claimed, has become disenchanted; Karl Marx described the lives of the vast majority of people in the modern age as a 'soulless condition'. In these circumstances, how are people creating a sense of meaning and purpose in their lives? I will examine the phenomena of paganism and Goddess religion as one means through which people, especially women, interested in constructing a relationship with the divine are doing so, despite – and perhaps because of – secularization.

Organized religion in Canada

Reginald Bibby has documented the decline in popular involvement in organized religion in Canada in two books (1987, 1993) based on his analysis of surveys he conducted among adults in 1975, 1980, 1985 and 1990 and among teenagers in 1984, 1988 and 1992, as well as the 1991 General Social Survey and census and Gallup poll data, both contemporary and historical. From these, he has produced a clear description of the broad trends in Canadian religious involvement over time, and it is to this description that I will primarily refer to reinforce that the secularization trend is proceeding in Canada in a way that would be familiar to sociologists in Britain and other European countries.

Bibby notes that nominal religious affiliation among Canadians is still high, with 87.5 per cent listing an affiliation on the 1991 census. On the 2001 census, this dipped only slightly, to 85.8 per cent. However, self-identification is only an indirect indicator of what is going on in the churches themselves. The proportion of the Canadian population holding church membership and the proportion attending weekly services on a regular or semi-regular basis, according to Bibby's research, have been declining since the end of the Second World War (1987: 12–16). In addition, those individuals most involved in, committed to, and financially supportive of Canadian churches tend to be those over 55. He notes that:

- more than 40 per cent are both local church members and weekly attenders, compared to around 25 percent of people in their late-30s to mid-50s and less than 20 per cent of Canadians under the age of 35.
- the major financial contributors to the churches are people 55 and older. In 1990, for example, they gave more than all other younger Canadians combined.
- almost five in ten of those who are 55+ say that religion is very important to them, versus just over two in ten of Canadians 35 to 54, and less than two in ten under 35. (1993: 96–97)

Further, as those older people who are currently most active in the churches age and gradually die off, it is unlikely that younger cohorts are going to become more religiously involved, pick up the slack and fill in the empty pews, in part because these cohorts were less involved in the life of the church with their families as children and are therefore less likely to reproduce the pattern in their adult families with their children. As one indication of this tendency, Bibby cites Gallup poll comparisons:

> In a 1957 Gallup poll almost three in four Canadians said they had gone to Sunday school when they were children; 60 per cent said they had attended regularly. As of the early 1990s, that figure has dropped to one in four. Consequently, the question of whether Canadians are *returning* to church is increasingly irrelevant; an evergrowing majority have *never* been actively involved (1993: 19).

He notes that from a purely demographic standpoint, organized religion in Canada is headed for serious difficulties if it expects to maintain itself in its current form.

Despite this, however, Bibby places little credence in the arguments made by theorists such as Stark and Bainbridge that in those areas where membership levels in traditional religions are low, membership in sects and cults will be stronger, due to the higher structural availability of potential recruits (1987: 212–213). Bibby notes that there may well be more people available to join such groups, but they still do not appear to be doing so in great numbers, certainly not in numbers that would suggest that religious membership overall is not in decline (1993: 48–58). Stark and Bainbridge's assertion may be correct, argues Bibby, but it is peripheral, as it seems unlikely that the new religions will make any inroads whatsoever in replacing the old ones.

However, despite a falling away from traditional religions and only a lukewarm interest in new ones, Bibby also documents what he interprets to be a strong interest in 'religious questions', including supernatural or paranormal events, what happens after death, and the existence of God, among both those Canadians who are involved in the churches, and those who are not. For example, according to his surveys:

- one in two Canadians claim they themselves have experienced precognition (1993: 119);
- one in two Canadians claim they themselves have experienced mental telepathy (1993: 119);
- the proportion of adult Canadians believing they will be reincarnated after death has risen from seven per cent in 1980 to 26 per cent in 1990 (1993: 127);
- the proportion of teenagers believing in reincarnation is even higher, 32 per cent in 1992 (1993: 127);
- four in ten Canadians agree that 'we can have contact with the spirit world' (1993: 131);
- slightly more than 20 per cent of Canadians believe that 'it is possible to communicate with the dead' (1993: 131);
- 90 per cent of Canadians maintain that either God is 'important' or is 'becoming more important' to them (1993: 129);
- 21 per cent of Canadians assert they have definitely 'personally experienced' God, while another 23 per cent in 1990 and 27 per cent in 2000 believe they may have had a similar experience (2002: 147).

Bibby takes this interest in supernatural and spiritual matters, combined with the documented decline in church membership and attendance, as evidence that organized religions are failing to maintain their position as the obvious and natural venues through which to pursue these interests. He attributes this in part to the secularization of society more generally, but also to the routinization in church organization which has served to move the focus of 'church life' from the spiritual life of the people to the organizational life of the church. He comments,

> There is good reason to believe that a considerable number of Canadians are failing to associate their interest in mystery and meaning with what religion historically has had to offer. ... In other words, Canadians are not in the market for churches. They are, however, very much in the market for the things religion historically has been about. (1993: 177)

The spiritual concerns – those concerning the nature of the relationship between the natural and supernatural worlds – that have been the traditional concerns of organized religion have become disembedded from church organizations and returned to the individual as matters of private contemplation as the churches have lost their status as special arbiters of truth and goodness. Bibby argues that this has occurred for a number of reasons. First, Canadians, he asserts, have responded to cultural pluralism by rejecting absolute truth claims and adopting a relativistic position, particularly where matters of morality, lifestyle and belief are concerned. He notes that on his 1990 survey, 65 per cent of adult Canadians agreed that 'everything's relative' and 50 per cent maintained that 'what is right or wrong is a matter of personal opinion'. Among teens in 1992, the proportion believing that right or wrong was a matter of personal opinion was 65 per cent. He also observes that adults and youths involved in religious groups were no less likely to espouse these views than other Canadians (1993: 67). Second, many of the most established Christian churches in Canada have lost credibility and the confidence of the Canadian population due to the ongoing sex and abuse scandals with which they have been associated. Last, increased secularization has resulted in many of the social improvement functions of the churches being either entirely taken over by governments or other non-profit organizations, or at very least, in competition for those sectors. Church membership has become one of many voluntary individual affiliations, competing not just with other potential religious identifications, but also with other social opportunities and service organizations.

Expert systems, authority claims and sequestration

The erosion of sweeping authority claims is discussed directly by Anthony Giddens (1991) as a feature of late modernity in the West. He asserts that traditional authority loses its overarching character in all spheres as knowledge systems become more abstracted from individuals, and is replaced by area expertise. This is especially damaging for religion, which sees the scope of what it can claim for itself dramatically reduced, while simultaneously being forced to compete with other 'expert' interpretations and explanations. Giddens also offers some explanation for the displacement of organized religion as a central location for the production of social identity, although only by extension, through his description of the sequestration of experience in late modernity.

Giddens argues that the day-to-day 'taken for grantedness' of modernity can only be achieved by the exclusion of those 'fundamental existential issues which raise central moral dilemmas for human beings' (1991: 156). He refers to the removal of phenomena such as madness, criminality, sickness, death and sexuality from the visible routines of ordinary life as a 'sequestration of experience'. 'The sequestration of experience means that, for many people, direct contact with events and situations which link the individual lifespan to broad issues of morality and finitude are rare and fleeting' (1991: 8). I would argue that those things that Bibby designates as 'supernatural experiences', such as a personal experience of God, also belong in the category of 'sequestered' experiences.

Secularization effectively removed mystical or supernatural experience from any central role in the organization of the public sphere, exactly as Bruce suggests (1996: 1), relegating spiritual experiences and their attendant moral questions to the institution of organized religion, much in the same way that madness was relegated to the asylum and illness and death to the hospital. However, the continued progress of secularization and the mainstream churches' attempts to accommodate themselves to an ever-increasingly non-religious public culture, have resulted in these experiences becoming further sequestered, moving out of the institutions designed to contain them and taking root in the most private sphere of all, the reflexively constructed narrative of the self.

As a result, spirituality – in the sense of connection between the natural and supernatural, and a quest for ontological security – has become a comparatively unregulated domain, not subject to the same sorts of structural constraints that surround, for example, an individual's participation in the economy. Individuals are free to grapple with existential and spiritual concerns, but are no longer compelled to do so by the social structure. The meaning of life has become entirely separated, in a structural sense, from the ordinary living of life, so that it is possible to do the latter without any necessary reference to the former. Individuals who are dissatisfied with this fundamental divorce must find a way to re-embed moral relevance into the process of living, and they must do so as individuals faced with competing options for generating purpose and meaning.

The difference between Bruce's assessment of this situation, and my own, is not in a dispute over the facts, but in our respective evaluations of the residual relevance of religion. Bruce focuses on the broad social effects of religion, following Durkheim (1915 [1995]), while I am more interested in the ontological, discursive and identity-formation functions of religion (or spirituality, if you prefer). I wish to examine the primary function of religion – the extent to which it is able to produce a feeling of connection between the natural and supernatural world – for the individual, rather than for the social group, as the whole notion of 'social group' has been problematized and complicated by the very conditions of modernity that Bruce elaborates (1996: 38–39).

It is in this context that the logic of neo-paganism becomes compelling for some, especially women, postulating as it does a spirituality based on a personal, individual, non-prescriptive relationship with an immanent and pervasive divinity. The emergence of spiritualities in which the individual, rather than the proximal social group in which the individual is located, is taken as the basic unit of analysis could be taken as an indication that the forces of secularization that first moved religious concerns out of the sphere of civil discourse and into the sequestered environment of institutional religion have now further disembedded those concerns, leaving them to be constructed wholly within the individual's own ontological discourse and reflexive biography. Because neo-paganism is fundamentally disorganized, having neither a centralized hierarchy nor canonical texts, its adherents are free to construct it according to their own preferences around a minimally specified framework. Therefore, it could be expected to flourish under conditions of secularization. Even Stark and Bainbridge (1987), sceptical as they are about an expansive future for new religious movements, acknowledge that secularization promotes religious innovation (307–311). Why women especially? Because it was women's voices that were most constrained by the existing religious structures, and during the same period that those structures were showing obvious signs of deterioration, the second wave of the feminist movement found its voice, and insisted on telling their stories differently.

Women, Paganism and the Goddess

In 1978, Carol Christ stood before a microphone at the University of Santa Cruz in California and delivered the keynote address to the "Great Goddess Re-Emerging" Conference. That address, "Why Women Need the Goddess", became one of the defining statements of the feminist spirituality and Goddess religion movements. It was a clear, well-reasoned elaboration of what a Goddess could do for women that neither the Father in Heaven, nor his church on earth, could. In her declamation, she builds upon anthropologist Clifford Geertz's definition of religion:

> A religion is 1) a set of symbols which acts to 2) establish powerful, pervasive and long lasting moods and motivations in men by 3) formulating conceptions of a general order of existence and 4) clothing these conceptions with such an aura of factuality that 5) the moods and motivations seem uniquely realistic. (Geertz 1973: 90)

Based on this, she argues that the utilization of exclusively male symbols and images for divinity has negative political, social and psychological consequences for women. She writes,

> Religious symbol systems focused around exclusively male images of divinity create the impression that female power can never be fully legitimate or wholly beneficent. This need never be explicitly stated ... for its effects to be felt. ... She may see herself as like God (created in the image of God) only by denying her own sexual identity and affirming God's transcendence of sexual identity. But she can never have the experience that is freely available to every man and boy in her culture, of having her full sexual identity affirmed as being in the image and likeness of God. (1979: 275)

Christ continues her argument by elaborating on four of the reasons she believes contemporary women need the Goddess as a potent and accessible religious symbol. She asserts that the Goddess legitimates women's power, women's bodies, women's wills and women's heritage and bonds with each other, independent of men. In effect, she is saying that the religions in which the majority of her listeners had been socialized (Christianity and Judaism) had never effectively performed what is supposed to be the primary function of religion – to relate the natural world of day to day experience and the supernatural world of divinity, mystery and power. They had not been able to do that because both these worlds had been constructed solely from the perspective of men, and excluded and marginalized women symbolically, socially, and spiritually. The spiritual visions were men's visions, and the institutions that enacted, embodied and regulated these visions were men's institutions.

The lack of a divine symbol with which/whom women can identify has been rectified by the proponents of contemporary pagan religions of most forms, from the relatively gender egalitarian British-origin streams of witchcraft and Druidry, to the radically feminist and separatist streams within feminist witchcraft and Goddess religion. Can the Goddess[2], as she is constructed within contemporary paganism and Goddess worship, escape the toll that secularizing forces have taken on mainstream religions? Will the number of people for whom paganism and Goddess worship provides a meaningful linkage between the natural and supernatural worlds inevitably diminish over time? I will argue not, precisely because of the way in which contemporary paganism is adapted to the conditions of late modernity.

Proportionally, according to Statistics Canada, paganism is the fastest growing religion in Canada. In 1981, there were 2,810 people recorded as being pagan on the census. In 1991, that rose to 5,530 and in 2001 to 21,085. In previous work, I have suggested that there is strong evidence to predict that, contrary to what secularization theorists might have us believe, the number of self-identified pagans will continue to increase in Canada, and, by extension, in the United States, since both countries experienced similar post-war population patterns (Reid 2005).

It is not difficult to ascertain that the majority of pagans are women. Most pagans will be able to tell you that anecdotally, and both research and census findings bear out those observations.

Table 6.1   2001 Census findings

Region	Pagans*	% Women	% Men
Canada	21 085	62.9	37.1
England and Wales	38 000	56.4	43.7
New Zealand	5 862	62	38

* The 2001 Census of England and Wales has two separate categories I have here combined as 'Pagan': Pagan (31,000) and Wicca (7000). These terms are used less interchangeably in the United Kingdom than they are elsewhere.

The United States' Census does not collect information on religious affiliation, but a number of research projects conducted through the 1980s and 1990s suggest a similar pattern of affiliation by sex as is seen in Canada and New Zealand.

---

[2]   The idea of 'Goddess', and of the nature of the divine in general, is constructed in a wide variety of ways, and this has always been the case in contemporary paganism. Some believe that divinity is personal, some an aspect of one's own higher self, some that all the various divine personalities are expressions of one ineffable divine force, some in a true and competitive polytheism. Nor do these interpretations stay consistent over time. Practitioners will describe their relationship to the divine and their beliefs about its nature differently, at different times and in different contexts.

Table 6.2   American findings†

Researcher	Survey Period	Sample*	% Women	% Men
Berger et al.	1993–1995	2089	64.8	33.9
Jorgensen & Russell	1996	643	56.8	42.3
Orion	1985	189	58	38

* Both Jorgensen and Russell and Orion distributed their questionnaires almost exclusively at mixed gender festivals. Berger *et al.* suggest that in so doing, they may have systematically biased their findings inasmuch as their research indicates that about half of all pagans they reached in their survey had not attended a festival in the previous year, and that men are more likely to attend festivals than women, and to attend more of them during the year (2003: 26). A mixed gender venue may also fail to capture those pagans who prefer to practice in women-only settings.
† Percentages do not add to 100 as some respondents gave answers that could not be definitively coded as male or female.

I conducted my own surveys among Canadian pagans in 1995–1996 (n = 187) and in 2005–2006 (n = 325). In each of these, the ratio of female to male respondents remained constant, at approximately three to one[3]. Furthermore, the first survey asked participants what they would list as their religion on the census; fully 25 per cent of my sample listed something that would not have been coded as pagan. This may account for some of the discrepancy between the proportions in my sample and those found by the census. What all of these findings clearly suggest however, methodological quibbling aside, is that women are drawn to contemporary pagan spiritualities, and furthermore that they are drawn in greater numbers than are men, lending credence to Christ's supposition that spiritualities prominently featuring a Goddess would speak especially strongly to women.

When I asked pagans during the 1995 survey what had initially appealed to them about paganism, as Christ would predict, the Goddess emerged as a significant draw.

Table 6.3   Initial appeals of paganism (Reid 1995–1996 data)

Quality	% of Respondents	% Women	% Men
Presence of the Goddess	24.6	30	12.5
Balance between God and Goddess	10.7	14	4.2
Positive image / valuation of women and their experiences	12.3	15.9	2.1

The idea of a powerful and, at the very least, equal Goddess, with all of the imagery and ritual elements associated with that, and all of the implied messages about the worth of women and their place in the world is clearly a strong initial attraction

---

[3]   While the raw percentages were marginally different, the difference was not statistically significant.

to paganism, more so for women than men. Another quality that was listed as an initial appeal much more often by women (14.5%) than by men (2.1%) was the empowerment of the individual to make choices about and/or changes in their lives. This supports Cynthia Eller's thesis that, relative to men, women experience a sense of disempowerment within and alienation from the conditions of their lives, which makes a practice that redefines them as central to the process of their own self-determination particularly appealing (1993: 209–212).

During the course of my follow-up interviews in 1998 (n = 18), every participant, male and female, brought the Goddess into the conversation somewhere. Often, it was when they were asked what made paganism different from other religions. Jon Bloch, in his analysis of interviews done with American neo-pagans and 'New Agers'[4] in the 1990s, also notes the prevalence of discussion of the Goddess and the divine feminine among his subjects (1998: 69–72)[5]. He observes a difference in the way in which his female and male subjects frame their explanations of the role and importance of the divine feminine. He suggests that while women are inclined to speak of Goddess spirituality in terms of larger gender inequalities and as a means of obtaining 'self-validation by having a female image of the divine with which to identify' (70), men are less likely to make reference to patriarchal social structures, and tend to discuss the Goddess 'more as an expressive or nurturing force that aided one's immediate self' (71). Bloch's observations about the way in which his female participants talked about the Goddess are congruent with both Carol Christ's and Cynthia Eller's discussion of the Goddess as a source of empowerment for spiritual feminists. 'What the goddess does for women is to give them power in their femaleness, not apart from it, to make womanhood itself a powerful quantity. It is a divine redemption of femaleness' (Eller 1993: 213). This sentiment is also apparent among my female interview participants:

> I think that Wicca, and I'm talking about British Traditional Wicca here, because that's what I know, gives women a forum where they can have a role that is feminine, but at the same time powerful. They don't have to trade their femininity for power and authority; the High Priestess, as the representative of the Goddess and as the first among equals, can embody both those aspects without there being a contradiction. I think that is a really strong appeal for women in the kind of society we find ourselves in, where there is such a dichotomy between femininity and power. (Andrea)

---

⁴ While Bloch largely conflates these groups, as do other authors such as Heelas (1996), most of those involved reject the notion that contemporary pagans and New Agers belong to the same group. Michael York, for example offers a list of characteristic outlooks that distinguishes between those who identify primarily with neopaganism, and those who identify primarily with the New Age (1995: 145–177). In my opinion, the ontological differences York identifies justify the treatment of contemporary paganism as a practice separate from the New Age, but with some overlapping features.

⁵ Bloch's interview format first allowed participants to talk freely about their spiritual journey, and then used set questions to encourage participants to explore particular themes. One of the prompts in the word association segment of the second stage of the interview was 'Goddess', so some of the discussion he records would have occurred in response to that prompt. However, he also mentions that all of his female subjects and five of his eleven male subjects mentioned the Goddess in the open, unprompted segment of the interview.

Although Andrea is involved in British Traditional Wicca, perhaps one of the most insistently gender-egalitarian forms of modern witchcraft, she expresses the same reaffirmation of her gender identification and reclamation of power for it that Eller describes as central to her exclusively 'spiritual feminist' respondents.[6]

Another interview participant spoke about her experience of the empowerment afforded to women through the invitation to think of divinity as both female and as immanent in what has become one of the classic rituals of Goddess religion.

> Many years ago at university, in one of the [women's studies] courses I was taking, (and this was the mid-1970s) one of the projects was to create the expression of a religious ritual or experience. And a half dozen of the women got together, and what they wrote was that their perception of a women's Goddess ritual would be. And they had all of us who chose to participate, which was most of us, in a circle, and you turned to the woman on your left, and you said 'Thou Art Goddess' and when you did this, you handed them what was basically a 1950s, silver-plated sugar bowl, with two handles. And as you handed it to her by one handle, she held the other, and you tipped it so that she could look in. And when you looked into the sugar bowl, the secret of the sugar bowl was that there was a little pocket mirror in the bottom, so when the woman next to you said 'Thou Art Goddess' and you looked in, you saw your own reflection. And that, really, to me is my best description of the experience of self-empowerment [through Goddess symbolism]. (Judith)

Many of the women I interviewed also chose to frame their speculation about the appeals of paganism to men through their own commitment to notions of gender equality and social change. One commented, 'I don't think all men want a patriarchal society, or expect power' (Bronwen). Another took a more Jungian approach,

> I think men become involved in Goddess worship because I think it harkens upon their own subconscious need – that there can be, and is, a feminine aspect to who and what they are, and a feminine that is around them to which they are not superior and cut off: another half. Goddess worship allows them to become more in tune with that. I think patriarchy has screwed up more men than it has women because men grew up and were taught men were superior, and therefore they have to act in certain 'manly' ways, which don't help them because they're not allowed to express or connect with their own femininity, which is essentially part of them, the anima and animus aspect again. They are not allowed to connect with that, but in Goddess worship, they are. (Beth)

Sometimes, women expressed both the sense of women's empowerment and the potential liberation of both men and women from the intellectual and spiritual limitations imposed by the dominant patriarchal system by asserting the necessity for a re-visioning of gender norms.

---

[6]   Eller defines 'feminist spirituality' in a very particular way that overlaps with some forms of contemporary paganism, and not others. She employs three criteria: that the movement is separatist, inasmuch as it is focused on and directed towards women; that it is centred outside of traditional religions; and that it is feminist, 'believing that either women's condition or the general state of gender roles in society as we find them are unsatisfactory or need to be changed' (1993: 7).

For both men and women, paganism requires an attitude adjustment – a re-visioning of themselves, and of what male is and what female is…. And I think that a primary difficulty that men have being involved in paganism … is that dislocation between what they experience in their spiritual lives and what the contexts of their lives in the outside world are. (Deanne)

It would certainly appear, at least anecdotally, that women do experience paganism and Goddess spirituality as something quite different from the patriarchal religious traditions in which most of them were raised,[7] and from which they became alienated. Women identified the external structure and embedded hierarchies of traditional religions as limiting to their personal freedom, autonomy, and spiritual expression and framed their own personal rejection of them in those terms.

… [paganism has] allowed me to grow as a person… in a way that I don't think that Judaism, that's the religion I was part of and the culture I was part of before I made the change, would have allowed me to… (Beth)

I saw no reason that as an adult heterosexual woman, I could not be religiously involved in the practice of my parish. When that was denied me, it was literally as though I'd been, you know, thrown out of doors. Um… I did feel dispossessed. I felt disinherited, and um, and it's wonderful that, uh, that my religious, how would you say, I guess, um, that I can more openly express the mysticism I do feel [in Goddess religion], let's put it that way. (Francine)

Beth and Francine's concerns, when elaborated, centre on their disempowerment as spiritually self-determining actors, by virtue of their sex, by the patriarchal religions in which they were raised.

Paganism and Goddess religion have, as Christ said they would, allowed them recognize in themselves a powerful image of the divine, which they perceive as having fostered their personal and spiritual growth in a way that their previous religious involvements, with their over-determined patriarchal norms, could not. Goddess religion provided women with symbols and narratives they could use to express their fundamental continuity with the sacred, rather than the ways in which they diverged from it. It made women protagonists in their own stories.

---

[7]   My own research indicated that 75 per cent of respondents were raised with at least a nominal religious identification. The religious traditions listed were overwhelmingly Christian; 92 per cent of those who indicated that they had been involved in other religions listed at least one Christian denomination in their backgrounds. Of 186 responses, 46 indicated no religion prior to their pagan one. 94 people indicated only a single religious tradition in their background: 34 were Roman Catholic; 48 were Protestant; 2 did not give a denomination; 3 were Jewish; and the remainder were other religions. 23 people indicated more than one denomination of Christianity and 22 listed a Christian denomination along with a non-Christian religion.

Conclusions

There are thousands of women who have found, and continue to find, their creative imagining of a Goddess to be motivating, inspiring, empowering and transformative, and their experiences can be neither denied nor refuted – but they must be contextualized and continually reflected upon so that this new spiritual direction does not come to reproduce the acknowledged limitations of the religions many of these same women left. One of the most important things that contemporary pagan religions have done is to release spirituality from its institutional cage. It is not, after all, as Bibby reminds us, an indifference to traditionally religious questions that has caused the decline in church membership and attendance and the rise of secularization, but the confluence of particular social, ideological and intellectual patterns.

The things that religion has traditionally been about, the creation of meaning and purpose, the legitimation of power and autonomy, and the celebration of some greater power in the universe to which the individual is meaningfully related, are the same things that Carol Christ suggests that women need from a Goddess religion that was barely fledgling when she first advocated it. Thirty years later, paganism and Goddess worship have a chance to escape the fate that has seen mainstream churches both shrink and become less relevant for their practitioners. They can potentially become a more broadly accepted spiritual alternative for both women and men by remaining true to the presuppositions that make them radical: that they are based on personal, individual, non-prescriptive relationships with an immanent and pervasive sacrality. The routinization and dogmatic pronouncements that characterize mainstream religious traditions have made it more difficult for them to adapt to the rapid social, intellectual and ideological changes of the past century, thus diminishing both their ability to stay relevant, and to attract and retain membership, as a segment of those within these institutions will resist changes to traditional ways of doing things.[8] Threats of the withdrawal of support of existing adherents must be balanced with the hope that changes will attract additional adherents, and address the concerns of adherents who believe that their tradition is 'out of touch' with the modern age. Paganism is congruent with the dominant cultural logic of pluralism and conforms to the limitations imposed by sequestration. Thus, it presents itself as a mode through which individuals can construct their spirituality that is not encumbered by the historical, ideological and physical trappings of the more mainstream religions, which have been forced by secularization to try to re-invent their own internal logic.

This is why it is of paramount importance that pagans remain reflexive about their beliefs, norms, practices, and myths, and resist the casual routinization, already visible in some spheres (Berger 1999: 100–114) that comes with the spiritually lazy desire to follow an already-charted path, rather than to continually re-invent the wheel. While pagans produce a great many books, courses and websites, almost all

---

[8]   See, for example, the struggles around the implementation of Vatican II, or the substantial, and ultimately schismatic resistance to the ordination of gays and lesbians in the United Church of Canada.

will tell you that reading books is not sufficient to be a pagan, because paganism is not so much about shared belief as it is about shared experience and a shared symbolic discourse. To be pagan is to feel a deep attachment to a potent force, both within and beyond one's self, and to perceive that attachment though the symbolic taxonomies of pagan discourse. It is ultimately the individual that is the basic unit of paganism – not the grove or coven or circle or amorphous 'pagan community', and certainly not the 'society', however defined. Paganism, witchcraft, and Goddess worship are vibrant and flourishing because they emerge uncoerced from the present-day experience of the individuals who have imagined them into being and who see through their symbolic lens. They are nourished in an atmosphere of hope for a better world, however unlikely pagans alone are to be able to bring that world into being.

We have come full circle, back to the fundamental agreement Steve Bruce and I have about secularization, and the fundamental disagreement we have about religion. Bruce writes,

> Belief in the supernatural has not disappeared. Rather, the forms in which it is expressed have become so idiosyncratic and so diffuse that there are few specific social consequences ... To pursue Weber's music metaphor, the orchestras and mass bands with their thunderous symphonies have gone. Handfuls of us will be enthusiastic music-makers but, because we no longer follow one score, we cannot produce the melodies to rouse the masses. (Bruce 1996: 234)

Rousing the masses is not what paganism, witchcraft or Goddess religion are about, or have ever been about. Christ does not suggest that women need a goddess to change the world – although she implies that might be the eventual end result of women transforming their perceptions of themselves. Asking if pagans and Goddess-worshippers would be able to successfully impose their vision of a better world on the societies in which they find themselves is setting up a straw man. Unlike the proponents of radical religious movements in the past, contemporary pagans do not want everyone to share their beliefs. Ideological hegemony is not among their agenda items. They are not even ready to compel other pagans to share their beliefs, except in the general sense of participating in the same pool of discourse. Bruce takes this as evidence of the lack of significance of contemporary pagan religions. I take it as their strength. Pagans are pagans in part, because they want to make the music, rather than to simply listen to it. It is nothing to them if you cannot hear the music or prefer another tune, so long as you do not try to prevent them from singing their souls forth into the soulless conditions of modernity.

References

Berger, Helen, *A Community of Witches* (Columbia, South Carolina: University of South Carolina Press, 1999).

Berger, Helen *et al.*, *Voices from the Pagan Census: A National Survey of Witches and Neo-Pagans in the United States* (Columbia, South Carolina: University of South Carolina Press, 2003).

Berger, Peter, *The Sacred Canopy* (New York: Anchor, 1967).

Bibby, Reginald, *Restless Gods* (Toronto: Stoddart, 2002).

Bibby, Reginald, *Unknown Gods* (Toronto: Stoddart, 1993).

Bibby, Reginald, *Fragmented Gods* (Toronto: Irwin, 1987).

Bloch, Jon, *New Spirituality, Self and Belonging* (Westport, CT: Praeger, 1998).

Bruce, Steve, *Religion in the Modern Age: From Cathedrals to Cults* (New York: Oxford University Press, 1996).

Christ, Carol, 'Why Women Need the Goddess: Phenomenological, Psychological and Political Reflections', in Carol Christ and Judith Plaskow (eds), *Womanspirit Rising* (San Francisco: Harper and Row, 1979).

Durkheim, Emile, *The Elementary Forms of the Religious Life.* Fields, Karen, ed. and trans. (New York: Free Press, 1915[1995]).

Eller, Cynthia, *The Myth of Matriarchal Prehistory* (Boston: Beacon, 2000).

Eller, Cynthia, *Living in the Lap of the Goddess* (New York: Crossroads, 1993).

Geertz, Clifford, *The Interpretation of Cultures* (New York: Basic Books, 1973).

Giddens, Anthony, *Modernity and Self-Identity* (Stanford: Stanford University Press, 1991).

Jorgensen, Danny and Russell, Scott, 'American Neopaganism: The Participants' Social Identities', *Journal for the Scientific Study of Religion*, 38(3) (1999): 325–338.

Luckmann, Thomas, *The Invisible Religion* (Houndsmills, Basingstoke Hampshire: Macmillan, 1967).

Orion, Loretta, *Never Again the Burning Times: Paganism Revived* (Prospect Heights, IL: Waveland, 1995).

Reid, Siân, 'Renovating the Broom Closet: Factors Contributing to the Growth of Contemporary Paganism in Canada', *The Pomegranate* 7(2) (2005): 128–140.

Reid, Siân, *Disorganized Religion: An Exploration of the Neopagan Craft in Canada,* unpublished Ph.D. thesis (Ottawa: Carleton University, 2001).

Stark, Rodney and Bainbridge, William Sims, *A Theory of Religion* (New York: Peter Lang, 1987).

Stark, Rodney and Bainbridge, William Sims, *The Future of Religion* (Berkeley: University of California Press, 1985).

Wilson, Bryan, *Religion in Secular Society* (Harmondsworth, Middlesex: Penguin, 1966).

York, Michael, *The Emerging Network* (London: Rowman & Littlefield, 1995).

Chapter 7

The Fusers: New Forms of Spiritualized Christianity

Giselle Vincett

'I'm a pagan and a Christian. I don't see any problems with that' (June).

'It's one of those strange things that…when I am with Christian women, I feel I'm very Goddess-ey, and when I'm with Goddess women, I feel I'm very Christian! [laughs] So it feels a bit on the edge of both' (Jan).[1]

Introduction

This chapter is based upon research with Christian and neo-pagan feminist women in the UK. One of the early results of my research was a clear indication that there was a significant segment of participants who saw themselves as incorporating elements of *both* Christianity and neo-paganism into their personal spiritualities. Some of these participants identify as Christian, some as pagan, others are consciously identifying as both, but all are strongly attracted to, and utilize elements of, both forms of religiosity. I call this group of people 'the Fusers'.

When I say that Fusers represent a new form of 'spiritualized Christianity', I am of course well aware that there have been, and continue to be, forms of Christianity which emphasize the spiritual. But in this context I use the term to refer to those recent forms of religiosity which usually set themselves up against traditional religion, and have been portrayed (positively or negatively) as part of a wider societal trend away from the churches (Bruce 2002; Martin 2005b; Woodhead and Heelas 2000 and 2005). Such alternative spiritualities are variously termed 'New Age' (Heelas 1996; Hanegraaf 1998), 'spiritualities of life' (Woodhead and Heelas 2000), 'subjective-life spirituality' or 'holistic spirituality' (Heelas and Woodhead 2005), or, somewhat more specifically, (neo-) paganism (Harvey 1997), 'nature religions' (Pearson et. al. 1998), and so on. All of these spiritualities generally identify themselves, and have been treated by researchers, as distinct from Christianity. Such spiritualities have identifiable characteristics, which locate the sacred and accord authority differently from traditional Christianity, and the above authors have attempted to map these differences. Fusers have many characteristics in common with the profiles of holistic

---

[1]   Names of participants have been changed, except where a participant asked to be identified using her real name.

spiritualities, but with the significant difference that Fusers attempt to hold together Christianity *and* neo-paganism.

It is my contention that Fusers are an important emerging religious group who help to answer the underlying questions of this volume and indicate one way in which Christianity is adapting in the face of secularization and a strong turn to new forms of spirituality. Below I sketch a profile for Fusers, and then look in more detail at how this group of people fuse Christianity and forms of neo-paganism.

Profile

In the research project of which the Fusers are a part, I examine how feminist women in the UK deconstruct pre-given notions of God and the sacred, and re-imagine the divine for themselves. The research is based upon participant observation of two ritual groups (one Goddess Feminist, one Christian) and 50 semi-structured interviews.[2] Of the total number of participants, approximately 12 are fusing. The number is approximate because the extent of fusing varies amongst participants. I visualize this variation as a continuum, on one end are those participants who identify as Christian but may utilize certain neo-pagan ritual techniques (for example). On the other end are those Fusers who identify as pagan, but are still strongly drawn to Christian ritual or figures such as Jesus or Mary. In the middle of the continuum are those who are fusing on several levels (for example, through group participation, celebration of festivals, personal ritual, deities).

There is little existing literature on the group of people I am terming Fusers.[3] One reason for this is the common assumption that new forms of spirituality do not mesh well with traditional religion:[4] Fusers have fallen through the gap between literature on the two poles, invisible possibly because when Fusers participate with a Christian or neo-pagan group, they are assumed to be no different from other members of those groups. Paul Heelas has noted that there are some Christian groups or individuals for whom it is difficult to decide whether they are Christian or New Age (he calls such Christians 'Pelagian') (1996: 116, 117), but he does not pursue the point. Heelas and Linda Woodhead in their Kendal Project (2005) were interested in the possibility of 'fusion' or 'hybridization' (2005: 32), but they emphasize that they found very little of this in their sample. In a later paper, Woodhead (2005) outlined their findings regarding what she termed 'boundary crossing', but again stressed that most participants were holding the two worlds separate (in Heelas and Woodhead's terms, those worlds are 'the congregational domain' and 'the holistic milieu'). Jone Salomonsen in her study of the Reclaiming Community (feminist Wicca) in San Francisco also notes the tendency of some Wiccans to have 'dual identities' (2002: 111). Additionally, I note

---

[2] The Christian ritual group leans toward fusing because several of its members are interested in exploring fusing options.

[3] See Kemp 2003 and Heelas and Woodhead 2005. The people Wade Clark Roof (1999) calls 'Spiritual Seekers' have some elements in common with the Fusers, but he emphasises that Seekers have left institutionalised religion (203), and are not 'theistic' (212). Many of my participants, by contrast, retain links with their churches and all are theistic.

[4] See for example, Heelas 1996: 23, 27 and Martin 2005: 156, 157.

increasing 'chatter' about Fusers on various forms of electronic communication,[5] including growing numbers of people testifying to their fusing identities.[6]

The continuing controversy in the sociological study of religion as to whether western societies are thoroughly secularized (Bruce 2006, for example) or whether there may be a trend towards (re)sacralization (Berger 1999 or Martin 2005a and b, for example) is fuelled by the sustained decline in church attendance figures (see Brierley 2001 for UK figures) and evidence that some forms of religiosity are growing and that religion is having a greater influence on 'secular' politics, especially since 9/11 and 7/7 (Berger 1999; Berger *et al.* 2003; Martin 2005a).[7] Proponents of secularization argue that pockets of religious groups and individuals are in the minority and that therefore their influence is insignificant (Bruce 2002, 2006); others argue that they are part of a cultural religion in the West, what Davie calls 'believing without belonging' (2002: 5). My own study can be seen as part of this debate, and I aim to show that even individuals who may appear to be secularized (for example, those Fusers who no longer attend a traditional church), may yet be active religiously in a meaningful way. Recent research by Day provides a useful distinction here: she distinguishes between those unaffiliated Christians who are, what she calls, 'Christian nominalists' (2006: 240), and those who although they do not attend church, remain engaged with religion and are what she calls 'Christian faithful' (273).

This study also fits in with the growing body of literature on women's religiosity, which helps to elucidate the 'gender gap' in Christian and alternative spiritualities in the West (for example, see Woodhead, Marler, and Houtman and Aupers in this volume). Additionally, my research dovetails with other research on groups which may be seen to be on the forefront of new forms of religion and spirituality in the West (Christian emerging churches, Christian feminist parallel churches,[8] neo-paganism), as such it presents an opportunity to study the dynamic development of religion, even in parallel with secularization.

The Fusers, like all of the participants in my larger study, are white and middle-class. They tend to be well educated, and many hold more than one higher educational

---

[5]   Members of several email lists to which I belong have observed the trend towards fusing over the last year: *natrel* consists of 'nature religion' scholars; *sofffia* (associated with the progressive Christian group Faith Futures Forward) is a list of feminist Christian women; and Lancaster University Pagan Social Club. These are closed lists.

[6]   There is also a similar group of people amongst my participants whom I call 'Quagans' (following the lead of one participant who self-identified as such). These people are neo-pagan Quakers in the unprogrammed liberal British tradition. They are neo-pagan in their spiritual beliefs, but Quaker in their lifestyle, ethics, and primary religious community (see Vincett in Dandelion and Collins, forthcoming). I interviewed four Quagans and have conducted on-going monitoring of Quagan blogs and email lists.

[7]   Two forms of Christianity in the West that have done well in the context of secularization are evangelical and charismatic denominations (see for example, Martin 2005a and b). Berger et al. (2003) as well as Reid (in this volume) provide evidence for the growth of neo-paganism.

[8]   I have used the term 'parallel church' to describe an organization which is Christian and may be linked with a particular Church, but which remains autonomous from the Church. Such parallel churches include, for example, the Catholic Women's Network.

degree. They range in age from their late twenties to their sixties, with the majority in their forties and fifties. They belong to the disenchanted generations who, under various influences,[9] question authority and hierarchy, are disaffected by the Church (even when they are active attenders), but who are searching for meaning (Berger 1974; Roof 1993; Lynch 2002; Heelas and Woodhead 2005). Participants are further united by their feminism, which drives their spirituality in their need to find ways of imagining the divine that are consistent with their feminist values.

All fusing participants were previously Christian, or were actively raised as such for at least part of their childhood. That is, no one in this study came to fusing from outside Christianity, even if they now identify chiefly as pagan.[10] Those still active within the Church are affiliated with a range of liberal denominations. One question that arises then is whether fusing may be seen as a permanent position or as a transitional phase in an individual's spiritual development. The answer has important ramifications for whether or not Christianity can incorporate alternative spiritualities into itself. I suggest that it depends on the individual: though one of my participants, June, sits firmly in the middle of the spectrum, I cannot imagine her trending further towards neo-paganism as she is committed to training for the priesthood (Anglican). On the other hand, Jan has left her previous position as minister (Baptist, then United Reformed) and says,

> I guess I've never been in a group that's exclusively Goddess oriented. And one of the things [pause] – I've often felt I would like to be [pause] because I've often felt like [pause] in most of the groups I've been in, I'm the one who is most – there are just one or two of us in that direction. And there's nobody who is kind of further on in that, if you know what I mean, to draw me more into it.

It would be very interesting to know whether in 10 years time, participants such as Jan have moved entirely out of the Church. Certainly, Rose Alba moved in and out of the Church for years before finally committing to identifying as pagan. Where

---

[9]   Woodhead and Heelas (2000) cover many of these influences: demythologisation and rationalization, detraditionalism (especially feminism), subjectivization, as well as events which served to undermine the authority or perceived relevance of the Church(es), such as the Vietnam war, or the sex scandals of the Catholic church.

[10]   Only one Fuser has a Catholic background or affiliation, the rest have Protestant backgrounds or affiliations, though several may be described as Catholicised Anglicans. It may be that Catholics do not feel the need to fuse because as Rose Alba (and several other participants) put it, 'you get some protestants …saying the Catholic Church basically might as well be pagan. And I think in a lot of ways that's true, you know!' However, Jone Salomonsen (2002) found in her study of feminist witches that it was the Catholics who were much more likely to 'balance a dual identity' (111) with Christianity and paganism, rather than those who were raised protestant whom she found were 'much more likely to 'trash' their religious heritage' (111). It would be interesting to know more about these Catholic Wiccans, particularly as Salomonsen suggests they are (with one exception) culturally Catholic (because of their family backgrounds), rather than actively practising Catholics. Jo Pearson on the other hand, has noted that 'Wiccans in Britain are overwhelmingly of Protestant religious background', but points out that this is consistent with the British population in general (2003: 175). It may be that my Fuser informants simply reflect the British protestant predominance.

it is a transition then, the movement appears to be unidirectional. As Kate (United Reformed) put it, 'there are people who have left Christianity behind to become pagan, and there are people who have left – well, no, I don't know anyone who has left paganism to become Christian [laughter]'!

Though my research was focused on women, I also interviewed two men who were partners of women in the study. Interestingly, both these couples were fusing. The men emphasized their attraction to female or feminine forms of the divine, their feminism, and the way they were drawn to socialising with women: 'I came over to Glastonbury [pause] and met these women who were taking Goddess seriously, and I was drawn to them like a magnet' (Sig), 'From my point of view [pause] I think there's a very strong feminine within me anyway…. Um and um I think most of my life I've sort of been in groups where I've been the one man amongst dozens of women' (Paul). Clearly further study is needed, but it may be that because these men already exist on the margins or borders of normalized masculinity and masculine roles, fusing is a spirituality which reflects the position they already inhabit in terms of gender role and performance. Indeed, as I shall outline below, the language and positionality of 'borders', 'margins', 'edges', was an important theme for all the Fusers.[11]

Dick Houtman and Stef Aupers (in this volume) suggest that women drawn to alternative spiritualities are highly detraditionalized (and post-traditional). Such people, they argue, question and deconstruct 'external and authoritative sources of meaning and identity'. I accept this, but think it important to point out that detraditionalization does not necessarily mean politicization: a woman may be forced into a post-traditional position without choice (by economic circumstance, for example). To consciously choose (as my participants do) such a position is another thing entirely. Feminist women (and men) are post-traditional – indeed, feminism may almost be defined as a deconstruction of traditionalism. It is not surprising then that the participants in my study all lean towards the subjectivization of experience which emphasizes the authority of the self (including those who identify solely as Christians). This does not however translate into a secularized worldview, nor does it translate into what Steve Bruce calls 'pick-and-mix' religion (2002: 105). Indeed, fusing participants are quick to stress that their spirituality is *not* 'mix and match' (Rose Alba). With Houtman and Aupers, I question the assumption on the part of some researchers that this position is antithetical to having a shared community, identity, or ethics.

Though Fusers conform to the turn to the subjective, and they are certainly syncretistic, participants have in many cases been practising a fused spirituality for years, and so clearly demonstrate a long-term commitment to fusing. In addition, they are often committed to daily spiritual praxis, and may have long-term group affiliations (both Church and/or small group). Because Fusers hold together Christian and neo-pagan elements, they must (even those who identify chiefly as neo-pagan)

---

[11]   For more on performance of gender see Butler 1990 and on masculinities see Connell 1987.

engage with, and in many cases negotiate with mainstream forms of religiosity. Indeed there are four Christian ministers amongst the Fusers.[12]

In this volume Linda Woodhead argues that detraditionalization has gender specific ramifications, and I suggest that it is this which helps to answer why post-traditional women may attempt to spiritualize Christianity. Having chosen in their feminism a detraditionalized position, many of my Christian participants (including some Fusers) hold on to the Church and God as constants in an otherwise constantly shifting world, but this does not mean they find the hierarchy or dogma of the Church acceptable.[13]

The Fusers represent an interesting problem: their position has been presented as antithetical to Church affiliation. David Martin writes that 'pagan naturalism ... [does] not leave space for the distinctive institution of the Church' (2005a: 157), and Heelas and Woodhead point to a 'deep incompatibility' (2005: 4) between the approaches to life associated with traditional Christianity and with 'spirituality'. Fusers are therefore an exception to the general rule that 'spirituality sets itself apart from ... the Christian churches' (Houtman and Aupers in this volume).

Analysis

The fusing position

Fusers, as the term implies, are interested in 'holding together'; they exist in the joint, the 'and', the margins, the edges where categories (usually treated as well-defined) blur. The apparently distinct worlds of Christianity and neo-paganism come together for the Fusers. Fusers bridge spaces, language, belief, symbols and concepts. To be marginal, or on the edge of something is to be so far from the centre of it, that one is close to whatever lies outside; it is a bridge position, whose vision encompasses both inside and outside. The creativity of such a position lies in the fact that it can draw inspiration from both sides (in this case, Christianity and neo-paganism). However, even a position on the margins, is still a position *in*, and many participants attend church regularly and consider themselves part of specific church communities. Others attend what I term 'parallel churches', small groups which are not necessarily tied to specific churches, but which are Christian in orientation and purpose.

Coming to fusing

Often Fusers were drawn into this position by a defining experience or period of crisis after which they made a conscious decision to move to a position on the margins. For example, Kate (late 20s, United Reformed minister) found her worldview was fundamentally changed when she returned to Britain from a year spent overseas:

---

[12] Of the ministers in this segment of participants, only one currently has a church appointment. One is retired (but still active), another is pursuing a Ph.D. and the last is in higher education.

[13] Woodhead has elsewhere attempted to sketch how different women legitimate, negotiate with or resist existing religious power structures (2007: 550–570).

I think there's something massively missing in the Church and the churches I've been part of, um [pause] in relation to the environment, just the ground we walk on. I spent a year overseas, mainly in Fiji and also Samoa, and a lot of the time [when I was there], I took my shoes off. And when I came back, and I had to put socks and boots on because it was so cold, and straight away I just felt like I was miles away from the earth, and all I had for like the first six months when I came back to Britain was [pause] I feel really far from the earth. And I'm walking on it with my shoes, and I can understand all that intellectually, but actually I don't feel [pause] connected in a *real* way. And – and that is – that is partly why I want to do something with my sister....

The disconnection from the earth that Kate identifies in the Church is brought to a crisis point for her by her experience of what it is like to be able to walk on the earth without anything *between* her and the earth (which she clarifies elsewhere in the interview *is* divine). This crisis drives her to experiment with ritual that celebrates the earth and nurtures our connection to it. Kate identifies neo-paganism as an earth-based spirituality, whose resources are easily tapped in order to feed her need for something she feels is missing from Christianity. Kate also tracks a shift in her understanding of God in her growing sense that the earth is not simply 'God's creation' but also 'is sacred, and is part of the divine' and 'therefore that involves worship. ... actually it seems like it's missing if it doesn't happen now, whereas a few years ago I never would have said that really'.

God expressed in many ways

Fusers attempt to hold together a theology of 'the One and the Many': though there is one God (variously described as the One, the Great Spirit, God, Earth Mother, oneness, Life Force), that deity/force/energy may be expressed in many different ways (i.e. through specific deities or places). Other Fusers tend towards a duotheism of God and Goddess, where all other male and female divinities are ultimately 'aspects' of God or Goddess. However, for Fusers, it is only *in conjunction with* the Many that the One retains its meaning, and its constancy.

Kate's immanent conception of the divine is consistent with 'spiritualities of life' (Heelas and Woodhead 2000), but rather than simply relocating the divine 'from Christian heaven to the deeper layers of self' (Houtman and Aupers in this volume), Fusers (*and* I would argue neo-pagans) locate the sacred much more broadly so that the whole of the earth and all its 'beings'[14] are sacralized. Such a radical immanence has interesting effects. Often I would ask participants whether 'that tree' outside was divine or part of the divine, or something else. Christian participants would say, 'well, part of what God is is the living-ness, the fact that things are alive' (Caroline); that is, a tree is part of God's Creation and is infused with God's creative power but is not sacred in itself. Conversely, fusing participants invariably gave an answer like this: 'Both. Both'.

The Fuser conception of God as One which is expressed in many ways is perhaps inevitable given their position, especially for those on the Christian end of the

---

[14]   Fusers attribute 'being-hood' to much more than humans or even animals, as Kate makes clear in the case of trees.

spectrum. These people must reconcile the monotheism of Christianity with their attraction to and experience of multiple expressions of the divine. The Fuser theology of One and the Many goes well beyond a traditional Christian Trinitarian concept of God: June (Anglican and pagan) celebrates Mary (mother of Jesus), but also a host of goddesses from Inanna to Gaia and Psyche. She elevates Eve 'who is now redeemed from being just Adam's wife, but as a creator in her own right'. Familiar Christian figures are raised to the status of aspects of the divine, and goddesses from other traditions are incorporated into God in syncretistic fashion.

Recently some scholars have pointed to a trend in neo-paganism towards polytheism (Jenny Blain web-based communication 2006;[15] Hardman 1995: xii; Harvey 1997). Fusers do not fall easily into such a category. When Fusers make reference to and/or celebrate many different 'aspects' of God in the space of one ritual, they *may* be said to be functionally polytheistic (as are some neo-pagans). However, most Fusers would be uncomfortable with being viewed as 'practically polytheistic' (i.e. polytheistic in praxis, but not theology), precisely because of their continuing ties to the Church. The Fuser links to the Church are bound up with a confessional identity (Woodhead 2004), which despite their emphasis on experience, places equal emphasis on belief.

Fused spaces and celebration

Fusers are confident about making their own spaces: physical, mental, and social. Mary put it like this: 'I need to find my own fresh ground', and 'I *make* Church'. This basic need and assumption that they could create new spaces for spiritual nourishment was common to fusing participants. All Fusers had multiple spiritual communities, which they held together in a 'network' (Mary). Such communities were varied, for example: traditional churches, ritual groups, and web-groups.

Fused spaces may also be creative spaces: Fusers emphasize experiential ritual as a way of expressing faith, and thus June *enacts* the figures mentioned above in a one-woman play she wrote called *Lunacy, or the Pursuit of the Goddess*. Ritual enactment of a deity is frequently found in Goddess Feminism (Griffin 1995; Rountree 2004), which has influenced June. Though Griffin and Rountree stress that ritual enactment is metaphor, my own experience with Goddess Feminist groups in the UK is that during ritual enactment a woman briefly embodies a goddess; that is, she *becomes* whichever goddess is being celebrated.[16] Ritual participants encounter a goddess amongst them, and thus a *particular* revelation of the divine. Such rituals 'redefine what it means to be female and to be spiritual' (Griffin 1995: 44). June, and most of the Fusers on the Christian end of the spectrum, would stop short of claiming such a radical

---

[15] The formation of the (British) Association of Polytheist Traditions in 2005, and their organization of a conference in 2006 at which J. Blain was a keynote speaker, is another indication of this trend. The polytheist traditions of the association are specifically neo-pagan and the group emphasises that "we see our gods as individual deities, not as 'aspects of the Divine'" nor as 'avatars of the Godhead'. www.manygods.org.uk.

[16] This is not simply playacting, although 'play' is an important part of neo-pagan ritual, neither is it spirit possession, but lies somewhere in-between the two.

embodiment when she 'puts on' a goddess in her play, but she does say, 'They're all images of God, they all contain important mythic truths about ourselves. So they're all images of God'. In other words, they too are particular revelations of God.

Images such as Eve and Mary, whom Fusers reconceptualize as goddesses, are easy to celebrate in Christian contexts and may be one reason that participants are particularly drawn to such figures. Paul and Sylvia (Christian and pagan) related to me their journey towards fusing, which was eventually confirmed and validated by a 'fused' figure[17]. Following their interest in Celtic spirituality, they 'were kind of introduced to – to St. Brigid'. At the same time, they were interested in exploring sacred landscapes. In the Orkney Islands of Scotland, Paul relates that they both felt 'there was this very, very strong feeling of being touched by the ancestors – called towards the Goddess'. Upon returning home, they 'sort of [pause] touched base and touched Brigid again, and she kind of said, "You do know I'm a goddess, don't you, and not just a saint?" [laughter] And it just sort of clicked and um I think from that point we decided that we would um celebrate the Celtic quarter days.'[18]

Similarly, Rose Alba (pagan, formerly Catholic) identifies Astarte as her favourite goddess. Rose Alba is interested in the idea that a lot of the titles associated with Astarte 'are of the Blessed Virgin Mary as well'. She considers Mary 'an aspect of Astarte' and admits that her images of Astarte are 'influenced very much by the statues of the Blessed Virgin'. In a daily invocation she wrote to Astarte, she 'includes quite a lot of the litany to the Blessed Virgin Mary'. I found the way that Rose Alba always referred to Mary, mother of Jesus, as the 'Blessed Virgin' important and indicative of her continuing love of both Mary and the Catholic Church, and therefore her fusing position.

All fusing participants celebrate festivals they consciously associate with neo-paganism. Often there was explicit reference to the overlay by the Church of Christian festivals on or near pagan festivals (such as Imbolc/Candlemas, Samhain/All Souls Eve and All Saints Day, winter solstice/Christmas). Jan mentioned that celebrating the winter solstice enables her to re-inscribe meaning to a festival which 'has lost so much meaning, even the radical and alternative meanings [of Christmas] have been done to death!' Other participants emphasized that they felt the neo-pagan ritual year was more closely tied to the rhythms of the earth: 'I know that I am much more influenced by the cycle of – of the seasons than I am by the Church's year. Um [pause] I love seeing it get lighter in the spring' (Andie, Unitarian).

For some Fusers, celebration of neo-pagan festivals are private affairs shared only with those closest to them. Others celebrate in small ritual groups that may identify as pagan or as Christian. For example, in my participant observation of a Christian women's ritual group, neo-pagan festivals were often celebrated. On Samhain one year (which coincides with the secular Hallowe'en), the women held a ritual entitled 'Reclaiming your inner witch'. Many elements of neo-pagan ritual were borrowed

---

[17] Fusers see figures such as Brigid, or even Mary, mother of Jesus, as fused figures containing elements from both Christianity and pre-Christianity.

[18] The festivals of which Paul speaks are Samhain (Oct.31), Imbolc (Feb.1), Beltane (May 1), and Lughnassa (August 1) and are standard festivals in the ritual year of many forms of neo-paganism (see for example, Starhawk 1999[1979]; Harvey 1997; Rountree 2004), which generally also include the solstices and equinoxes for a total of eight yearly festivals.

here, such as 'casting' a circle (a particular way of creating ritual space), invoking the directions, and dismissing those present with a neo-pagan blessing. These were combined with a Christian influenced litany.

Still other participants mentioned using techniques learned from neo-paganism, such as energy raising, in Christian ritual. Mary (Anglican minister) said,

> A lot of my understanding comes from writers like Starhawk, etc. ...I guess the Goddess Feminist stuff has freed me to find the Christian Feminist! And I really find that if I process this stuff into Christian terms, Christian women know it, it's very powerful because it's true to their own body experiences.

One of the ways that Mary 'processes' neo-pagan techniques is by an emphasis on energy and the body. She says, 'I often use my sexual energy to be creative, and I know I lead liturgy from my uterus! [laughter]'. In this way, participants fuse even in non-fusing contexts.

The most common way of ritualising in a fused manner was through circle dance, which many Fusers practised regularly. As Jan says, 'The other source of [my neo-pagan influence] um is circle dancing. ... some of the events I've been to, um they all celebrate the solstice or the equinox, or Samhain, and use goddess imagery in that'. She later says, 'I think of God or Goddess, [pause] more in terms of activities', a favourite one is 'God dancing, and dancing on the edge, but its also us dancing with God'. In circle dance, Jan (and other informants like her) ritualizes her image of the divine; she dances with the divine and with other people in a profoundly relational embodiment and enactment of the divine and the human. She also says, 'dancing on the edge is a lot about balancing feminism, Christianity, Goddess/God. Um, and it's that edge. But I think it's also the sense of the unknown, of risk, or not quite knowing where we're going, of trying new things'.

Compare this ritualized expression of balancing on the edge (a popular metaphor amongst Fusers) with Paul and Sylvia's use of it. Paul and Sylvia were also very involved in circle dance, but in addition expressed and ritualized their fusing through pilgrimage to 'edge places':

> Paul: [Brigid] seemed tantalisingly on the threshold between paganism and Christianity. ...there's this liminality about Brigid um – and I've always been drawn to liminal places.
> Sylvia: On the edge, yeah.
> ...Paul: I love the edge places. That's why we're always trying to get to the Hebrides and to Orkney, and places that are right on the edge um because I think you experience something different at the edge than you do in the centre. ...because I – on the whole, all the really creative stuff I think happens on the edges, it doesn't happen on the centre.
> Sylvia: On the edges.

David Martin notes: '...the search for a personal path and the mystical may also express itself in the liminal experience of pilgrimage to sacred sites, Christian and pagan, which grows in popularity year by year' (2005a: 157). I agree that this is a key reason why my participants are so drawn to pilgrimage, but pilgrimage is also a safe way of ritualizing in a fused manner (sites are often sacred to both Christians and neo-pagans)[19] without necessarily needing to come out of the spiritual closet. In the same way, circle dance enables participants to use dances, songs, and symbols that they identify as pagan in source and meaning, in a context that may be 'legitimately' Christian.

Mystical experience

More than half of my fusing participants mentioned that they had had mystical-type experiences, especially visions. It is perhaps because Fusers are happy to break down boundaries which surround self-hood, gender, the world and the divine, that they so often have these sorts of experiences. Megan (Anglican), who is an artist, started to have visions at the age of 33 when she had a crisis stemming from childhood sexual abuse. It is in her visions and in the paintings she makes of them that she fuses. She says, 'I think the Goddess is fine as an image. My paintings are very goddess-y. My latest one, which I did at Easter, is called 'She is risen!' It's three women coming out of one'. Megan paints the Christian trinity in female terms because, 'you know, for me I would say Christ. I wouldn't want to say Jesus. But the Christ is female for me'. As Megan points out, the female trinity in her painting may also be read as the neo-pagan trinity of maiden, mother, crone which the Goddess expresses: 'we need to get back to that image…'. Similarly, Sara related these powerful experiences to me,

> We did IVF a few times and… they do implantation and that hurts – anyway, I was in the hospital room and I saw these specks of light…it was quite a spiritual moment for me because I felt… um I felt that I was in the presence of God and that God was in me, around me, I was of it, it was of me, there was an intimate connection um almost as if um I had a form that didn't – it was quite a magic moment. Um and I remember writing my paper on the Goddess and I got to the point where I really felt the same sort of thing…this intimate connection um with a very benevolent force that was in me, outside of me, and again there was no… there wasn't that division between self and other.

Conclusion

Fusers thus inhabit an unusual space. It is space that is neither here, nor there. It is a space that holds together difference, and it is the crossing-over point(s) between differences. This point, however, is not fixed, but is itself constantly shifting: its make-up constantly changing, and differing from person to person. Fuser multiple spiritual communities, multiple 'aspects' of the divine, multiple sources of inspiration, etc. all point to the fact that they do not exist entirely in any one place, and that they stress the mulitiplicity of relations; Fusers exist in the crossing over points. In this way, Fusers are not so fragmented as to exist in all points at once, or so shallow as to exist in a partial mixture of these places (i.e. pick and mix). Instead, Fusers *inhabit* the 'inter', the between, that which holds together.

---

[19]   For example, Kildare in Ireland is associated with Brigid, and draws both Christian and neo-pagan pilgrims (personal experience and Monaghan 2003).

References

The Association of Polytheist Traditions. www.manygods.org.uk (Accessed February 13, 2007).

Berger, Helen A., Leach, Evan A., and Shaffer, Leigh S. (eds), *Voices from the Pagan Census: a National Survey of Witches and Neo-Pagans in the United States* (Columbia, SC: University of South Carolina Press, 2003).

Berger, Peter, *The Sacred Canopy, Elements of a Sociological Theory of Religion* (Garden City, NY: Doubleday, 1967).

Berger, Peter (ed.), *The Desecularization of the World: Resurgent Religion and World Politics* (Grand Rapids, MI: W.B. Eerdmans, 1999).

Brierley, Peter (ed.), *UK Christian Handbook: Religious Trends 3 (2002–2003)* (London: Christian Research, 2001).

Bruce, Steve, *God is Dead: Secularization in the West* (Oxford: Blackwell, 2002).

Bruce, Steve, 'Secularization and the Impotence of Individualized Religion', *The Hedgehog Review: Critical Reflections on Contemporary Culture: After Secularization*, 8(1&2) (2006): 35–45.

Butler, Judith, *Gender Trouble: Feminism and the Subversion of Identity* (New York: Routledge, 1990).

Connell, Robert W., *Gender and Power: Society, the Person and Sexual Politics* (Cambridge: Polity, 1987).

Dandelion, Pink and Collins, Peter J. (eds), *A Sociology of British Quakerism* (Aldershot: Ashgate, forthcoming).

Davie, Grace, *Europe: the Exceptional Case: Parameters of Faith in the Modern World* (London: Darton, Longman & Todd, 2002).

Day, Abigail, *Believing in Belonging in Contemporary Britain: A Case Study from Yorkshire*, unpublished Ph.D. thesis (Lancaster: Lancaster University, 2006).

Eller, Cynthia, *Living in the Lap of the Goddess: the Feminist Spirituality Movement in America* (Boston: Beacon, 1993).

Griffin, Wendy, 'The Embodied Goddess: Feminist Witchcraft and Female Divinity', *Sociology of Religion*, 56(1) (1995): 35–48.

Griffin, Wendy (ed.), *Daughters of the Goddess: Studies of Healing, Identity and Empowerment* (Walnut Creek, CA: AltaMira, 2000).

Hanegraaf, Wouter J., *New Age Religion and Western Culture: Esotericism in the Mirror of Secular Thought* (Albany, NY: State University of New York Press, 1998[1996]).

Hardman, Charlotte. 'Introduction', in Harvey, Graham and Hardman, Charlotte (eds), *Pagan Pathways: a Guide to the Ancient Earth Traditions* (London: Thorsons, 1995): pp. ix–xix.

Harvey, Graham, *Listening People, Speaking Earth: Contemporary Paganism* (London: Hurst & Co., 1997).

Heelas, Paul, *The New Age Movement* (Oxford: Blackwell, 1996).

Heelas, Paul, 'Challenging Secularization Theory: the Growth of 'New Age' Spiritualities of Life', *The Hedgehog Review: Critical Reflections on Contemporary Culture: After Secularization*, 8(1&2) (2006): 46–58.

Heelas, Paul and Woodhead, Linda, *The Spiritual Revolution: Why Religion is Giving Way to Spirituality* (Oxford, UK and Malden, USA: Blackwell, 2005).

Kemp, Daren, *The Christaquarians? A Sociology of Christians in the New Age.* (Sidcup, Kent: Kempress, 2003).

Knott, Kim, *The Location of Religion: a Spatial Analysis* (London: Equinox, 2006).

Lynch, Gordon, *After Religion: "Generation X" and the Search for Meaning.* (London: Darton, Longman & Todd, 2002).

Martin, David, 'Secularisation and the Future of Christianity', *Journal of Contemporary Religion*, 20(2) (2005a): 145–160.

Martin, David, *On Secularization: Towards a Revised General Theory* (Aldershot: Ashgate, 2005b).

Monaghan, Patricia, *The Red Haired Girl From the Bog* (Novato, CA: New World Library, 2003).

Pearson, Jo, Roberts, Richard H. and Samuel, Geoffrey, *Nature Religion Today: Paganism in the Modern World* (Edinburgh: Edinburgh University Press, 1998).

Reid, Síân, *Between the Worlds: Readings in Contemporary Neopaganism* (Toronto: Canadian Scholars Press Inc., 2006).

Roof, Wade Clark, *Generation of Seekers: The Spiritual Journeys of the Baby Boom Generation* (San Francisco: HarperSanFrancisco, 1993).

Roof, Wade Clark, *The Spiritual Marketplace: Baby Boomers and the Remaking of American Religion* (Princeton NJ: Princeton University Press, 1999).

Rountree, Kathryn, *Embracing the Witch and the Goddess: Feminist Ritual-Makers in New Zealand* (New York: Routledge, 2004).

Rountree, Kathryn, 'The Past is a Foreigners' Country: Goddess Feminists, Archaeologists and the Appropriation of Prehistory', *Journal of Contemporary Religion*, 16(1) (January 2001): 5–28.

Salomonsen, Jone, *Enchanted Feminism: The Reclaiming Witches of San Francisco* (New York: Routledge, 2002).

Starhawk, *The Spiral Dance: A Rebirth of the Ancient Religion of the Great Goddess* (San Francisco: HarperSanFrancisco, 1999[1979]).

Woodhead, Linda, 'Church on Sunday, Yoga on Monday?', (Unpublished paper, 2005).

Woodhead, Linda, 'Gender Differences in Religious Practice and Significance', in James Beckford and N.J. Demerath III (eds), *Handbook of the Sociology of Religion* (London: Sage, 2007: 550–570).

Woodhead, Linda, *An Introduction to Christianity* (Cambridge: Cambridge University Press, 2004).

Woodhead, Linda and Heelas, Paul (eds), *Religion in Modern Times: An Interpretive Anthology* (Oxford: Blackwell, 2000).

Chapter 8

'Because I'm Worth It': Religion and Women's Changing Lives in the West

Linda Woodhead

> I am writing these words in a bar in London in the spring of 1997. I'm drinking a glass of beer and watching people go by the window. This is a simple, easy pleasure... I am wearing a trouser suit, and my hair is loose... I can take real pleasure in the clothes I buy... I will pay for my drink with my own money, that I earn from my own work.
>
> Natasha Walter (1998: 254–255)

The distinctive conditions, constraints and commitments of women's lives are beginning to be taken more seriously as we struggle to understand the nature and causes of the rapid religious change which has taken place in western societies since the 1960s. One approach is to argue that the speeding-up of secularization, particularly disaffiliation from Christian churches, can be explained by the fact that women's lives came to approximate men's more closely. As women entered the workforce in growing numbers they became subject to the same 'disenchanting' forces that men had encountered with the onset of industrialization (Woodhead 2005). Another argument suggests that the sexual revolution played the decisive role. As women claimed ownership over their own bodies and sexuality, so they abandoned the subordinate, male-referential forms of femininity which had previously defined their lives. Since such femininity had been identified with Christian piety since the nineteenth century, its abandonment involved a decisive break with Christianity (Brown 2001).

What both these arguments have in common is the assumption that there was a decisive change in women's lives after the 1960s which had a negative impact on religious adherence. In this chapter I propose a more complex understanding which acknowledges that important transformations took place in women's lives after the 1960s, but denies that these amount to a 'revolution' in which genuine equality between men and women was achieved (for a thorough review of the evidence, see Walby 1997). Traditional forms of 'women's work' and aspects of traditional femininity have persisted – partly because there has been no revolution in patterns of masculine work, identity and privilege – resulting in what Arlie Hochschild (1990: 11ff.) calls a 'stalled' gender revolution. The consequences for religion are correspondingly complex, and mean that we cannot simply assume that male experience is the 'leading edge' of a secularization process with women falling into line once they come under the sway of the same processes of modernization.

Attempts to relate more nuanced understandings of change in gender relations to religious change are beginning to be made – not least in this volume. In Woodhead (2007a), I consider the implications of the stalled gender revolution for the differentiated decline of Christianity and for the rise of holistic forms of spirituality. Here Penny Marler offers a detailed review of labour market and familial change, and shows how women's ambivalent relationship to domesticity impacts on Christian affiliation and spiritual seeking. Also in this volume, Houtman and Aupers ask whether women's being 'haunted more severely [than men] by problems of meaning and identity' may help account for their preponderance in new forms of spirituality. In this chapter I take forward this general line of enquiry by focusing on modes of selfhood engendered in contemporary women's working and intimate lives, and considering how they may relate to projects of the self authorized by religious and spiritual practices and communities in the West. I will draw on a number of data sources, including interviews and participant observation carried out by myself with women in Kendal, Cumbria (UK) and Asheville, North Carolina (USA) between 2000 and 2006.

The late modern project of the self

The late modern condition can be characterized by the extensive and intensive way in which the self becomes disembedded from established traditions, roles, regimes and rituals. Even if this is a social process, brought about by a nexus of factors including the modes of production and consumption characteristic of late capitalism, it is integral to it that it is *read* as a matter of individual choice and responsibility. Indeed the tendency to interpret social processes in individualized terms becomes sign, symptom and cause of the process of individualization itself. Representations of the self as free, responsible, self-propelled, self-made and independent become dominant, and 'standard biographies' and given 'roles in life' give way to 'elective' or 'do-it-yourself' biographies (Beck and Beck-Gernsheim 2001: 24–25). As a host of best-selling autobiographies remind us, even the most brutally dominated childhoods must be transcended by force of self-directed will.

Modernization thus involves a shift whereby, perhaps for the first time, the 'individual' becomes a value, rather than a cautionary tale of sad, lonely, dangerous or idiotic deviation from the general. The gradual acceptance of human rights legislation with its deep-seated assumptions about human dignity, equality and basic entitlements marks and solidifies this process. But late modernity goes beyond 'first modernity's' stress on given, general, human worth and entitlement. 'Material' imperatives give way to 'postmaterialist' ones of self-development and self-fulfilment (Inglehart 1990). Uniqueness and non-identity become key values, and the task of continually differentiating one's life from others becomes a measure of success in the project of generating authentic 'expressive' selfhood (Taylor 1989, 1991).

Thus late modernity spawns dominant modes of selfhood which stress individual worth, entitlement, self-propulsion and independence. This is not because the anomic individual is set free in a world of normless possibility, but because – on the contrary – guidelines, targets, demands and 'opportunities' spread their tendrils as never before. Unlike roles and rules which call for passive acceptance, this new regime compels self-organization and the constant exercize of choice and self-assertion. This is particularly true because of the differentiated, fragmented and often contradictory nature of the institutional guidelines in which lives are enmeshed. Individuals are forced to become 'reflexive', to gain new knowledges, explore new possibilities, make constant choices, negotiations and compromises. The discontinuity and dissonance between different sets of guidelines, rather than the dominance of unified sets of rules and expectations, is what forces 'the self' to become self-aware and self-reflexive (Giddens 1991; Bauman 2005).

Whilst it may have hegemonic status, the entitled, reflexive, self of late modernity is nevertheless a fragile project which is inflected by gender, class and ethnicity, and which can only ever be partially inhabited. It requires particular social and material conditions for its realization – or even approximation. As Taylor (1991) has emphasized, projects of unique selfhood are risky because they require *recognition*, and such recognition can fail. Whilst they may present themselves as self-determined and self-referential, our sense of valued unique selfhood is constructed by way of quotidian interactions with others. A sense of self-worth is not self-created, but relational, and depends upon others' willingness to make space and make time, to listen, acknowledge and recognize. That, in turn, is related to one's access to resources – to social, political, cultural and economic capitals. Successful projects of selfhood depend, importantly, upon access to fulfilling, socially valued, and well-paid work. They depend upon having money (and/or credit) for oneself, as well as upon being able to make time for oneself and space for oneself. Most fundamentally, they depend upon bodily health and integrity and a sense of ownership of one's own body. Indeed, the domination or alienation of one's body, including one's sexuality, constitutes perhaps the most serious of all obstacles to the creation of a sense of unique, bounded and valuable selfhood under one's own control.

Late modern femininities

For the current generation of white, middle-class women in the richer economies of the West, a femininity shaped around an independent, entitled, self-propelled self has greater purchase and legitimacy than for any previous generation. Whereas women of earlier generations could only dream of 'a room of one's own' (Woolf 1991), women who have come of age since the 1960s can buy property for themselves with money they have earned and credit to which they have equal access with most men. Though men might dismiss it as trivial, the experience which Natasha Walter writes about in the quotation which opens this chapter is revolutionary for women, because it entails occupying public space legitimately and without depending on male permission; feeling entitled to occupy such space; taking time, leisure time, for oneself; buying consumables for oneself with money one has earned oneself; enjoying no company but one's own; not depending on male permission. Whereas such activities – 'going down the pub' or club and other self-pleasuring leisure events – have always been legitimate for men of all classes, for women they are unprecedented.

What has changed is not merely that, as gender-blind sociological literature puts it, women have become disembedded from 'tradition' and 'traditional roles', but – more precisely – that they have begun to escape masculine domination. Whereas before women were confined to masculine-dominated space (the father's house, the husband's house, the boss's workplace), were generally dependent on a male wage, lived in societies in which all positions of authority were occupied by men (policeman, headmaster, clergyman, medical and legal professionals etc.), and were educated in traditions which made such domination appear natural and/or God-given, today women can 'do things for themselves' without having to refer or defer to men. Their ability to do so is, importantly, undergirded by laws enacted throughout the course of the twentieth century relating to property, citizenship, and equality. The result, psychologically, is a growing sense of self-worth and entitlement, the sense that 'I am worth it' and perhaps that 'I don't have to put up with that'. For women, then, late modern projects of the independent, entitled self represent a far more revolutionary break with the past than do male projects of the self. For late modern men, sitting outside a pub having a drink is 'more of the same', for women it is a new experience (Beck and Beck-Gernsheim 2001: 75).

For many women, however, the project of independent, entitled selfhood remains fragile and elusive. This is due not only to its shallow roots in the past, but to its shaky situation in the present. For many non-white women the project may be elusive due to some combination of factors including economic deprivation, lack of connection to 'white' social networks, racial discrimination, and religious and cultural factors favouring masculine domination. For white working-class women, 'respectable' femininity is likely to be conceived less in terms of independence than in terms of life lived for others (Skeggs 1997). Given the rise in single-parenthood – which actually means single-motherhood – the 'others' may no longer be men, but children and other dependents. Working-class women are also more likely to be involved in forms of paid employment which involve bodily and emotional care work, such as teaching assistantships, care for elderly people, cleaning, housework and childminding. Such care work is unlikely to support a strong sense of independent, entitled selfhood. As Armstrong (2006) discovers, whilst both middle- and working-class women are likely to have to take prime responsibility for child care and domestic work, working-class women are less likely to find this a threat to their sense of identity because their femininity is more fully identified with mothering, caring, and providing rather than with independent achievement.

Even the ability of white middle-class women to pursue projects of independent, unencumbered selfhood are compromised, however, by a range of factors, most notably by men's failure to take on an equal share of childcare and domestic work (Brannen and Moss 1991; Hochschild 1990; Beck and Beck-Gernsheim 2002: 101–118). The tension between living 'life for oneself' and a 'life for others' can be acute for women educated on equal terms and with equal expectations with men, who then find themselves 'drowned' by responsibilities of care for others. Thus middle-class women often find their lives caught in a web of contradictions between two incompatible modes of selfhood – the independent, entitled self and the other-referential, caring self. The contradiction is reflected in a wider cultural confusion about femininity and women's roles. On the one hand, the 'homey', 'wholesome' woman who bakes, sews and welcomes all into her cosy home; on the other hand the successful businesswoman, briefcase in hand, 'showing the boys how to do it'. The contradiction even shows up in the European Values Surveys, which find that around 80 per cent of Europeans agree with the statement that a pre-school child will suffer if his mother works *and* the statement that a working mother can have 'as secure and warm a relationship with her children as a mother who does not work' (Halman, Luijkx and Zundert 2005: 36).

The upshot is that for late modern women, unlike men, there is really no culturally acceptable form of selfhood in terms of which lives, dreams and aspirations can comfortably take shape. The figure of the independent career women is surrounded by moral ambiguity, and concern about her 'unnatural' private life and wellbeing is never far from the surface – as an interview in *The Observer* put it:

> Who could forget Nicola Horlick, dubbed 'superwoman' 10 years ago for being able to combine an adrenalin-charged City career with bringing up a big family? Well, she's changed – this is a different woman, calmer, comfortable in her own skin, with more time to talk and laugh a little. (25 September 2005)

But if 'career woman' is an ambiguous femininity, so too is wife-and-mother. Although the 1950s stay-at-home 'mom' may still dominate the imagination, women who actually chose to stay at home rather than to work are castigated for being social security scroungers (working-class women) or pampered 'yummy mummies' taking up too much space with their 'Chelsea tractors' and sponging off men. As Nirpal Dhaliwal put it in the *Sunday Times* 'Style' magazine:

> Nothing hardens my resolve to abstain from parenthood more than the herds of posturing yummy mummies who congregate to slurp lattes and share the tedious details of their offspring's development. I can feel my sperm count falling through the floor just thinking about these idle heifers and their conceited, boring lives. (28 January 2007)

Dhaliwal's comments are typical of a nearly ubiquitous tendency to characterize women who display even the slightest desire to embrace a project of self-development as 'pampered', 'selfish' and 'narcissistic'. This reveals the continuing influence of a double standard of selfhood, in which men are admired for pursuing independent selfhood, whilst women are expected to orient their lives around others as much as, or more than, themselves. Acceptable forms of femininity are those which are considerate, polite and deferential; ready with a shoulder to cry on and a listening ear; neither pushy nor ambitious; putting one's own needs second. As Hochschild puts it,

> We have a simple word for the product of [women's] shadow labour: 'nice'. Beyond the smaller niceties are the larger ones of doing a favour, offering a service. Finally, there is the moral or spiritual sense of being seriously nice, in which we embrace the needs of another person as more important than our own. Each way of being nice adds a dimension to deference... Almost everyone does the emotion work that produces what we might, broadly speaking, call deference. But women are expected to do more of it. (1983: 166)

A similar double standard continues to operate in relation to the body and sexuality, where acceptable femininities are those which make themselves physically attractive and pleasing to men. A number of studies have noted the recent growth in importance of this facet of late modern femininity (Walby 1990; Wolf 1991). It is 'policed' by way of derogatory terms old and new such as 'dog' and 'minger', and by accusations that women who do not present themselves as 'up for it' (sex with men) are uncool, uptight, and 'no fun' (Levy 2005). As well as fuelling spending on clothes and beauty products, the imperative to look attractive at all times has led women to undertake increasingly radical and expensive measures to discipline and alter their bodies, whether by exercize and beauty regimes or by more radical means – from cosmetic surgery to forms of dieting so extreme that they become pathological and sometimes fatal (Knapp 2004). Women may be allowed to enter public space as never before, but the pressure on them to look attractive to men when they do so continues to prevent them doing so on their own terms.

Consequences for religion

The contemporary contradictions of femininity are nicely captured by the hugely successful L'Oréal advertising campaign 'Because I'm worth it', launched in 1973 and still running today. On the one hand, the slogan captures just how much has changed for women as they have been allowed access to male projects of independent, self-referential, entitled selfhood as never before. On the other hand, the very necessity of having to *make* such an assertion and, more importantly, to *prove* one's worth by buying expensive beauty products in order to make oneself more attractive and 'worthy' indicates just how fragile the sense of entitlement may be. Turning now to the realm of religion, I will explore some implications for western religion and religious change.

Christianity

The most important change to be explained is, of course, the decline of Christianity in Europe and North America. Whilst established theories of secularization which invoke modernizing processes such as rationalization, bureaucratization or differentiation may help explain aspects of general Christian decline, they fail to explain why – for example – church attendance grew in the 1950s only to decline so dramatically after the 1960s.[1]

---

[1]   As writers like Bruce (2002) have documented in detail, almost every aspect of organised Christian life that can be quantified can serve as a measure of decline – whether ordinations of clergy, baptisms, confirmations, Sunday School attendance, church membership, or church attendance. To take just the latter, and to use Britain as an example, the picture is one of growth between 1800 and 1840, lower growth between 1840 and 1910, slow decrease after 1910, and accelerating decline after and 1970 (Currie, Gilbert, and Horsley 1977: 21–38). Britain is not the most secular of European countries: that honour goes to (in ascending order of secularity) to Hungary, France, Czech Republic, Finland, Sweden, Denmark (*Social Trends*, No. 36). In the USA Christianity remains significantly more buoyant than in most

Attention to shifting femininities can enhance our understanding of such changes. As a general principle, we can postulate that religion is likely to appeal widely to women – and win the support of men – when it supports and complements modes of femininity which have wide social acceptance or desirability (Woodhead 2007b). Historically, Christianity has flourished when it has supported a patriarchal gender order and accompanying masculinities and femininities (just as it has done well when it has supported the established social order, political order and economic order). But if the gender order begins to falter, then the religion which sanctifies it is likely to suffer as well. Given Christianity's constitutive relation to 'tradition' and its male-dominated and cumbersome organizational forms, it is hard for it to change quickly and decisively enough to embrace new gender orderings – especially when changes take place as quickly as they did after the 1960s.

Thus one reason that Christianity grew in the 1950s but declined thereafter may be that its alliance with femininities of service, self-sacrifice and domesticity, which served it well in the unusual circumstances of the immediate post-war period (May 1988), became a handicap as women were increasingly influenced by late modern projects of self-propelled, independent, 'worthy' selfhood. There is limited, but growing, evidence from in-depth qualitative research to support this thesis. Mary Beatham's (2003) interviews with Catholic women aged over sixty remind us just how integral the churches had been in reinforcing femininities of service to others, particularly men. As the women recalled:

> You fulfilled your duty as a good Catholic girl, dutifully committing yourself to your family, as your mother did, sublimating your own desires for the needs of the greater good, of everyone else, and you just got on with it. (2003: 24)

> To work was to pray… We offered it up, and gave thanks to God… it was nothing out of the ordinary to be doing your washing and reciting the rosary at the same time! (2003: 25)

> It wasn't unusual to 'go without' myself in order that the family had something to eat or to wear. My mother often had to make sacrifices when I was a child, doing without herself so dad could have a hot meal. (2003: 26)[2]

Interviews with this generation of women also reveal that a self-sacrificial Christian femininity was bound up with a sexual ethic which made it hard not only for women to imagine they had any rights in a sexual relationship, but to even admit to sexual desire. Their bodies were, in almost every sense, not their own but the property of men, whether the Holy Father (the body as a 'temple of the Holy Spirit'), the Divine Son (Jesus the bridegroom), or flesh-and-blood fathers and husbands. The negation

---

of Europe. Levels of commitment to churches and churchgoing remain higher, and religion has a stronger presence in the culture and in personal and political life. Nevertheless, some significant decline in churchgoing does seem to have taken place. Reliable recent research suggests that attendance levels are currently around 22–24 per cent in the USA (Marler and Hadaway 2000: 42) and that they have fallen from around 40 per cent in the early 1960s (Hadaway, Marler and Chaves 1998; Presser and Stinson 1998).

[2]   See also the interview-based research with Christian women by Clark-King (2004) and Porter (2004).

of women's 'own' sexual and bodily needs and desires was effected as much by silence as by explicit restrictions. Compared with the relatively high visibility of topics like (male) masturbation and 'how far can you go' (in 'making love to' a woman), female sexuality remained a silenced subject in church circles. Unwritten codes concerning appropriate suitable clothing (demure), language (pure) and dating rituals (where the woman was responsible for enforcing propriety) reinforced the male prerogative.

There is also interview-based evidence of a recognition of the change in feminine identity which occurred between this generation and their daughters and grand daughters. As one woman puts it:

> It was the same for everyone... and you accepted it...you saw it [domestic work] as a privilege, like you'd been given an 'exulted' role in your own home! [laughter]... not that young girls, even my own daughter, would see it like that today! She'd laugh at the idea. They would say we were being duped. Maybe we were. (Beatham 2003: 25)

Or, as another informant remarks:

> It's easier to with hindsight to see what had happened. Today women do what they believe is best for themselves and their families, as they should...they don't have all the guilt and conscience stuff... I envy them that. (Beatham 2003: 40)

This generation of women retained their church connections. Many of the next – baby boom – generation ceased to attend church. Some speak about their defection in ways which make it clear that a changing sense of identity was at play. To quote one middle-aged Lancashire woman whom I interviewed, and who had ceased going to church in her forties:

> they were standing up in church and reading passages, you know, what was it, something about being masters and slaves and basically saying 'you shall be subservient', I thought this doesn't make any sense to me. I might just have drifted along like that, we took the kids to Church Parade on a Sunday... it seemed so empty, so hypocritical really... I couldn't believe values like respectability and family life... I just wanted to do my own thing: I wasn't having anyone telling me what to do.

As women of the baby boom generation and since have embraced ideals of self-directed, fulfilling, worthy selfhood, some thus seem to have turned away from femininities orientated around deference, self-sacrifice and male-referentiality. Some, like the woman above, make a conscious choice to break with a commitment to churchgoing. More defect in their early teens, once they are old enough to 'make up their own mind'. Having never made an adult commitment to Christianity, they often have little to say about their reasons for defection, other than they find church 'boring', 'irrelevant', 'not for me', and that there are 'more exciting things to do'. These 'more exciting things' tend to be activities which give greater scope for autonomous self-exploration. Even those women who remain loyal to church are likely to have less time to give, and less willingness to perform, the traditional roles which keep churches going – whether looking after the priest, delivering leaflets, cleaning the brass, making the tea, or supporting 'women's organizations' under the oversight of a male clergyman. Some, as we found in Kendal, attend in spite of much of what goes on in church. As one woman we interviewed put it,

> I'm not looking for community... I've no desire to join in any of the groups... because I like to go to church for me, it's my personal time... what religion is for me is my space, my time... I find the building allows me to focus better... it's a place I don't have to think about the washing up or the cooking or the gardening or anything else...And the service can wash over...it does allow that. I just find some of the incidentals very irritating.

This quotation reminds us that it is too simple to assume that women have simply abandoned the churches as they have embraced a project of unencumbered selfhood incompatible with self-sacrificial Christian femininity. For some, particularly those who rejected the family ideal and embraced a full-time career, this may be true. But, as I have argued throughout, the more common scenario is likely to be one of ambivalence about identity, as women find themselves caught between incompatible modes of selfhood and life-commitments. In this context, Christianity can still exercize an appeal for women who embrace the project of entitled, independent selfhood without severing all connection with 'traditional' femininities. The informant from Kendal quoted above uses church mainly as a space to escape from domestic chores and make space for unique selfhood. Others whom we interviewed use church as an arena in which to cultivate and celebrate their familial, domestic femininities, even though they no longer believe their 'whole' selves to be defined by them. Still others devote some time to church, often in retirement, because they support the sense of community which it supports, and are happy to perform the 'woman's work' required to sustain it. Some speak, revealingly, of 'nostalgia' as part of what sustains their commitment.

   This affirmation of a 'part time' or partial domestic femininity which does not, however, rule out the simultaneous embrace of a more independent, entitled selfhood, is most likely to prove compatible with membership of liberal, mainline churches. A 'full time' commitment to domestic selfhood is catered for in more conservative churches. Indeed, the relative success of conservative evangelical Protestantism in the last part of the twentieth century may be accounted for in large part by its ability to cater for a 'niche market' of women – and men – who wish to affirm gender roles based around male headship and female domesticity. Such allegiance may be interpreted as an attempt to find hospitable spaces for the cultivation for a form of femininity which is now widely denigrated in wider western society. However, as a number of recent studies show, even within these most gender-conservative milieus, women are actively negotiating selfhood in ways which enable them to claim some aspects of an entitled, independent selfhood (see, for example, Brasher 1998 and Griffith 1997). Even the most conservative churches have accepted the necessity, even the right, of women's paid employment, and accept that women as well as men have a right to seek personal and financial fulfilment and happiness (Hunter 1987; Smith 2000). The bargain (or 'covenant') they offer is that women can expect male protection and fidelity in return for traditional, unpaid, female domestic labour. The deal comes with a number of benefits, including release from confusion about femininity, the significant support networks of the church and the church community which often provide counselling and childcare, and the respect of other women and men within the community.

'Alternative' spiritualities

If mainline churches in the West seem to mirror the contradictions of contemporary femininity by maintaining rituals, liturgies, language and institutional arrangements which reinforce masculine domination and male-referential femininities whilst simultaneously teaching the equal dignity of all human beings, alternative spirituality seems to offer more creative solutions to the problem. For those who wish to abandon male-defined forms of identity more wholeheartedly, but without abandoning the sacred, contemporary forms of spirituality may offer an attractive alternative. No longer quite as 'invisible' as Thomas Luckmann's (1967) eponymous book title would suggest, such spirituality now includes a vast and rapidly-changing range of activities ranging from Reiki to Buddhist chanting, Interfaith ceremonies to Tai Chi (Heelas and Woodhead 2005). Accumulating evidence suggests that such spirituality has been growing rapidly since the 1980s (see Houtman and Aupers in this volume and Heelas and Woodhead 2005).

Attempts to explain the growth of such spirituality have already acknowledged its ability to cater for the late modern project of independent, entitled, unique selfhood. Heelas (1996) argues that the New Age movement succeeds because it sacralizes the self, and labels contemporary spirituality 'self-spirituality'. What such an account fails to explain, however, is why women are preponderant in such spirituality, with up to 80 per cent of those involved in Kendal at least being white, middle-class women aged over forty (Heelas and Woodhead 2005). But we can make this 'gender puzzle' disappear if we acknowledge that the late modern project of the self is mediated by gender, age, class and ethnicity, and that women engage with it in very different ways from men. Thus the virtual absence of elderly, non-white, and working-class women from alternative spirituality can be explained by the fact that their lives offer no space or purchase for the project of independent, unencumbered selfhood. And the preponderance of white, middle-class, middle-aged women can, in turn, be viewed in the context of a desire to access resources which are readily available to them, but help them negotiate dilemmas of selfhood which frame their lives.

Contemporary forms of alternative spirituality seem to serve this need particularly well by virtue of their ability to combine an emphasis on unique individual selfhood with a 'holistic' approach. Although such spirituality is increasingly internally differentiated and now embraces neo-paganism, New Age, metaphysical seeking, and health-oriented practices, the 'holistic' emphasis is common throughout. It emphasizes unity, connectedness and wholeness, first, by insisting that the individual self is a unity of 'mind, body, spirit', and second, by stressing the individual's essential connection with, and enmeshment within, a web of relationships. At the same time, it affirms the existence of a unique 'core' self which is inherently sacred – and whose potentials it promises to release. The effect is to offer a framework in which the choice between 'a bit of a life for oneself' and 'living for others' can be negotiated to suit particular circumstances and priorities. Because the balance between the whole/relationality and the unique/individuality can shift, different forms of alternative spirituality may thus prove helpful workshops of selfhood for both (a) women seeking to embrace more of a 'life for myself' and (b) women – and men – who are already engaged in late modern projects of individual self-realization and who wish to cultivate 'relational' and 'dependent' aspects of selfhood.

In our research in Kendal we found more of the former than the latter. As I have documented in more detail elsewhere, many practitioners and clients emphasized how they were dealing with 'issues of self-esteem and self-confidence' and trying to overcome a tendency to lose oneself in relationships (Woodhead 2007a). One woman said she had 'sacrificed myself and sacrificed my truth for the sake of relationships', whilst another said:

> [I had to learn] to know myself. That was important because I wasn't a full person. I couldn't separate from other people and felt like everyone else was leaning on me and pushing me down. I tried to solve everyone's problems.

The gender dimension, and the issue of masculine domination, was often made explicit. Several women spoke about spending twenty years or so subordinating their own lives for husband and children, others spoke of disastrous relationships with men, of trying to escape from having 'my life journey around relationships with men', or of dealing with sexual and other forms of abuse by men. We observed a class on 'Energy Management' whose facilitator warned that 'the most common area in which we allow damage to our energy field is when we are too invested in wanting to "help"... and end up sacrificing our own life force for the other person'. She emphasized that the proper, spiritual goal is 'to find your own truth' by 'feeling what's right for *you*'.

Thus holistic forms of spirituality cater directly to some women's desire to construct more robust, independent, entitled forms of selfhood by way of a range of teachings and, more importantly, practices. They promise: 'happiness', 'wellbeing', 'transformation', 'helping you to heal and empower yourself'; 'discovering your potential to grow', 'being yourself', 'self discovery' (headlines from a selection of flyers picked up in Glastonbury, UK in August 2006). Some involve 'talking cures' in which individuals are encouraged not only to explain their discontents and disease, but also to articulate their hopes and desires. More importantly, they use the body as a means to explore hurts, pains, and negative emotions and engender a sense of identity, value, and entitlement (Sointu 2006). Having one's body touched physically marks out one's boundaries and hence one's independent identity and unique selfhood. The mere fact of taking this time for oneself, paying for it, and entering an all-woman or woman-dominated space is also directly empowering for many women (and nearly impossible for most working class women). As one of participant in holistic spirituality in Kendal put it, 'A lot of it is having the time out where no-one can make demands on you. It's total "you" time'. Revealingly, others, including some churchgoers, criticize self spirituality as self-indulgent, 'navel-gazing', and indulgent – i.e. subversive of more traditional, Christian, other-regarding forms of femininity.

Given its constitutive dialectic between self and other, however, alternative spirituality is also capable of shifting the emphasis in order to allow individuals engaged in competitive projects of selfhood to engage with and perform more affective, relational and 'holistic' aspects of selfhood. Where it occurs, growing male engagement in holistic spirituality may well be related to this dynamic, and – although much more research is needed – I have heard men speak of engaging in such spirituality as a means of becoming more 'connected' to their partners, more committed to relationships, more 'in tune' with their feelings and the natural world. Likewise, women who have pursued 'masculinized' forms of independent selfhood perhaps at the expense of family and relationality, may find in alternative spirituality (if not in mainline Christianity) opportunities for the exercize of more relational, mutual aspects of selfhood. In Asheville, for example, a wealthy professional women in her early thirties who had recently suffered a miscarriage spoke to me of how the experience had made her turn away from the Presbyterian church and its male God, and embrace a more feminized, 'compassionate' understanding of the divine: 'more of a mother, care-taker of our earth and creator, I just think of that as a woman, and birthing'. At the same time, she had decided to pull back from full time professional work in order to work shorter hours and carry out non-profit work for underprivileged children, and to devote more time to (alternative) spiritual exploration. She was, in other words, using spirituality as a resource for the exploration and enactment of a form of unique selfhood in which there was more of a balance with a caring, relational mode. Later that same summer of 2006 I was carrying out research in Glastonbury, and noticed just how central the construction of 'female-centred' rituals has become in alternative spirituality. One booklet I picked up offered rituals for:

Intention to conceive/conception
Blessingway in pregnancy
Birth/Baby naming/Baby blessing
Becoming a parent/grandparent
Miscarriage/Stillbirth/Abortion
Weaning/First Steps/First School Day
First blood/Puberty/Coming of age
Menopause/Becoming a crone.

Thus the dialectic between self and other, individual and whole, independence and mutual dependence which lies at the heart of holistic spirituality gives it a flexibility in relation to contemporary experiments with selfhood which lends itself to a range of 'solutions' to the dilemmas which are currently experienced by many middle-class women. At one end of the spectrum it may sacralize the achievement of independent, 'successful' selfhood by offering tools and techniques for individual empowerment and self-advancement. At the other, it may become embodied in small, tight-knit elective communities dedicated to worship of the Goddess, eco-friendly lifestyles, or political protest. And in the currently more well-populated middle ground one is more likely to find white, middle-class women whose children have left home, and who seek human and divine help in achieving a balance between 'living for others' and 'a bit of a life for myself'.

Conclusion

This chapter aims to take forward an increasingly lively debate about gender-inflected causes of religious change in the West. My suggestion is that attention to issues of identity, selfhood and subjectivity both within and outside religious institutions has the potential to illuminate recent developments, but that such potential is only realized when the mediations of late modern projects of selfhood – particularly in relation to gender – are taken seriously. More concretely, I suggest that we need to pay attention to the dilemmas of selfhood which entangle contemporary generations of women caught in a stalled gender revolution. I have tried to show that the ability of different forms of religion to resource women in dealing with these dilemmas may have a significant bearing on their success.

Although the study of secularization has traditionally been theory heavy and evidence light, it will be obvious that more research is needed to test the theory I am proposing. I have drawn attention to suggestive correlations, but much more (methodologically challenging) work is required before a causal link can be more plausibly established. A complication is that religious growth and decline seem to be determined by a whole range of converging causes, and it is extremely hard to gauge which carry the most weight. I have no wish to suggest that gender is the only relevant factor, though I do believe that it is a particularly important and neglected one, and that it has become ever more important in a western context in which religion has shed many of its ethnic/nationalistic, political and economic functions.

Finally, though it may not need emphasizing, the scope of this paper has been limited to a discussion of religion and femininity. I hope it goes without saying that the study of religion and masculinity is also needed, and that it too has the ability to advance our understanding of religious change in modern times.

References

Armstrong, Jo, 'Beyond "Juggling" and "Flexibility"': Classed and Gendered Experiences Combining Employment and Motherhood', *Sociological Research Online*, 11(2) (2006).

Bauman, Zygmunt, *Liquid Life* (Cambridge: Polity, 2005).

Beatham, Mary, 'Woman, Who are You?': A Study into the Feminine Identity and Role of Women in the Catholic Church'. Unpublished M.A. Dissertation (Lancaster: Lancaster University, 2003).

Beck, Ulrich and Beck-Gernsheim, Elisabeth, *Individualization: Institutionalized Individualism and its Social and Political Consequences* (London: Sage, 2001).

Brannen, Julia and Moss, Peter, *Managing Mothers: Dual Earner Households after Maternity Leave* (London: Unwin Hyman, 1991).

Brasher, Brenda, *Godly Women. Fundamentalism and Female Power* (New Brunswick, NJ: Rutgers University Press, 1998).

Brown, Callum, *The Death of Christian Britain: Understanding Secularisation, 1800–2000* (London: Routledge, 2001).

Bruce, Steve, *God is Dead. Secularization in the West* (Oxford: Blackwell, 2002).

Clark-King, Ellen, *Theology by Heart: Women, the Church and God* (Peterborough: Epworth, 2004).

Currie, Robert, Gilbert, Alan and Horsley, Lee, *Churches and Churchgoers: Patterns of Church Growth in the British Isles Since 1700* (Oxford: Clarendon Press, 1977).

Dhaliwal, Nirpal, 'I Hate Yummy Mummies', *Sunday Times*, 28 January, 2007.

Giddens, Anthony, *Modernity and Self-Identity: Self and Society in the Late Modern Age* (Stanford, CA: Stanford University Press, 1991).

Griffith, R. Marie, *God's Daughters: Evangelical Women and the Power of Submission* (Berkeley, CA: University of California Press, 1997).

Hadaway, C. Kirk, Marler, Penny Long, Chaves, Mark, 'Over-reporting Church Attendance in America: Evidence that Demands the Same Verdict', *American Sociological Review*, 63(1) (1998): 122–130.

Halman, Loek, Luijkx, Ruud, and van Zundert, Marga, *Atlas of European Values* (Tilburg University and Leiden: Brill, 2005).

Heelas, Paul, *The New Age Movement* (Oxford: Blackwell, 1996).

Heelas, Paul, and Woodhead, Linda, *The Spiritual Revolution: Why Religion is Giving Way to Spirituality* (Oxford: Blackwell, 2005).

Hinsliff, Gaby and Hill, Amelia, 'Why the Have-it-all Woman Has Decided She Doesn't Want It All', *The Guardian Observer Magazine*, 27 November, 2005.

Hochschild, Arlie, *The Managed Heart* (Berkeley, CA: University of California Press, 1983).

Hochschild, Arlie with Machung, Anne, *The Second Shift: Working Parents and the Revolution at Home* (Berkeley and London: University of California Press, 1990 [1989]).

Hunter, James Davison, *Evangelicalism: The Coming Generation* (Chicago: University of Chicago Press, 1987).

Inglehart, Ronald, *Culture Shift in Advanced Industrial Society* (Princeton, NJ: Princeton University Press, 1990).

Kindred, Glennie, and Garner, Lu, *Creating Ceremony* (Wirksworth: Kindred, 2002).

Knapp, Caroline, *Appetites* (New York: Counterpoint Press, 2004).

Levy, Ariel, *Female Chauvinist Pigs: Women and the Rise of Raunch Culture* (New York: Free Press, 2005).

Luckmann, Thomas, *The Invisible Religion* (London: Collier-Macmillan, 1967).

Marler, Penny Long and Hadaway, C. Kirk (2000), 'Attendance', in Wade Clark Roof (ed.), *Contemporary American Religion*, vol. 1: 40–42 (New York: MacMillan, 2000).

May, Elaine Tyler, *Homeward Bound* (New York: Basic Books, 1988).

Porter, Fran, *It will not be Taken Away from Her: A Feminist Engagement with Women's Christian Experience* (London: Darton Longman and Todd, 2004).

Presser, Stanley and Stinson, Linda, 'Data Collection Mode and Social Desirability Bias in Self-Reported Religious Attendance', *American Sociological Review*, 63(1) (1998): 137–145.

Skeggs, Beverley, *Formations of Class and Gender: Becoming Respectable* (London: Sage, 1997).

Smith, Christian, *Christian America? What Evangelicals Really Want* (Berkeley, CA University of California Press, 2000).

Sointu, Eeva, 'The Search for Wellbeing in Alternative and Complementary Health Practices', *Sociology of Health and Illness*, 28(3) (2006): 330–349.

Social Trends No. 36, National Statistics (Basingstoke: Palgrave MacMillan, 2006).

Taylor, Charles, *Sources of the Self: The Making of the Modern Identity* (Cambridge: Cambridge University Press, 1989).

Taylor, Charles, *The Ethics of Authenticity* (Cambridge, MA: Harvard University Press, 1991).

Walby, Sylvia, *Theorizing Patriarchy* (Cambridge: Polity, 1990).

Walby, Sylvia, *Gender Transformations* (London: Routledge, 1997).

Walter, Natasha, *The New Feminism* (London: Little, Brown, 1998).

Wolf, Naomi, *The Beauty Myth: How Images of Beauty are Used against Women* (London: Vintage, 1991).

Woolf, Virginia, *A Room of One's Own* (New York: Harcourt Brace Jovanovich, 1991).

Woodhead, Linda, 'Gendering Secularisation Theory', *Kvinder, Køn og Forskning* (*Women, Gender and Research*), 1–2 (2005): 24–35.

Woodhead, Linda, 'Why So Many Women in Holistic Spirituality?' in Kieran Flanagan and Peter Jupp (eds), *A Sociology of Spirituality* (Aldershot: Ashgate, 2007a).

Woodhead, Linda, 'Gender Differences in Religious Practice and Significance', in James Beckford and N.J. Demerath (eds), *Handbook of the Sociology of Religion* (London: Sage, 2007b).

Young, Iris Marion, *Throwing Like a Girl and Other Essays in Feminist Philosophy and Social Theory* (Bloomington and Indianapolis: Indiana University Press, 1990).

PART 3
Islam

Chapter 9

Counting Women with Faith: What Quantitative Data can reveal about Muslim Women in 'Secular' Britain

Serena Hussain

Patterns of Muslim settlement in Britain

Although there has been a Muslim presence in Britain for hundreds of years (Sherif 2002) the Muslim community grew significantly from 1960 onwards as a result of a labour shortage during post World War II. Britain invited citizens of the Commonwealth to fill vacancies, resulting in many of today's British Muslims being of South Asian descent. A clear demonstration of the growth of British Muslims since the 1960s is the rise in the number of mosques. In 1963 there were only 13 mosques registered in Britain. The number grew to 49 in 1970 and doubled in the space of five years to 99 in 1975, and again to 203 in 1980. It almost doubled yet again to 338 in 1985 (Vertovec 2002). Ansari (2004) describes the large scale Muslim settlement to Britain as occurring in two broad phases: firstly 1945 to the early 1970s and then from 1973 to the present. However it is argued here that it is more useful to have a three-fold division (Hussain 2005):

i) 1945 to approximately 1970 – which predominantly consisted of young male migrant workers
ii) 1970 to approximately 1990 – where communities were formed as a result of wives joining husbands and British born children.
iii) 1990s onwards – a period of settlement characterized by young single men, asylum seekers and refugee communities rather than economic migrants.

The first phase was to fulfil the needs of Britain's expansion of production, which called for large numbers of migrant workers, many of whom were Muslim. The main pull factor for Muslim migrants in taking up undesirable employment opportunities was the financial gain. The pay in Britain for manual labour was up to 30 times greater than for equivalent jobs in some of their countries of origin (Shaw 1988). However it is clear when considering events occurring prior to or during peaks of migration that poverty was not the main motive for uprooting and settling overseas.

The partition of India, and to a lesser extent Cyprus, created a sense of 'motion' among communities, which promoted the migration of Muslims to Britain. For the majority of Pakistanis, originating from Azad Jummu and Kashmir, the building of the Mangla dam in 1960 left some 250 villages submerged, displacing 100,000 'Mirpuris' who might previously have been cautious about migrating when offered the opportunity by the British government to assist in rebuilding the economy. Similarly the Bengali Muslims who moved from Sylhet to Assam prior to partition did so in order to take up more advantageous land tenure; however once Assam became a province in the new India they returned to Syhlet as refugees, finding themselves with little or no other opportunities for economic betterment. However Lewis (2002) argues that migrants did not come from the poorest areas but rather prosperous farming areas and places with a tradition of emigration.

Many of those who arrived initially as pioneers were joined by members of their villages and 'biraderi' or kin networks, who often helped motivate prospective migrants to take the risks involved. This process is often described as 'chain migration'. Ballard (2004) argues that the majority of migrants made their journeys to specific localities for settlement as a result of acquiring information of the opportunities within those towns and cities prior to migration. The knowledge of such opportunities was passed back to the villages left behind through channels of kinship, friends and clientship. Ballard writes: 'As a result what may seem at first sight to be mass migratory movements invariably turn out on closer inspection, to be grounded in a multitude of kin- and locality- specific processes of chain migration' (2004: 1). It is therefore not uncommon to find communities who resided in the same villages re-established in neighbourhoods within the UK. Unsurprisingly due to the availability of work in the industrial sectors, early pioneers headed for some of the main industrial conurbations and when joined by other migrants, Muslim communities began to emerge in areas such as Greater London, the South East, West Midlands, West Yorkshire and Lancashire in England and in Scotland, central Clydeside, the ports of South Wales and in Northern Ireland's capital, Belfast.

In the early 1960s, legislation (influenced by growing racial tensions) to halt the inflow of migrants paradoxically led to an enormous rush to 'beat the ban' and migrants saw this as a crucial period in which to take the decision to migrate and bring over their families. Once the legislation was in place the stream of migrants decreased, although this was far from the end of Muslim settlement in Britain. Bangladeshis continued to arrive into the 1970s, but in addition to those from South Asia, who were primarily economic migrants, a different type of migration phenomenon occurred from this period. Those coming from the Middle East to Britain appeared to have a much more diverse profile, originating from various national and class backgrounds. There were Arabs who had taken advantage of their financial gain from the oil crisis of 1973–1974 and invested in property and businesses in Britain seeing it as a safer option than their home countries, which were undergoing uncertain political developments and regime changes. In addition, Muslim professionals, also facing political unrest, took advantage of employment opportunities in their fields in Britain.

The number of refugees began to grow as a result of ethno-religious and communal conflicts, famines and natural disasters. Refugees came from areas such as Somalia and East Africa as well as the Middle East. But from the 1990s there began a much more apparent arrival of asylum seeker communities, which has resulted in a hostile culture towards asylum seekers in the UK (Lewis 2005). Many applications for asylum from Bosnia were due to civil unrest and the partition of the former Yugoslavia. These Muslims differed significantly from previous Muslim communities: firstly, they were not economic migrants and therefore taking up positions within the labour market was not their primary motivation for migrating (it was instead fleeing from persecution); and secondly this group are ethnically European. There have been steady establishments of other Muslim communities who arrived as asylum seekers. These include Kurds, Afghans – for whom asylum applications steadily rose by over a thousand per year from 1996 (675) to 2001 (8920) – and more recently Iraqis (for whom the number of asylum applicants rose from 930 during 1995 to 14,570 for 2002)[1] (Heath, Jeffries and Purcell 2004).

As described above Muslim settlement in Britain occurred periodically in that different communities arrived in higher concentrations according to the pull-push factors facing them at any given time. This has resulted in communities being formed along ethnic lines that have come to be concentrated in different parts of Britain. Clearly chain migration played a key role in the development of 'pockets' of communities and the reproduction of village and kin networks. These have further been strengthened by transnational marriages where spouses are often from the area of original migration (Ballard 2004). Lewis (2002) argues that Muslim communities in Britain were extremely successful in reproducing many of their traditional cultural and social norms, and this is as much the case for Muslims from the Middle East as for South Asians. Religion therefore initially had little impact on their decisions to settle and the way they organized themselves in Britain.

Muslims in private and public

Prior to the 1970s, culture and ethnic or national origin occupied the way in which Muslims participated in the public sphere. The indigenous majority and the institutions of wider society viewed them overwhelmingly in these terms and not primarily as members of a religious minority. Now, Muslims have been firmly placed on the map and their presence most certainly acknowledged, but what processes occurred for these communities to be viewed progressively more so in terms of their religious affiliation rather than their ethnicity? Weller argues that during the 1960s, proponents of the secularization thesis believed that through a combination of technological advances, philosophical rationalism and the development of consumer society, religion would overwhelmingly be removed from the public into the private sphere, becoming akin to a 'leisure activity' (Weller 2004: 5).

However migrant groups had begun to add new fervour to religion, not following the shift described by Weller. Prior to being publicly acknowledged or endorsed, many of these new communities placed far greater importance on religious practice in their day to day lives than the indigenous majority. Results from a large scale survey of ethnic minorities in the United Kingdom, the Fourth National Survey of Ethnic Minorities, conducted in 1994, found that:

---

[1]   These figures for asylum applications exclude dependent children.

While only 5 per cent of Whites aged 16–34 said religion was very important to how they lived their lives, nearly a fifth of Caribbeans, more than a third of Indians and African Asians and two thirds of Pakistanis and Bangladeshis in that age group held that view. (Modood *et al.*1997: 356)

As agendas widened, minority communities began to assert their rights to religious observance in both the public and the private domain. Modood, the principle author of the study writes,

Equality is not having to hide or apologise for one's origins, family or community but expect others to respect them and adapt public attitudes and arrangements so that the heritage they represent is encouraged rather than contemptuously expected to wither away. There seem, then, to be two distinct conceptions of equal citizenship, each based on different views of what is 'public' and 'private'. These two concepts of equality may be stated as follows:

•   The rights to assimilate to the majority/ dominant cultures in the public sphere; and toleration of difference in the private sphere;
•   The right to have one's difference recognised and supported in both the public and the private sphere. (1997: 358)

For some groups the separation of religion from the public and private domains was particularly problematic. Muslims, for example, do not regard religion as compartmentalized and detached from other aspects of life but rather as a central reference point which enters all aspects of their lives – political, social and economic. There were increasing concerns over whether their faith would eventually become so marginalized and acculturated by the dominant ethos of modern western cultures and whether integration, pluralism and economic advancement were too high a price if the Muslim belief system was part of the trade off. Salvatore argues that in Europe the acceptance of Islam within the public sphere faces greater stigma than other religions. He maintains: 'The secularly minded stigmatise "insurgent Islam" as a kind of anti-modern mobilization. Many perceive Islam to be less as the backward culture of the "other" than as a "return to the Middle Ages", an egregious error from the authoritarian lacking clear separation between religion and politics' (Salvatore 2004: 1014). In Yousif's critique of liberal democracy (2000), he argues that in Europe some religious minorities are more equal than others and there are many examples of how Muslims are particularly marginalized by the state. Merry (2004: 127–128) picks up on Yousif's critique and contends:

It is equally true that applications to establish Islamic places of worship and schools have met with considerable resistance, even in countries that openly support the freedom to establish denominational schooling…Yousif is right that Muslim communities must, in many instances, prove that their activities are aimed more at "cultural preservation" and not at explicitly religious objectives, seems an untenable double standard.

The point made about separating or rather disguising the 'religious' element under the 'cultural' or 'ethnic' identity has become increasingly challenging for Muslims who contest the notion that religion in the West, based on the liberal notion of freedom, is constrained to a personal affair, distinct from the more 'rational' aspects of public life. In this view, the more secular structure of British society, compared to Muslim countries has, far from providing affirmation for a religious worldview, tended to portray it as progressively more irrelevant. Modood *et al* write, 'Religion is perhaps the key area where the minority groups manifest a cultural dynamic which is at least partly at odds with native British trends' (1997: 356). Global and local level events such as 9/11 and the London bombings on 7 July 2005 have added volume to the voices of those questioning whether Muslim communities really can adjust to and integrate within European societies. However as Salvatore writes, 'The question is rarely raised as to whether the institutions and ideologies of Europe can adjust to a modern world of which culturally diverse immigrants are an integral part' (2004: 1013). As Muslims in Britain demonstrated greater levels of religiosity than the indigenous majority, secularization clearly does not apply to this community in the same way as it has done for larger society.

Difficulties in measuring 'religiousness' for Muslims

Pre-census attempts at estimating the number of Muslims in the UK often raised the question of who should be counted as a Muslim. Debates about Muslim identity have centred on whether being a Muslim should presume the profession and practice of Islam or if an 'attachment' in a cultural or geographical sense is sufficient. A key issue when considering whether to only count those who are Muslims 'religiously' is to what extent religiosity can be measured due to the lack of an appropriate yardstick to measure religiosity and decide whether an individual is sufficiently practicing as a Muslim or not. At an individual level the five fundamental tenets or 'five pillars'[2] of Islam could be used. Sanders (1997) explored these conceptual difficulties and produced a religious index which inserted people into various positions on a range, from inert origins in a faith to active worship. House (1997) recognizes that even those who are 'not practicing' or Muslims in the latter sense, adopt the status of Muslim as a socio-political identity. She calls these Muslims 'sociological Muslims'. Tietze (2000) however argues that it is seldom the case that a Muslim who feels strong enough to assert a Muslim identity would not practice any tenets of the faith, or at the very least celebrate the festival of Eid and attend the mosque for Eid prayers out of a sense of community or tradition. A Muslim may not pray five times a day but, if approached by a researcher during Ramadan, may be fasting and praying the obligatory prayers and the additional Tarawee and Tahajjud prayers every evening in congregation at the mosque. This would no doubt result in the researcher ticking enough boxes on any chart measuring practical worship to designate the participant as a practising Muslim.

Tietze (2000) contends that this separation or distinguishing between believing and belonging is a result of processes of the rationalization of religious traditions, a

---

2   The 'Five Pillars' of Islam are: the declaration of faith in One God and of Muhammad being the final Prophet of God, praying the five daily compulsory prayers, fasting during the month of Ramadan, performing the pilgrimage to Mecca providing the means to do so are available, and giving charity to the poor.

symptom, he argues, of secularization. Counting attendance at religious institutions or places of worship as an indication of practicing is problematic for Muslims, and particularly for Muslim women. Muslims are not compelled to perform prayers in mosques with the exception of one Friday prayer (Juma) which is not obligatory for Muslim women and children or for men facing practical difficulties in attending the congregational prayer. However, even assuming it were possible to measure religious observance using such means and criteria, it would almost certainly only capture a small proportion of those who would identify themselves as Muslims. Despite it being difficult to 'quantify' religiosity through practical worship, there is evidence that demonstrates that religion plays a much more significant role in the lives of many minority communities when compared with their White counterparts. This is particularly true for those from South Asia. Modood *et al.* write about their findings from the Fourth National Survey of Ethnic Minorities: 'The South Asians' identification and prioritization of religion is far from just a nominal one. Nearly all South Asians said they have a religion, and 90 per cent said that religion was of personal importance to them' (1997: 306). Therefore although religious identity or affiliation is not synonymous with belief, for Muslims it is extremely difficult to separate the two.

Women and religiosity

The position of women is a significant area of discussion surrounding faith communities and integration (or lack thereof) into wider society, challengers of imposed secularization (such as the banning of religious symbols) and outward expressions of religiosity within the public sphere. The position of Muslim women in particular has gained significant attention within public discourse and is a subject of focus when debating whether religion still occupies a central role in the lives of some communities in Britain. Against this backdrop this essay sets out to explore whether it is possible to establish whether Muslim women are more religious than women from other faith communities. Although discussed in the section above it is difficult to measure levels of religiosity for Muslims, there are symbols by which it is possible to visibly demonstrate one's commitment to practicing one's faith. For Muslims an example of such a symbol is the head covering or *hijab*. There is no official data on how many Muslim women in Britain wear the hijab and it is therefore extremely difficult to use hijab as a variable for deciphering levels of religiosity for Muslim women.

Being less acculturated is not synonymous with being less secular; however, as the majority of Muslim women originate from cultures that are more religious than the indigenous British, and demonstrate less acculturation than women of other minority faith groups, one can assume that their beliefs about women's roles are more in keeping with those of the society from which they originate. As perceptions of gender roles are largely governed by religious doctrine within these societies (for example Pakistan and Bangladesh), it will be possible to demonstrate that religious teachings about the role of men and women will influence Muslim women's positions in Britain. This study will examine variables associated with measuring acculturation, such as looking after the home and family on a full-time basis and not engaging in employment outside of the home, and whether these can be used to demonstrate greater levels of religiosity expressed by Muslim women. In doing so this chapter provides a profile for Muslim women living in England and Wales using quantitative data, exploring their positions within the private and public domain (through levels of economic inactivity) and comparing data with that of women from other faith groups.

Creating a profile for Muslim women in Britain

Quantitative data will be used in order to explore whether Muslim women are more likely to remain within a domestic context and less likely to engage in paid employment outside the home. Attempts to contribute to the debate on the social position and participation of Muslim women, or women from any other faith community, for comparative purposes, have been difficult due to a lacuna of quantitative data on religion. There have however been some valuable sources of individual level data providing information on religion, such as Fourth National Survey of Ethnic Minorities (Modood *et al*, 1997). Prior to the availability of data on Muslims, data on Pakistanis and Bangladeshis was generally used due to the majority of these ethnic groups adhering to the Islamic faith. However these two ethnic groups constituted 60 per cent of British Muslims, with the remaining 40 per cent falling into other commonly used ethnic categories such as 'White'. This includes an array of Muslim ethnic and national groups, such as indigenous Muslims who have converted to Islam, Eastern European Muslims (for example Bosnian refugees) and even those from the Middle East. In 2001 after years of campaigning and lobbying by various faith groups, including the Muslim Council of Britain, a question on religion was included in the National Census. This was the first time such a large and comprehensive data collection exercise on religion had been attempted since 1851.

The question on religious affiliation was voluntary as a result of rigorous debate in the House of Commons (Hussain 2005). The question as it appeared on the Census form for England and Wales asked: 'What is your religion?' There were seven options provided on the form and eight categories in the output data. These included a single Christian category (for all Christian denominations), Muslim, Buddhist, Sikh, Hindu, Jewish and 'Any Other Religion' for those stating a religion which did not fall within these categories. There was also an output column in the tables for those who stated that they did not belong to any religion and as the question was voluntary, a column containing data on those who refused to answer the question.

Using the 2001 National Census data (Office for National Statistics 2003) an attempt to create a 'profile' for Muslim women is provided below. In doing so the position of Muslim women is compared with women from other communities with regards to their prevalence in gender specific roles. Analysis of the 1999 Health Survey for England (Erens, Primatesta and Prior 2001) has been conducted in order to supplement the census data. The primary function of the data from this survey is to allow for multivariate analyses and intra Muslim analysis which is not possible using pre-crosstabulated aggregate data.

Marriage and children

The family as an institution is of significant importance for Muslim communities, just as marriage is normative for Muslims (Hassouneh-Phillips 2001). Husain and O'Brien (2000) argue that due to the many influences and factors at play for Muslims living in a non-Muslim setting it is difficult to speak of a single Muslim family type. Here it is argued that socio-cultural norms regarding family structures in countries of origin are influenced not only by family models and laws in the country of residence but also by socioeconomic restraints and other external factors such as housing size. Islamic tradition does however provide definitions of what a family is and in the simplest sense a family consists of members related by a direct bloodline or marital relationship. This does not exclude the idea of the contemporary nuclear family unit and is open to the possibility of various family types, including polygamous or extended families (Husain and O'Brien 2000; Ballard 2004). Yet in reality spousal relationships within Muslim communities are based on traditional family roles common to most capitalist societies, that of the male breadwinner and the female nurturer and child-rearer (Sonuga-Barke and Mistry 2000; Husain and O'Brien 2000; Hassouneh-Phillips 2001). Although the 'old fashioned' or traditional family type is found amongst other South Asian communities, in their study of South Asian Muslim and Hindu mothers, Sonuga-Barke and Mistry (2000) find that Muslim women are living in more traditional families with more traditional and restricted roles within the family than Hindu women.

The 2001 Census data (Office for National Statistics 2003) and the 1999 Health Survey for England (Erens, Primatesta and Prior 2001) were examined to explore whether Muslim women have more gender specific roles (as mothers and wives) than women from other faith groups. Census table S151 on family composition shows that almost half of all Muslim households are described as married couple households.[3] This compares with 54 per cent of Hindus and 52 per cent of Sikhs. The national figure for this type of household is 37 per cent, as demonstrated in Figure 9.1. Muslims are therefore the third most likely to report this household type, which is essentially a 'nuclear' family type household.

When broken down by age however, analysis of the 1999 Health Survey for England shows that for those reporting to be either currently married or ever married, of people aged 16–24 Muslims are more likely to be married than Sikh and Hindus. Of this age cohort 34 per cent of Muslims were currently or had been married compared with 21.5 per cent of Sikhs, seven per cent of Hindus and three per cent of Christians. Of those aged 25–34, 93 per cent of Muslims compared with 84 per cent of Sikhs, 79 per cent of Hindus and 44 per cent of Christians reported this marital status. Analysis of the next age cohort, 35–44, shows that the proportions of people who had been married for Hindus, Sikhs and Muslims are very similar, with all three groups reporting close to 98 per cent. This compares with 72 per cent of Christians in

---

[3]   A married couple family consists of a husband and wife with or without their child(ren). In most tables, the term 'married couple household' is used to describe a household that comprises a married couple family and no other person. www.statistics.gov.uk/census2001/pdfs/glossary.pdf

this age category. The proportions of married people in all other age cohorts remain smaller than these three groups. It is clear from the analysis that Muslims do have higher rates of marriage amongst the younger age cohorts compared to all other faith groups.

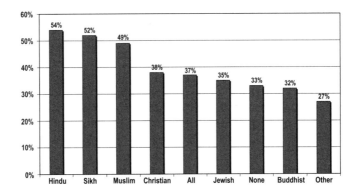

Figure 9.1   Percentage of married couple households by religion for England and Wales. Taken from the 2001 National Census

The findings from the data are clearly in keeping with some previous studies (Heath and Dale 1994). The three predominantly South Asian groups appeared to be similar in terms of marriage and cohabitation; however Muslims showed a clear trend towards entering into formal marriages at younger ages, as revealed in the Fourth National Survey of Ethnic Minorities. The surveys under study have limited data on divorce and it is not possible to discuss divorce and legal separation to any meaningful extent.

Fertility

The data shows that Muslims have the highest proportion of children, and the Census illustrates that 34 per cent of Muslims are aged 0–15. Although Muslims make up three per cent of the total population of England and Wales, Muslim dependent children make up five per cent of all dependent children in England and Wales. In other words, one child in every 20 in England and Wales is a Muslim.

Figure 9.2 shows data from commissioned Census table M293. Sixty-three per cent of Muslims households contain dependent children; this is the highest percentage of households with dependent children for all groups and double the proportion containing dependent children nationally. In addition table 151 on household composition demonstrates that proportionately Muslims have the highest percentages for two or more children in every household type apart from cohabiting couple households (although Muslims still have a higher percentage with two or more children in such households compared with Hindus, Sikhs and Jews).

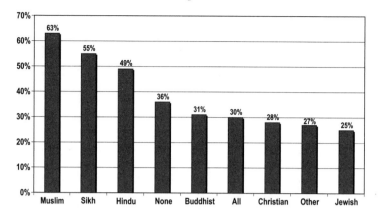

Figure 9.2   Percentage of households containing dependent children by religion for England and Wales. Taken from the 2001 National Census

The 1999 Health Survey demonstrates that Muslims were also most likely to have three or more children per households. In addition Muslim women were proportionately more likely to be pregnant at the time of the survey than women from any other group, although closely followed by Sikh women (5.5 per cent and five per cent respectively). The percentage of Christian women who reported being pregnant at the time of the survey was just over three per cent.

Census table M287 also demonstrates that Muslims also have the highest proportion of households with three or more infants (aged 0–4 years old). Twenty-three per cent of Muslims had three or more children in this age range compared with seven per cent of all people, five per cent of Hindus and nine per cent of Sikhs. Muslims therefore do have the highest proportion of households with the largest numbers of children. Of course, the fact that Muslims are younger in comparison to other groups means that they are more likely to be of child-bearing age, and as a consequence more likely to have children. Therefore part of the higher fertility rates is age related.

Muslims, gender roles and acculturation

A running theme when discussing Muslims has been their roles within their communities and wider society. It has been argued that Muslim women are likely to take on the role of wife and mother (both accepting formal marriages as normative and having higher and longer sustained periods of reproduction) and that this is influenced by acculturation (Sonuga-Barke and Mistry 2000) and educational attainment (Heath and Dale 1994). There are several indicators for acculturation available from the data under study. The 2001 National Census (S153) provides data on economic activity, broken down by sex, and provides data on reasons for economic inactivity.

Although both Muslim men and women have the highest rates for economic inactivity, Muslim women are nearly twice as likely to be so as both Muslim men and all women (70 per cent, 36 per cent and 41 per cent aged 16–75, respectively). As already stated Muslims have slightly lower married couple households, higher cohabiting couple households and higher proportions of one parent households as Sikhs and Hindus. If this were an indication that Muslims are slightly less inclined towards 'traditional' family types, economic inactivity may be an indication of gender specific roles within these communities. 41 per cent of Sikh and Hindu women are economically inactive compared with 26 per cent of Hindu men and 27 per cent of Sikh men. Hindus, Sikhs and all other women are therefore 1.6 times more likely to be economically inactive than their male counterparts. This compares with Muslim women who are twice as likely to be economically inactive as Muslim men. Therefore in absolute terms and as regards to male female ratios, Muslim women are more likely than any other group to be economically inactive.

The 1999 Health Survey asked whether or not women had ever been in paid employment or been self-employed. Seventy-five per cent of Muslim women in this sample answered 'no' compared with 45 per cent of Hindu and 35.5 per cent of Sikh women. 12.5 per cent of Christian women.

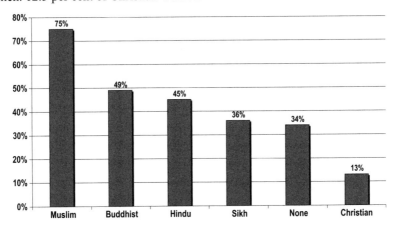

Figure 9.3   Percentage of women who reported never having been in paid employment. Taken from the 1999 Health Survey for England

English language proficiency can be used as an indication of level of participation within the public sphere, being a prerequisite to most employment. Muslim women were least likely to report English as a spoken language, when compared with women from other faith groups. Seventy-three per cent of Muslim women could speak English compared with 76 per cent of Buddhist, 81 per cent of Sikh and 90 per cent of Hindu women.

A more specific indicator of gender roles however is that of caring or looking after the home. The Census data shows that 18 per cent of Muslims are looking after home or family compared with seven per cent nationally (aged 16–74). Muslims have the highest proportion of people in this category. When broken down by sex, both Muslim men and women (three per cent and 34 per cent) are three times more likely than all men and all women to be caring for the home and family (one per cent and 12 per cent). When broken down by sex and age however, Muslim women aged 16–24 are five times more likely to be looking after the family or home than women of this age group nationally and have the highest percentage of women in this category across all faith groups. For women aged 25–74 Muslim women also have the highest proportion looking after family and home; the figure is 29 per cent – nearly three times greater than the national figure for women of this age range.

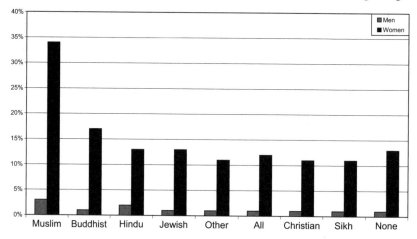

Figure 9.4   Percentage of men and women who are looking after the home or family on a full time basis by religion in England and Wales. Taken from 2001 National Census

Here again Muslim women have the highest proportion across all groups looking after the family or home and a third of all Muslim women aged 16–74 are in this category. This indicates a significantly greater preference or trend for women from this community.

The data shows a greater trend among Muslims towards what would be commonly referred to as traditional gender roles, in so far as a smaller proportion of Muslim women are economically active and therefore leaving the 'bread winning' largely to men. Of course the high proportion of female economic inactivity could be seen to reflect the high proportion of economic inactivity for Muslims as a whole, but, as stated, Muslim women are twice as likely to be economically inactive as women from all other faith groups who are already 1.6 times more likely to be so than their male counterparts. Higher proportions of both Muslim men and women reported looking after the home and family. However when broken down by age Muslim women when compared with other women showed greater female/male ratios looking after the family and home compared to the other groups. In addition a question on housework asked in the 1999 Health Survey demonstrated that Muslim men were least likely to have reported doing any housework in the month prior to the survey. Muslims therefore do appear to show greater differentiated roles: women tend to occupy the role of nurturer/home keeper rather than being breadwinners or contributors to breadwinning.

Women, the public sphere and secularization

The data clearly demonstrates that Muslim women have more defined gender roles in terms of being more likely to remain within the home and less likely than women from all other faith groups to be economically active. When looking at differing levels of religiosity there have been links made between levels of economic inactivity for women and levels of faith. For some this is associated with less exposure to secularly influenced public institutions. In attempting to explore the differential impact secularization has had on the religious beliefs and practice of men and women in the West, Woodhead (2005) examined data on church attendance linking lower proportions of attendance by men with the development of modern industrialized society. According to theories on secularization, as propagated by Weber (1996), Marx (2003) and Berger, Berger and Kellner (1974), religion has occupied a vulnerable place in society since the onset of modern industrialization. This is largely as a result of the incompatibility, in this view, of mystery and meaning (as propagated by religion) and rational scientific modes of thought. In the business of economic production religion comes to be seen as an obstacle to progress. Woodhead (2005: 25) explains:

> The result is a world which is governed and shaped not by sacred meaning but by the harsh and impersonal standards of a 'rationalised' and 'bureaucratised' order whose only aim is greater productive efficiency. Human beings become cogs within machines that neither appreciate nor accommodate their feelings of hope, desires and dignity. Their soft selves are crushed and constrained to fit into thee hard and impersonal structures of the factory, the office and the organisation.

It is argued that men were more likely to become disenchanted with religion due to their greater exposure to 'primary institutions' such as the workplace, legal and associated institutions, the political establishment and higher education, as it was men who participated in the public world of paid work. Women who were located primarily within the domestic context, however, had far less exposure to this mode of thought and were less driven by the need for efficiency and production. This allowed spiritual meaning to be attached to their daily practices and gave them more opportunity than men to engage within religious ritual and practice. In keeping with this theory, the increased participation of women within the public sphere through paid employment outside the home would result in growing disillusionment with religion and a decline in rates of church attendance for women as well as men.

Muslims, however, far from becoming more secular as a result of greater time spent on British soil and exposure to some of the harshest labour conditions, have not chosen to identify themselves less in terms of religious affiliation. On the contrary second and subsequent generations of Muslims who have been through the education system and had exposure to institutions in the same way that young people from the indigenous population have, are asserting a more vocal religious identity.[4] As

---

[4]   An opinion poll of British Muslims conducted in 2006 by GfK-NOP for Channel Four found that Muslims from the younger generations were more likely to express a desire for greater religious presence within the public sphere.

suggested by Woodhead (2005) the lack of exposure to the public sphere for women may contribute to greater levels of religiosity found among Muslim women and if extended further, through the emphasis placed on the family and community, to the greater levels of religiosity expressed by Muslims as a faith community.

Although the data does indeed provide a clear profile in terms of activity, does this necessarily confirm that women are more religious as a result of remaining at home? Woodhead was able to use data on Church attendance to make the link, but for Muslims measuring belief or practice rather than simply affiliation, which is what the data used here does, is particularly problematic. Higher levels of economic inactivity among women are associated with religiosity by other theorists also. Van de Kaa (1987) argues that communities who adhere to religious teaching more than others demonstrate greater economic inactivity among women. If Muslim women are less likely to work than women from other backgrounds it could be argued that this impacts on their social trajectory, hindering full participation of the entire community within British society and the adoption of British cultural norms – including secularization.

Bowen (2004) argues that the greater levels of economic inactivity present among Muslim women are likely a result of Islamic doctrine. The principle of western law has been based on the rights and obligations of each individual. Islamic law however, in contrast, takes the family unit as the primary unit of responsibility rather than the individual. Although Bowen primarily refers to women living within Muslim countries, it is assumed that this is also the case for Muslim women living as minorities in non-Muslim countries. Therefore if as suggested by Woodhead (2005) the greater prevalence of women within the domestic context contributes to their levels of religious belief and practice, the lack of exposure to the public sphere for Muslim women is likely to result in them remaining more religious. This coupled with the emphasis placed by Islam on the unit rather than the individual, as expressed by Bowen, could suggest that Muslim women's religiosity provides a strong enough alternative and forum against the disenchantment resulting through exposure to the public sphere for members of their families and communities also.

Yet there is growing evidence to suggest that greater exposure and participation of Muslim women within the public sphere does not influence levels of religiosity nor encourage greater secularization. It is generally accepted that among most Muslim communities women are required to dress modestly. Some Muslim societies adopt a strict interpretation, believing that women should not expose any parts of their bodies except the oval of their face and their hands. Despite this, depending on cultural practice, dress and tradition, women cover in varying degrees. For example, women from South Asia largely wear loosely draped scarves, without a preference for a particular colour. Within Iran and Saudi Arabia however, most urban women wear a long covering which starts from the top of the head and covers the entire body. The most common colour for such a covering is black.

The style of hijab worn by the modern younger Muslim woman within western societies has less to do with following the traditions of their communities and more to do with asserting an authentic Muslim identity. Salvatore explains: 'This new veiling has been interpreted as "accommodating protest", a notion that stresses its contradictory yet also active character' (2004: 1025). What is particularly noteworthy about this style of hijab is that it is more likely to be worn by younger Muslim women, who are educated and who have regular experience within the public sphere. Many sociologists (Werbner 1998; Mandaville 2003; Ballard 2004) have argued that the hijab has been part of an intergenerational struggle for younger women to assert a more authentic, educated version of Islam than that of their parents' generation. This suggests that for Muslim women there is no evidence to support the contention that greater participation in the public sphere is likely to result in a process of secularization for them or the wider Muslim community. It is likely that, rather than becoming more secular, as more Muslim women participate within the public sphere, including taking up paid employment outside the home, religion will still remain a central aspect of their personal and where possible public persona, as has been the case with their male counterparts.

Key to understanding why Muslim men have not lost their religious identities as a result of exposure to public organizations and institutions within Britain (although as suggested this has yet to be seen for Muslim women to the same extent), is that the Islamic world had very different historical reactions to modernity compared with Christianity. Whereas in the West religion was relegated into the private, in the Islamic world religion was largely reformed and rethought as a consequence and reaction to experiences of colonialisms, decolonialism, building of nation states and for minorities, carving out a space within their host society. Salvatore (2004: 1016) describes this process:

> A whole spectrum of differential (and often competing) personalities, groups and movements, inspired by reform blueprints (Arabic *islah*), contributed to the redefinition and collective pursuits of moral and social goods that went well beyond the secularly-minded delimitation of religious practice centred beliefs and basically located in the private sphere.

The fact that Muslims as a community are under focus more than ever before suggests it is likely that this carving out will continue to influence both Muslim women and men in asserting their Muslimness. Werbner (1998: 24) states: 'more than anything, identities constitute subjective narratives of virtue and moral commitment'. As religious identity is under threat through negative portrayals of Muslims as terrorists and discussions about Muslims being unable to integrate within western society, the 'clash of the civilisations[5]' thesis is more likely to be relevant to the shaping of Muslim identity and belief than the secularization thesis.

Conclusion

At the beginning of this chapter it was argued that Muslims in Britain demonstrate higher levels of religiosity than the indigenous population. Despite periods of settlement for the majority of Muslims in Britain dating back to the 1950s, the identification with Islam still remains and secularization appears to not have impacted

---

[5] Huntington's theory of the 'Clash of Civilisations' describes how the western and Islamic civilisations are incompatible.

this faith community in the same way that it has wider society. When attempting to explore whether it is possible to utilize large scale data on Muslim women to measure their religiosity, variables measuring acculturation were analyzed. The findings show that Muslim women of all generations were more likely to demonstrate profiles which conform to traditional gender roles associated with Islam.

A possible explanation for secularization having less impact on Muslims in Britain was the lack of exposure women have with the public sphere, which has been argued by those such as Woodhead (2005) to result in a greater ability for women to practice their faiths and not become influenced by secular primary institutions. As stated during this chapter a useful measure of religiosity is the donning of religious symbols such as the hijab. Although there is no data available on numbers of women who wear the hijab within the realm of official statistics, researchers such as Wernber (1998), Mandaville (2003) and Ballard (2004) have commented on the increasing number of young Muslim women adopting the hijab despite having social interaction with wider society and primary institutions. There may of course be young Muslim women who as a result of exposure to primary institutions choose to become less religious. Unless levels of religiosity were measured this would be difficult to ascertain through data that is available at present. Analysis using religious identity and level of qualification or occupational status would not necessarily demonstrate whether there was a correlation between being exposed to secular institutions and being less religious, as many Muslim women may still identify themselves as Muslims in the more sociological sense described earlier. Therefore qualitative research would be far more meaningful in attempting to ascertain whether Muslim women are influenced by daily exposure to secular institutions than those who largely remain within the domestic realm.

Although it is interesting to draw parallels between the experiences of women from other communities, in doing so there emerge clear reminders that Muslim women also face a very different set of issues with regards to their faith than the women Woodhead (2005) described. External forces of Muslim prejudice, a legacy of colonialism together with the current climate of tensions due to actual and attempted terrorist acts mean that the religiosity of both Muslim women and men is likely to come across difficulties through exposure to secular institutions within the public sphere, but not in the way described by the secularization thesis discussed in this chapter. In this view it is more useful to explore types of religiosity and whether differing emphasis is placed on certain forms of worship for both the genders as a result of their greater location within either the public or private sphere. In engaging within the public realm, is worship manifested in the form of political engagement for men and the visualizing of Islamic symbols for women? Is worship for women who are primarily or exclusively based within a domestic context linked with the more traditional forms of 'Sufi' spiritual devotion found to be more prevalent among women in many Muslim societies (Mernissi 1987)? Gendered forms of worship (as a result not only of exposure and day-to-day location in the home or in a secular workplace but also as a way of making sense of the current tenuous position Muslim communities find themselves in) would be particularly relevant when looking at how the position Muslim women are in impacts on their lives and those of their communities. Over and above this however, Muslims and wider society need to ask why Muslim women are located within the private domestic domain to a greater degree than other minority women, and whether this is due to preference or constraints within the public sphere that are particularly unaccommodating to women of faith.

References

Ansari, H., *The Infidel within: Muslims in Britain since 1800* (London: Hurst and Co., 2004).

Ballard, R., *Riste and Ristedar: The Significance of Marriage in the Dynamics of Transnational Kinship Networks* (University of Manchester: CASAS, 2004). http://www.art.man.ac.uk/CASAS/pdfpapers/ristedari.pdf.

Berger, Peter, Berger, Brigitte and Kellner, Hansfried, *The Homeless Mind: Modernization and Consciousness* (Harmondsworth: Penguin, 1974).

Bowen, J., *Islam, Law, and Equality in Indonesia: An Anthropology of Public Reasoning* (Missouri: Washington University, 2004).

Erens, Bob, Primatesta, Paola and Prior, Gillian (eds), *Health Survey for England: The Health of Minority Ethnic Groups '99* (London: The Stationery Office, 2001).

Heath, S. and Dale, A., 'Household and Family Formation in Great Britain: The Ethnic Dimension', *Population Trends*, 77 (1994): 5–13 (London: Office for National Statistics).

Heath, T., Jeffries, R., and Purcell, J., *Asylum statistics: United Kingdom 2003* (London: Home Office, 2004).

Hassouneh-Phillips, D., 'Marriage is Half of Faith and the rest is fear Allah: Marriage and Spousal Abuse among American Muslims', *Violence against Women*, 7(8) (2001): 926–946.

House, J., 'Muslim Communities in France', in G. Nonneman (ed.), *Muslim Communities in the New Europe* (Reading: Ithaca Press, 1997).

Huntington, S., 'Clash of Civilisations: The Next Pattern of Conflict', *Foreign Affairs*, 72(3) (1993): 22–28.

Husain, F. and O'Brien, M., 'Muslim Communities in Europe: Reconstruction and Transformation', *Current Sociology*, 48(4) (2000): 1–13.

Hussain, S., *A Statistical Mapping of Muslims in Britain*, unpublished Ph.D. thesis (Bristol: University of Bristol, 2005).

Lewis, B., *What Went Wrong?* (Oxford: Oxford University Press, 2002).

Lewis, M., 'Hostility to Asylum Seekers has risen most among the Middle Class', *The Guardian*, 29 June 2005. http://society.guardian/co.uk/asylumseekers/comment/0,8005,1517104,00.html.

Mandaville, P., 'Towards a Critical Islam: European Muslims and the Changing Boundaries of Transnational Religious Discourse', in S. Allievi and J. Neilsen (eds), *Muslim Networks and Transnational communities in and across Europe* (Leiden: Brill, 2003).

Marx, Karl and Engels, Friedrich, *The Communist Manifesto*. Reprinted in David McLellan (ed.) *Karl Marx: Selected Writings* (Oxford: Oxford University Press, 2003).

Mernissi, F., *Beyond the Veil: Male-female Dynamics in Muslim Society* (Indianapolis: Indiana University Press, 1987).

Merry, M., 'Islam versus (Liberal) Pluralism? A response to Ahmad Yousif', *Journal of Muslim Minority Affairs*, 24(1) (2004): 123–139.

Modood, T., Berthoud, R., Lakey, J., Nazroo, J., Smith, P., Virdee, S. and Beishon, S., *Ethnic Minorities in Britain: Disadvantage and Diversity* (London: Policy Studies Institute, 1997).

Office for National Statistics, *Census 2001: National Report for England and Wales* (London: The Stationery Office, 2003).

Salvatore, A., 'Making Public Space: Opportunities and Limits of Collective Action among Muslims in Europe', *Journal of Ethnic and Migration Studies*, 30(5) (2004): 1013–1031.

Sanders, Åke, 'To What Extent is the Swedish Muslim Religious?', in Steven Vertovec and Ceri Peach (eds), *Islam in Europe: The Politics of Religion and Community* (Warwick: Centre for Research in Ethnic Relations, University of Warwick, 1997).

Shaw, A., *A Pakistani Community in Britain* (Oxford: Blackwell, 1988).

Sherif, J., 'Historical Roots of Islam in Britain', in Muslim Council of Britain, *The Quest for Sanity* (London: Muslim Council of Britain, 2002).

Sonuga-Barke, E. J. S. and Mistry, M., 'The Effect of Extended Family Living on the Mental Health of Three Generations within Two Asian Communities', *British Journal of Clinical Psychology*, 39 (2000): 129–141.

Tietze, N., 'Managing Borders: Muslim Religiosity among Young Men in France and Germany, in A. Salvatore (ed.), *Muslim Traditions and Modern Techniques of Power: Yearbook of the Sociology of Islam 3* (London & Hamburg: LIT Verlag, 2001).

Weber, Max, *The Protestant Ethic and the Spirit of Capitalism*. First published 1930 HarperCollins Academic, trans. Talcott Parsons (London: Routledge, 1996).

Weller, Paul, 'Identity, Politics, and the Future(s) of Religion in the UK: The Case of the Religion Questions in the 2001 Decennial Census', *Journal of Contemporary Religion*, 19(1) (2004): 3–21.

Werbner, P., 'Diasporic Political Imaginaries: A Sphere of Freedom or Sphere of Illusions?', *Communal/Plural: Journal of Transnational and Cross-cultural Studies*, 6(1) (1998): 11–31.

Woodhead, Linda, 'Gendering Secularisation Theory,' *Køn og Forskning* (Women, Gender and Research), 1–2 (2005): 24–35.

Van de Kaa, P., 'Europe's Second Demographic Transition', *Population Bulletin*, 42(1) (Washington DC: Population Reference Bureau, 1987).

Vertovec, S., 'Religion in Migration, Diasporas and Transnationalism', *Research on Immigration and Integration in the Metropolis*, University of British Columbia Working Paper 02–07, (2002).

Yousif, Ahmad, 'Islam, Minorities and Religious Freedom: A Challenge to Modern Theory of Pluralism', *Journal of Muslim Minority Affairs*, 20(1) (2000): 29.

Chapter 10

'Real' Islam in Kazan: Reconfiguring the Modern, Knowledge and Gender

Sarah Bracke

Articulating religion

Secularization theories, as an academic effort to elaborate how religion and modernity relate, are a significant site in the (discursive) production of secular modernity.[1] The secularization paradigm consolidated by such theories holds a mythical quality, which shows in the ways the paradigm's claims resist operationalization and empirical research defies its assumptions. Critical engagements with the paradigm engendered theoretically more sophisticated accounts of secularization: we are told that secularization should not be taken to mean religious decline, but rather refers to systemic changes such as the process of functional differentiation or the privatization of religion. More recently, scholarly attention to the secular has turned to exploring its epistemological assumptions. This critical move is not only concerned with investigating discourses or ideologies (of secularism) but also modern behaviours, knowledges and sensibilities as well as secular forms of governance (see notably the work of Talal Asad 2003).

Inspired by a critique of established modes of thinking and framing religion and the secular, this essay looks into narratives of religious revival from the feminist standpoint impulse of thinking from women's lives. Why and how is it that secularization theories do so poorly in accounting for the lives and subjectivities of pious women? If questions concerning the relationship between religion and modernity were thought from the perspectives of women's lives, what would that reveal about hegemonic notions of religion and modernity?

My engagement with these kinds of questions is grounded in conversations and interviews with young Muslim women gathered during a period of intensive fieldwork in the city of Kazan (Tatarstan, Russian Federation) in the winter, spring and summer of 1998.[2] The case-study contributes to thinking about European predicaments from minoritarian contexts. Situated in the Russian Federation on the European side

---

[1]   I am grateful for careful and generous readings by Nadia Fadil and María Puig de la Bellacasa.

[2]   Kazan is the capital of Tatarstan, an autonomous republic within the Russian Federation. Tatarstan is a multi-ethnic republic: the two main ethnic groups are Tatars and Russians (respectively 48.5 per cent and 43.3 per cent of the population), traditionally connected to respectively Sunni Islam and Russian Orthodox Christianity.

of the Ural Mountains, Tatarstan is Russia's prominent East or Orient (Neumann 1999); Tatarstan has occupied, and continues to do so, a crucial role in Russian history and geo-politics, and in Russian negotiations of its European belonging. In the differentiation between what is Tatar and what is Russian, boundaries between Europe and Asia, West and East, Christianity and Islam are played out. Moreover, Tatarstan represents one of those locations in Europe where Islam has a history of settlement (from the tenth century onwards) which precedes the Christianization of the region (in the sixteenth century) by many centuries. Last but not least, the post-communist context of Tatarstan provides us with a history of religion under secular modernity that differs substantially from West-European histories. This chapter's discussion of economies of subjectivity in relation to religion, knowledge and gender is structured as follows: the first part engages with three influential accounts of women and Islam/Islamic revival in Tatarstan, which are subsequently juxtaposed with accounts from young Muslim women.

Through modern eyes: women, religion, knowledge

> *A common-sense tale of modernity.* As I sought a better understanding of the constitution of the religious field in Tatar society, I engaged in many conversations about religion. In such conversations, I would most often introduce my research interest in vague and general terms as an investigation about 'women and religion'. With few exceptions, interlocutors would insist that the city of Kazan was the wrong place for such an investigation. To gain some insight in the question of woman and religion, and of religion in general for that matter, I was told, *you will have to go to the babushki in the villages.*[3]

This wide-spread common-sense account about the location of religion in Tatar society resonates with a familiar story of secularization: a story that holds that religion withered away from the heart of modern society and its remnants are to be sought in the margins of contemporary life. In the case of Tatarstan, modernization and urbanization took place in the context of the Soviet regime under which religious institutions and expressions were strictly regulated and generally suppressed.[4] The glasnost and perestroika of the Gorbachev era and the subsequent dismantlement of the Soviet regime brought along a proliferation of religious activities, including

---

[3]   I have adopted a methodological device of putting narratives produced in the process of ethnography in oblique print and in continuous text. This device is borrowed from Susan Harding (2000), who deploys it to explore belief as a language of faith which expresses a way of inhabiting and making sense of the world.

[4]   Religion was regulated through the Law on Religious Associations (1929), which allowed believers to worship in a building registered for the purpose, while outlawing any expression of religious faith elsewhere. This legislative framework remained largely unchanged untill the 1990s, and needs to be considered in its relation to the policy on religion: the registration of places of works hip was for instance usually denied. While the policy first seemed to be aimed at exterminating religion, during the war time it changed to keeping religious institutions above ground, but under close supervision. This mode of relations between state and religion continued throughout the postwar period only to be interrupted by Krushchev's anti-religious campaign and the increased repression in Brezhnev's declining years.

religious charitable and welfare work, evangelism, organization of religious education, printing and distributing religious literature, and the (re)opening of churches and mosques. In post-communist times religious practices and expressions gained visibility in the city of Kazan. Surely my interlocutors could not have failed to notice this; in fact, on other occasions some of them lamented the new 'fashion of religion'. But in a peculiar way those observations did not interfere with the hegemonic knowledge about secularization which locates religion in the margins of (how) modern society (should look).

This common-sense account did not prove to be very reliable as an indication of where religious revivals and dynamics are located in contemporary Tatar society. But it did turn out to be a heuristic device for grasping how a symbolic economy of centre and margin operates in Tatarstan. What does the suggestion to look away from the city and turn towards babushka in the countryside point to? Babushka is an archetypical Russian representation and trope by excellence; Nancy Ries (1997) qualifies her as a 'mythical formula' embodying stoic endurance and survival. She is the crucial protagonist of many traditional fairy tales, and she continues to appear in many contemporary narrations of life. Her association to all things religious hint at both survival and marginality: religion survives, hidden away from public and urban sight, in the hands and hearts of old peasant women, and thus it has withered away from the heart from modern life.

An investigation into the gendering of narratives of secularization requires us to look at what gets articulated in this figure. Articulation refers here to an approach (notably elaborated by Stuart Hall) that invites us to inquire *how* and under which circumstances certain linkages or connections are made, how certain ideological elements achieve unity in certain conditions – a discursive unity that reflects the articulation of several elements, that can be re-articulated in several non-determined ways (Hall 1996).[5] The figure of babushka connects rurality, old age and gender to religion. Moreover, as my interest in 'women and religion' would rather consistently be understood as one in 'women and Islam', (Tatar) ethnicity and Islam were crucially part of the articulation.[6]

What holds this articulation together is a notion of tradition, and more specifically tradition as the binary opposite of modernity; that is, not merely antithetical or 'pre-existing' to modernity, but simultaneously constructed and produced by it. Within such an understanding of tradition, religion gets positioned as something modernity is *not*. Religion has indeed been one of the principles by which modernity tried to recognize itself and to specify its own difference (Jameson 1991: 387). In other words, it became part and parcel of a constitutive 'outside' or 'other' of secular

---

[5] Articulation, following Stuart Hall, refers to 'the form of the connection that can make a unity of two different elements, under certain conditions. It is a linkage which is not necessary, determined, absolute and essential for all time. You have to ask, under what circumstances *can* a connection be forged or made? So the so-called 'unity' of a discourse is really the articulation of different, distinct elements which can be re-articulated in different ways because they have no necessary "belongingness".' (Hall 1996: 14)

[6] My investigation was equally focused on women involved Russian Orthodox revivals, but that part of the research turned out to be more difficult as women were less willing to participate. (Bracke 2004).

modernity – the other without which secular modernity could not be nor recognize itself. It is crucial to note how religious traditions are positioned differently in this respect. Christianity served at once as a 'religious other' to the emergence of modern society as well as provided the cultural repertoire for the hegemonic formation of the secular. Islam got framed not merely as a religious but also as an Oriental other, and the density of this articulation ascribed Islam with a radical otherness to modernity (Bracke and Fadil 2006).

These narratives of modernity not only presume and sustain binaries such as traditional/modern, domestic/public, past/future, and so on, but they also gender them (Hodgson 2001). The prominence of babushka, the old Tatar/Muslim peasant woman, in the contemporary tale of religion in Tatarstan, speaks of the *fleshing out*, of the particular embodiment or incarnation of that which is not modern.

The emergence and constitution of the discipline of Sociology is deeply informed by such kind of articulation, which can be traced in foundational sociological texts and paradigms that put religion central in their accounts of the genesis of modern society. In Ferdinand Tönnies' *Gemeinschaft und Gesellschaft* (first published in 1887), for example, the transformations of western society in the nineteenth century are conceptualized in terms of the transition from Gemeinschaft (community) to Gesellschaft (society, also association). Gemeinschaft is depicted as a 'natural' condition of organic unity of human wills in which differentiation occurs following 'natural' patterns (notably sexual difference). The development of Gesellschaft is staged as a truly tragic conflict that brutally disrupts the 'natural and ideal equilibrium' of Gemeinschaft, and profoundly marks the consciousness of the modern subject. Albeit tragic, there is no doubt that rational will, responsible for breaking up Gemeinschaft, has developed because of its superiority. Tönnies' account of modernization in fact constructs and draws upon a 'feminized opposite' of modern society: Gemeinschaft (characterized by 'natural will') is associated with women and Gesellschaft (characterized by 'rational will') with men. Rational will generates a different mode of communication and interaction: it gives birth to 'public opinion' which is rationally and scientifically grounded and comes out of discussion and reflection, and stands in contrast to traditionally handed-down belief which characterizes communication within Gemeinschaft. Belief, Tönnies argues, is characteristic of the common folk while disbelief is characteristic of the scientific and educated classes: women are believing, men disbelieving (Tönnies 1955: 186).

While the centrality of religion in accounts of modern society decreased, and got confined to the subdiscipline of Sociology of Religion, this kind of articulation continued to be rehearsed. In *The Sacred Canopy*, which theorizes secularization as a process of functional differentiation in which a religious worldview ceases to be the overarching framework but instead becomes only one of the institutions (or functions) within society, Peter Berger (1969) emphasizes that secularization is not uniformly distributed within modern societies. There is a pattern of 'internal differentiation' of secularization; in other words, the process of secularization affects various groups in society in different ways. Among the axes of differentiations Berger lists sexual difference, age, urban vs. rural, modern industrial occupations vs. traditional occupations, and different religious traditions – the way these are marked as either 'more secular' or 'more religious' is familiar by now. While lacking in empirical rigour, this account became a landmark within the secularization paradigm. Berger finds that church-related religiosity is strongest on what he calls 'the margins' of modern industrial society, and thus this vision of secularization consolidates notions of what and who is central and marginal to modern society.

A social scientific view on Islamic revival. In a study about Islamic revival in Tatar society Rozalinda Musina (1997) reveals that women are prominently present in the mosques, medresses (Quranic schools) and revival movements. During a long conversation[7], Raifa Urazmanova and Rozalinda Musina, researchers at the Academy of Sciences of Tatarstan, asserted that women were the dominant force of Islamic revival: women attended more religious classes than men, and the two social scientists also had the impression that male students graduating from the medresses were less knowledgeable about Islam than female students. Speculating about the underlying reasons for this strong female participation and domination, they believed there might be a female inclination to 'fanaticism', which they related to (socially constructed) factors such as a lower level of intellectual development, a tendency to teach and instruct others (related to motherhood) and a higher degree of emotionality (in contrast male restraint).

This social scientific account based in empirical research confirms the presence of Islamic revival in the city Kazan, and in particular the emergence of new movements around mosques and medresses. It thus addresses Islamic revival in a way the common-sense account failed to do. It also offers a number of sociological observations about the revival: the scholarly and scriptural character of Islamic revival, and the participation of women, who are positioned as a dominant and more 'knowledgeable' force of the revival. This observation does not stand in isolation; women's presence within contemporary Islamic revival and their relation to knowledge is repeatedly noted (see for example Göle 2003 for Turkey; Jonker 2003 for Germany; Jouili and Amir-Moazami 2006 for Germany and France). The twist, however, lies in how these observations are related to each other: the emphasis on a knowledge-oriented religiosity does not do away with a modernist belief-knowledge binary. The social scientific account dismisses this Islamic revival as fanatical, but not through an argument with respect to knowledge. Rather, the emphasis on its feminization that establishes the point about fanaticism. The knowledge sought and fostered in the Islamic movement is ultimately emotional and fanatic, it is suggested, in a line of reasoning that relies on the gendered character of the belief-knowledge binary to make the point: this is knowledge connected to women who, through their socialization, have less developed intellectual capacities and are thus more prone to religion.[8] The prominence of women in Musina and Urazmanova's account of Islamic revival thus seems to have a double function. It resuscitates an understanding

---

[7]   Our meeting, together with my colleagues Aurora Álvarez Veinguer and Zulfiya Fathkullina, took place in March 1998, at the Academy of Sciences of Tatarstan.

[8]   Yet another well-rehearsed articulation, constitutive of the modern public sphere. In her investigation into the making of the modern French Republic, Joan Scott (1996) elaborates upon how the figure of the pious superstitious 'handmaiden of the priest' operated as one of the tropes depicting women as inimical to the newly emerging republic. The belief in women's tendency to religiosity, she argues, rested on the one hand upon older notions about female superstition, irrationalism and fanaticism, which somehow got articulated with more

of female religious subjectivity as fanatic and haunted by false consciousness – a technology, one could say, which regulates access to modern subjectivity and citizenship. At the same time, women's presumed tendency to fanaticism serves to position, contain and ultimately dismiss Islamic revival. Although this social scientific account acknowledges Islamic revival whereas the common-sense account fails to do, it provides yet another modernist vision of societies' centre and margins.

> *A male Islamist view on Islamic revival.* Kazan State University (KSU), as a centre of intellectual production in Tatarstan, was one of the places where such tales of modernity and secularization were sustained and reproduced. One day I encountered Renat in the Centre for Sociology of Culture at the KSU, where he was using the computer facilities. We struck up a conversation and soon enough it became clear that Renat held an marked Islamist discourse (including, among other things, advocating an application of the Shari'a), and was involved in gathering people and establishing Islamic youth groups, while dreaming about setting up an Islamic political party in Tatarstan. In the course of the fieldwork I had come to formulate my research interest in terms of religion as it re-appeared in 'the centres' of society: in the city, among the highly educated and the young. While perceived as contradictory or paradoxical in terms of a hegemonic tale of secularization, this account was met with much recognition by Renat, who offered to be an informant for the project. One element of the investigation, however, deeply disturbed him: the focus on women. Clearly, he argued, this would undermine the whole project. Men, he insisted, were the dominant force of Islamic revival in Tatarstan. As we moved hence and forth between his reasons to reject and mine to insist on the focus on women, Renat asserted that in any case it would be more difficult to find women who were into *real* Islam. When I argued I had reasons to believe otherwise, he came to what for him was the heart of the matter: women's relationship to knowledge. True Islam is about knowledge, he argued, and clearly boys and men took that more seriously and were more inclined to knowledge and rationality. Girls and women did not fail to be good *believers*, he argued, but they failed more easily to be good *scholars*, and hence had more difficulties in being 'real' Muslims.

Renat's account of Islamic revival in Tatarstan was marked by an articulation that transgresses the tradition-modern binary. The transgression revolved around situating knowledge at the heart of *real* Islam – an emphasis which encompassed a more traditional insistence on knowledge in Islam but was equally insistently modern in its emphasis on information, science and 'contemporary' knowledge. Renat in fact did not have a high esteem for belief. He did not go as far as to dismiss it all together, but he left little doubt that *real* Islam should be characterized in terms of the pursuit of knowledge and religious scholarship. Thus a modern binary knowledge-belief, with its devaluation of the latter, served in Renat's account as a terrain upon which to re-articulate or reposition Islam: no longer on the side of babushka's belief, but in the heart of a contemporary knowledge society.[9]

---

modern arguments about women's lack of secular education and psychological arguments about women's submissive nature.

[9]   Renat had graduated in computer sciences, and in one of his more theological elaborations he insisted that God nowadays was information: *In the beginning there was the Word and the Word was God. And the Word is Information, so God is Information.*

Once more the gendered character of a modernist knowledge-belief binary was put into play. In order to position the Islamic revival in which Renat partook as an Islam of knowledge, women (associated to belief and irrationality) had to be (symbolically) excluded, despite their visible presence and participation. To do otherwise, as Renat suggested, would disqualify the whole project – a statement that did not only hint at my investigation into Islamic revival, but indeed at the Islamist project Renat conceived of.

Getting real: new Islamic subjectivity

In between attributions of invisibility, fanaticism and a more traditionally believing (in opposition to knowledgeable) mode of religiosity, how did pious Muslim women position themselves? From many conversations and interviews I had within a network of pious female students at the KSU – which was relatively small at the time of fieldwork – and their friends at the Mukhammedia Medresse, I could discern the following contours of an emerging religious subjectivity.

Their narratives of self and of religious trajectories were invested in the construction of a genealogy, that is, an understanding of a recovery of struggles together with the rude memory of their conflicts (Foucault 1980). Under the Soviet regime Islamic creeds and practices had effectively become subjugated knowledges, and the real concern of subjugated knowledges, Foucault insists, is a historical knowledge of struggles. In telling the story of how Islam became meaningful in their lives, the young women were plotting a story of survival, filled with wonder and marvel at the way in which, beyond the contingencies and idiosyncrasies of their own stories, Islam was transmitted. *I am so surprised how Islam survived in all this,* Naila put it, as she spoke of almost empty shelves in the religion section of libraries. Religious transmission took place underground, in the secrecy of the private sphere or, in Naila's words, *behind closed curtains.* Some of my interlocutors mentioned of a number of extraordinary people (women) – *Rashida Iskhakim, even during Stalinist times, under the threat of being imprisoned, she was teaching anyway* – and all drew attention to the quotidian survival by ordinary nameless people (women).

This is where babushka majestically reappears. Beyond a trope of stoic endurance, she provides a myth of origins in the genealogy composed through the young women's stories – a genealogy which positions the generation of their parents as atheist, lost and beyond redemption. Babushka was the one who planted the *seeds of Islam* in their lives. This is how Liaisan remembered growing up with her grandmother:

> I always saw [babushka] reading namaz [praying], saw her... everything whispering. And I remembered some words, these words. And then she read some old books, which seemed to me... well, they seemed to be very interesting. And sometimes she told me about 'the last day', and how awful it would be. So those kinds of things, which seemed to be very interesting for children. In a sort of fantastic way.

Moreover, the young women's symbolic reliance on babushka was marked by a significant re-appropriation. Babushka is a *Russian* archetype, a discursive stance within Russian language through which Russianness is reproduced (Ries 1997).

Appropriating (Tatar) babushka to narrate a continuity with an Islamic heritage is a striking move. Rather than reproducing Russianness, the trope of babushka in this case asserted the survival of a Tatar and Islamic culture/world under Russian (first Christian, then communist) domination. As the figure of babushka provided an anchor in their narratives of self, the women were able to claim a continuity with a religious tradition, while at the same time revisit and re-articulate the stereotypical representations of Tatar babushki caught up in the hierarchies of a modern economy of 'self' and 'other'. The re-articulation took place through a recourse to knowledge. In the context of minimal and sometimes non-existent formal religious education and institutions, babushka emerged as the 'knowledgeable' woman: she was associated with reading books, knowing (some) Arabic, reciting the Quran.

Babushka's significance within this genealogy should, however, not be mistaken for a model for the young women's religiosity or a reflection of their experience of Islam. After emphasizing babushka's importance in how they came to Islam many young women at some point admitted, in a rather low-key way, that babushka's religious knowledge remained rather basic. In Gulsum's words: "In principal I didn't know about Islam, just like all Soviet children. Yes, of course, babushka was saying something. But on a very basic level".. Endje, whose grandfather had been a mullah and whose babuskha was involved in the mosque, could not simply call the religious knowledge of her grandparents 'basic'. She formulated the difference in another way. "I discovered many things for myself. Now I understand that what my granddad and babushka knew is not enough for me". Gulnara characterized babushka's belief and knowledge as *not up to date*. Basic, not enough, not up to date. To distinguish their own religiosity from babushka's, the women most often used the expression *real* Islam. The reconfiguration they designated by that name reflects a new and self-conscious articulation between an Islamic tradition and legacy on the one hand, and notions of the modern on the other. The way in which this reconfiguration took place can be grasped by what Lara Deeb (2006) calls 'authentication', that is, an open ended process of seeking for correct meanings and understandings of various religious and social practices and beliefs, which is driven by textual study and historical inquiry, as well as a particular notion of rationality.

What, according to the young women, did *real* Islam consist of? A first vital impulse marking their experience of Islam was an emphasis on knowledge, scholarship and spiritual renewal. Islam they found in Kazan was an Islam of knowledge, of *decent Islamic teaching* as Nailia put it.[10] The importance of the pursuit of religious knowledge occurs in conjunction with a move to the city: all young women I spoke to had in fact grown up in a village or small town. They consistently situated their first genuine interest in Islam after having moved to Kazan for the purpose of higher education.

---

[10]   A speech by the first deputy mufti of Tatarstan signals how real Islam, and in particular its focus on knowledge, scholarship and interpretation, is perceived as a threat to the established Islamic authorities. 'Obsolete Methods of ijtihad [critical reasoning, interpretation] lost their actuality a long time ago and will not revive because they have fulfilled their function [...] there is not need to cardinally change the orthodoxy of Islam in order to make it up-to-date.' Valiulla Yakupov at a conference on Islam in Tatarstan, Kazan, April 1–2, 2004.

Somehow all mullahs are only self-taught in our place. Yes, they are either self-taught in our place or they do not have enough knowledge. And so, all of this has not been very strong. They taught us mostly on the level of namaz [salat] and Uraza [Ramadan]. But here, I came here already... well, I do not know, it is more on a spiritual level, so to speak. And here I am in a sense is stronger, higher, and somehow spiritual knowledge is stronger.

Moreover, the emphasis on religious knowledge was strongly articulated with the necessity for secular knowledge and education. As Gulnara put it:

How it happens usually... people just, they well, they just stay in one sphere... But it should be otherwise. One should know everything, one should be widely educated. An Islamic scientist said: 'Do not try to comment on the Quran, if you don't know at least 40 sciences.' Therefore it is necessary to try somehow, to try to improve one's own abilities and knowledge. Even the Prophet told us: Study is compulsory for you from your birth till your death. And you must try to get knowledge in all possible ways. He said, even if you have to go to China to get it.

It should be noted that their educational (and professional) ambitions were situated in a post-communist context of increased unemployment and decreased job opportunities for women as part of the new free-market, as well as a marked fall from the 1990s in both absolute numbers and proportional rates of female students within institutions of higher education. (Dmitrieva 1996).

A second impulse of *real* Islam concerned the relation between religion and ethnicity. From the vantage point of real Islam the young women developed a critique of being Muslim in a 'nominal' way, which implied a 'traditional' and/or 'ethnicised' understanding of Islam. Their critique was marked by a dissociation of the categories of Muslim (religious) and Tatar (ethnic). Havva found herself struggling to make appropriate distinctions.

Well, since childhood, since childhood I knew about Islam only from my babushka. But none of my relatives were... well, were Muslims. Well,... they haven't been real Muslims. So, I mean... they were... as if they have been considered as Muslims. But generally... this is a common feature among Tatars, we can say that... but they never follow the prescriptions given by Islam.

While she began claiming that none of her relatives were Muslims, the claim felt uncomfortable and not quite right. As Tatars, her relatives are considered *as* Muslims, and Havva did not want to dismiss or give up that articulation entirely. But she was equally not prepared to accept the automatic nomination of Tatars as Muslims, as she felt that being a Muslim should imply religious observance. This is where the qualification of '*real* Muslims' came in: it allowed her to speak about Islam in a different way than the wide-spread nominal understanding of Muslim in Tatarstan, while at the same time she did not have to deny that her relatives were Muslims. In another conversation Havva specified, with more confidence in the categorical distinctions she relied on: "[There is a wide-spread opinion] that who belongs to our ethnic group believes. They think they are Muslims, but they don't hold to the norm that is ascribed to real [in English] Islam".

The distinction between tradition and religion was connected to an impulse of conceiving communities and social ties in novel ways. Once more migration to Kazan played a crucial role. Urban space offered possibilities to create new communities unhindered by social norms of villages or small towns, the women insisted. The city offered them 'freedom of religion'.

> I mean every religion, Jewish, Christian or Muslim... is free and you don't attract people's attention. Everybody thinks, whatever you want, just do it. They say that all the time. Just do it. And when I want to go to the mosque to pray... nobody asks you 'What are you doing here?' Kazan is a big city... The people understand everything that is not the case in the villages or in small towns.

Alfyia continued to assert that religion was in fact not so wide-spread in the villages – a perspective which obviously clashed with the common-sense understanding of religion in Tatarstan. She was of course well aware of such representations; her comment reflected the extent to which she had appropriated an understanding of *real* Islam as her way of viewing the world.

Moreover, the young women's articulation of real Islam reflected a process of individualization in which an emphasis on a personal relationship to God and personal decisions prevailed (see also Amiraux 2001). Their position vis-à-vis a traditional Tatar way of wearing a headscarf, leaving a good part of the back of the head uncovered, illustrates the point. The women impatiently rejected this custom, as they considered it a sign of religious ignorance. At the same time they were very respectful towards 'real' Muslim women who for some reason did not wear a headscarf, including three friends at the core of their community. All of them, including those who did not cover, believed that a real Muslim woman should be covered. But they insisted that it was a *personal decision* that should be taken in conditions of religious *knowledge* – two crucial elements which they positioned in contradiction with ignorance or (ethnic) tradition. In this respect their religious experiences was less characterized by symbols of identity or belonging (although these dimensions were part of the practices and communities the women engaged in), but rather by the appropriation of certain modes of self governance, geared towards shedding off custom and ethnic particularity and grounded in knowledge and personal decision-making in the field of the religious.[11]

Coda: gendering the secular, modernizing the religious

At the end of a long collective interview, as a way of wrapping up the conversations, Elmira insisted: "I want to say that we found in religion something contemporary and new for ourselves". The quest for knowledge, shedding off traditional, ethnic or

---

[11]   The universalizing logic of real Islam was far from acceptable to all forms of Islamic revival in Tatarstan; it notably clashed with a more wide-spread nationalist religious revival. Two elderly Tatar ladies with a renewed interest in Islam, which lead them to take various religious classes, and whose heads were covered in a traditional Tatar way, expressed their disagreement like this: "If we are Tatars and live in Tatarstan, and if this is how our ancestors did it, then why all of a sudden should we adopt Arab fashions?"

customary elements, redoing communities and social ties away from the small town social norms, the freedom of the city. All of these conjure a sense of the modern, and it was with that sense – not against it – that the young women sought a way to be a *real* Muslim, a way that would situate them right in the middle of contemporary life instead of at its margins, like babushka's religiosity did.

The fact that women are important forces in a process of re-articulating Islam (which could be grasped through Deeb's notion of 'authentication') begs us to understand the gendered stakes of that process. Theories, narratives and formations of secular modernity are gendered; they are made of various dense connections between women and religion, which are notably played out in relation to a hegemonic knowledge-belief binary. This is illustrated by my analysis of the babushka trope, but I have argued that such an articulation equally informs social scientific accounts of Islamic revival (as women's presence serves a point about fanaticism) or a male Islamist account (as Islamic revival is anchored in the realm of knowledge through dismissing the importance of female believers). The different stakes of these accounts influence the very perception of women's presence within Islamic revival, and even more so their role and agency. Young pious Muslim women in Kazan, on their side, insisted on positioning themselves as knowledgeable female religious subjects, and by doing so, transgressed notions of secular and religion, and in particular the modern/traditional binaries that cross them.

References

Amiraux, Valérie, *Acteurs de l'islam entre Allemagne et Turquie: Parcours militants et expériences religieuses* (Paris: L'Harmattan, 2001).

Asad, Talal, *Formations of the Secular: Christianity, Islam, Modernity* (Stanford: University of Stanford Press, 2003).

Berger, Peter, *The Sacred Canopy: Elements of a Sociological Theory of Religion* (New York: Anchor Books, 1969).

Bracke, Sarah, *Women Resisting Secularisation in an Age of Globalisation. Four Case-studies within a European Context*, unpublished Ph.D. thesis (Utrecht: Utrecht University, 2004).

Bracke, Sarah and Fadil, Nadia, *Islam and Secular Modernity under Western Eyes: A Genealogy of a Constitutive Relationship* (European Institute Firenze, Working Paper, 2006).

Deeb, Lara, *An Enchanted Modern: Gender and Public Piety in Shi'i Lebanon* (Princeton: Princeton University Press, 2006).

Dmitrieva, Elena, 'Orientations, Re-orientations or Disorientations? Expectations of the Future among Russian School-leavers', in Hilary Pilkington (ed.), *Gender, Generation and Identity in Contemporary Russia* (London: Routledge, 1996).

Foucault, Michel, *Power/Knowledge, Selected Interviews and Other Writings, 1972–1977*, (ed.) Colin Gordon (Brighton: Harvester, 1980).

Göle, Nilüfer, *Musulmanes et modernes: Voile et civilisation en Turquie* (Paris: Editions La Découverte, 1993).

Hall, Stuart, *Het minimale zelf en andere opstellen* (Amsterdam: Sua, 1991).

Hall, Stuart, 'On Postmodernism and Articulation: An Interview with Stuart Hall', [Edited by Lawrence Grossberg] in David Morley and Kuan-Hsing Chen (eds), *Stuart Hall: Critical Dialogues in Cultural Studies* (London: Routledge, [1986]1996).

Harding, Susan, *The Book of Jerry Falwell: Fundamentalist Language and Politics* (Princeton: Princeton University Press, 2000).

Hodgson, Dorothy, *Gendered Modernities: Ethnographic Perspectives* (New York: Palgrave, 2003).

Jameson, Fredric, *Postmodernism, or, The Cultural Logic of Late Capitalism* (London: Verso, 1991).

Jonker, Gerdien, 'Islamic Knowledge through a Women's Lens: Education, Power and Belief', *Social Compass*, 50(1) (2003): 35–46.

Jouili, Jeanette and Amir-Moazami, Schirin, 'Knowledge, Empowerment and Religious Authority among Pious Muslim Women in France and Germany', *The Muslim World*, 96 (2006): 617–642.

Musina, Rozalinda, 'L'islam et la communauté musulmane au Tatarstan aujourd'hui', in Stephane A. Dudoignon, Dämir Is'haqov et Räfyq Möhämmätshin (dir.) *L'Islam de Russie: Conscience communautaire et autonomie politique chez les Tatars de la Volga et de l'Oural, depuis le XVIIIe siècle* (Paris: Maisonneuve and Larose, 1997).

Neumann, Iver, *Uses of the Other: 'The East' in European Identity Formation* (Manchester: Manchester University Press, 1999).

Ries, Nancy, *Russian Talk: Culture and Conversation during Perestroika* (Ithaca: Cornell University Press, 1997).

Scott, Joan, *Only Paradoxes to Offer: French Feminists and the Rights of Man* (Cambridge, MA: Harvard University Press, 1996).

Tönnies, Ferdinand, *Community and Association* [Gemeinschaft und Gesellschaft]. (London: Routledge and Kegan Paul, [1887] 1955).

Chapter 11

Being Muslim and Being Canadian: How Second Generation Muslim Women Create Religious Identities in Two Worlds

Rubina Ramji

Introduction

The Islamic diaspora in western countries is often viewed as a homogenous entity. Issues of nation, class, education and ideology are often overlooked when dealing with the notion of a collective identity. Social structures such as race, nation, and religion play a strong role in the way Muslims are influenced by the views of the dominant culture in which they find themselves. This research study[1] strives to understand how diverse Muslim groups from different classes with different cultural, ethnic and national backgrounds self-identify themselves within a Canadian context.

As Anne Sofie Roald (2001: 3), author of *Women in Islam: The Western Experience*, states, 'widespread migration initiates processes of change in Muslims' understanding of the Islamic message', as the introduction of new cultural paradigms sometimes challenge, or on the other hand reinforce, traditional solutions to problems. Religious identity can be said to manifest itself in different ways: at the group level, at the individual level or both, depending on how religion and religious sentiments are defined.

Although many studies in the European context tend to find that Muslims turn to a Muslim identity because of their contact with their 'host' cultures, this research deals with a different group of immigrants. North American research on immigrants also tends to focus directly on the first generation immigrant population, often with little regard to the role of religion (see, for example, Berns McGown 1999; Bramadat and Seljak 2005; Coward and Goa 1987; Coward *et al.* 2000; Janhevich and Ibrahim 2004; McLellan 1999; Rukmani 1999; Shakeri 1998). Therefore there is a gap in

[1]   Religion among Immigrant Youth in Canada is a research project funded by the Social Sciences and Humanities Research Council of Canada. The author collaborated with Peter Beyer (principal investigator), Shandip Saha, and Leslie Laczko at the University of Ottawa, Nancy Nason-Clark at the University of New Brunswick, Lori Beaman and Marie-Paule Martel Reny at Concordia University in Montreal, and John H. Simpson, Arlene Macdonald, and Carolyn Reimer at the University of Toronto. This research study on Muslim women is part of a larger study that has been undertaken which focuses on second generation immigrants from Buddhist, Hindu, and Muslim backgrounds and who currently reside or study in the urban regions of Toronto, Montreal, and Ottawa-Gatineau.

understanding the long-term implications of migration to Canada, and the effects that migration has on religious identity.

Muslim immigration to Canada

Canadian society has become increasingly religiously diverse in the past thirty years due to immigration patterns.[2] Also, Canada's approach to diversity is to foster a culture of inclusion through its core values of equality, accommodation and acceptance (Biles and Ibrahim 2005). Within this Canadian context, religion has remained important in relation to the creation of identities, boundaries and group solidarities. In fact, research in Canada has shown that recent immigrant children and youth who have lived in Canada for less than a decade are twice more likely to attend religious services in comparison to their Canadian-born complement (Biles and Ibrahim 2005).

The Canadian Muslim community grew rapidly after the 1970s, building mosques and establishing trans-ethnic communities across Canada (McDonough and Hoodfar 2005). Canadian immigration policies have allowed Muslims from almost every part of the Muslim world to migrate to Canada, and many tend to be from middle- and upper-middle-class families. In fact, the number of Muslim immigrants to Canada has doubled each decade since 1981 (Statistics Canada 2003). Thus the foreign-born Muslim population in Canada is diverse, multi-ethnic and multilingual. Given the fact that many Muslims have lived in Canada for a few decades, the population of Canadian born Muslim youth has substantially grown. These younger Muslims, not having a direct ethnic identity to build upon, have had to define Islam and its practices for themselves, in juxtaposition to the ethnic cultural values they have received from their parents.

Research focus: second generation Muslim women in Canada

The Muslim women focused upon within this study are not being confronted by a new culture, but rather have been raised within, and feel completely at ease in, Canadian culture. They have been raised to contend with a variety of identity dimensions in their lives, those of their Islamic faith, their parents' ethnic cultural heritage and their exposure to the values and practices of Canadian culture through school, politics and the media. The approach to these individuals in the study has to take into account the culture of both the parents and the youth in order to better understand the diverse conflicts and tensions faced by these second generation Muslims as they develop their religious identities in a Canadian society.

---

[2] Multiculturalism is a key element to Canada's immigration and citizenship policies. The Canadian Multiculturalism Act (1988) places great emphasis on the freedoms of citizens to practice their religion without prejudice or interference. The Multiculturalism Act states: 'the Government of Canada recognizes the diversity of Canadians as regards race, national or ethnic origin, colour and religion as a fundamental characteristic of Canadian society and is committed to a policy of multiculturalism.'

This research project examined the involvement of second generation immigrant Muslim female youth, aged 18–27, who had at least one immigrant parent and were either born in Canada or who arrived in Canada before the age of ten. These participants came from Muslim backgrounds, and were currently living or studying in the urban areas of Toronto, Ottawa and Montreal. The interviewees were asked to participate in a semi-structured interview which took place within a three hour time span. Participants for this study were recruited almost entirely on university campuses and community colleges; as research has revealed, at least 80–95 per cent of the youth with which the project is concerned possess a postsecondary education (Beyer 2005). The interviews were conducted over a two-year period beginning in September 2004 and concluding in April 2006.

The purpose of the research was to investigate the participants' involvement in religion and attitudes towards religion. The question of religious identity or lack thereof was central to the investigation. Interviewees were asked about their upbringing within their inherited religious identity, their own involvement in that religion if any, the adoption of any religious practices and unconventional practices they may have acquired. They discussed how their own views and practices differed from the parental generation (the first generation of immigrants), and how they situated themselves within Canada and the wider world.

In terms of identity, definitions of what makes someone Muslim vary from discipline to discipline. Åke Sanders from the Institute of Ethnic Religions in Gothenburg, Sweden has created a four-category classification of what makes someone a Muslim. A Muslim can either be an ethnic, a cultural, a religious or a political Muslim. A person belonging to an ethnic group in which the widely held belief of the population is Muslim can be considered an ethnic Muslim. A cultural Muslim is someone who is socialized in a Muslim culture. A religious Muslim would be considered a person who performs the Islamic commands, and a political Muslim is a person who claims that 'Islam in its essence primarily is (or ought to be) a political and social phenomenon' (Sanders 1997: 184–185).

Although these categories might be useful at the level of quantifying population information, for this particular study it is imperative that the interviewee's own self-definition be utilized in the classification. This study looks at orthopraxis (actions of obligation), intentions, familial and institutional influences, as well as levels of belief.[3]

Therefore, given the information that was provided by the participants during the interviews, the Muslim women within this study can be separated into four categories using the basis of self-definition and identification.[4]

---

[3]   Islamists, particularly the Salafists, tend to look at the level of one's Muslimness (Roald 2001).

[4]   92 people were interviewed who considered themselves to have Muslim backgrounds. Of the 92 participants, 58 were female and 34 were male.

Participant categorization

The four categories fashioned from the 58 female participants' own perceptions are: the '*Salafists*' (three), the *highly-involved* (25), the *moderately-involved* (22), and the *non-believers* (eight). The term Salafist, as it is used here, refers to participants who espouse forms of Islamic Sunni ideology and practice that they consider a 'pure' form of Islam. Salafists believe that the Prophet Muhammad's life serves as a perfect example of how Islam should be lived and practiced. According to the Salafi practitioner, the *Quran* and *ahadith* should not be viewed in innovative ways, and therefore they often hold conservative or traditionalist views about Islam. The highly-involved participants want to follow the tenets of Islam strongly as they consider it to be a central aspect of their lives. They attempt to pray five times a day, fast during Ramadan, give to charity and search for ways to be more religiously minded, but they are less insistent on the unique correctness of their interpretation of Islam. They are significantly more irenic in their attitudes. The moderately-involved group are those who know the tenets of Islam and follow some of the practices of their faith such as celebrating Eid, but they tend not to pray or attend mosque regularly. They continue to identify themselves as Muslim but religion is not a central aspect of their identities or their lives. The non-believers generally define themselves as atheists or have some belief in a creator but do not attribute their beliefs to any religion. None of them had converted or adopted another religious tradition. They acknowledge that they are Muslim by family and cultural background.

Patterns of involvement

From the distribution across the categories, a few conclusions can immediately be drawn. Firstly, a high percentage of second generation Muslim females in Canada have a strong involvement in their religion. The second generation is not losing their religion to secularism. Secondly, a large percentage of the female participants between the ages of 18–20 continue to maintain their faith from a moderate to a very strong level. From these conclusions, other significant details have been exposed to make these representations more complex.

Faith

As was observed very early on in the study, the beginning of the level of involvement in their faith was measured, and a vast majority of the women stated that their involvement had begun in childhood as expected, but that their level of involvement had increased since then. This also includes the majority of the moderately-involved. Of the ten women who stated their level of religious involvement was higher than their parents today, one (out of three) was a Salafist, six (out of 25) were highly-involved, and three (out of 22) were moderately-involved. Interestingly, the numbers for the same level of involvement and lesser level of involvement in the religion were almost identical. Twenty-six participants stated that they continued to practice and believe at the same level as their parents. Twenty-one participants felt that their level was lower than their parents, but quite of few of them said that they hoped to increase their level of practice after completing their education.

From the interviews with the Muslim women, several major themes emerged for each subgroup. These concern gender relations, the role of religious institutions compared to individualistic ideas, the types of religious practice, parental influences, moral questions and religious versus non-religious activities.

Two dimensions of the research project aims came out clearly in the data: participants clearly articulated how they were constructing their individual religious identities and what place institutional forms had in these constructions. Throughout the interviews, participants were very specific in the ways they constructed their identity, above all in relation to their parents and friends. Also, certain institutions played strong roles in either constructing religious identity, such as internet forums, or reinforcing those identities, such as university-based Muslim Student Associations.

Gender relations

Gender relations are a common theme in the process of identity formation. The restrictions placed upon females regarding dating, and even friendships with the opposite sex, were discussed by most of the participants interviewed. None of the Salafist youth dated, but were highly involved in volunteer activities in their communities including being counsellors at summer camps and even being part of the university campus radio show on Islam. Only five of the 25 highly-involved participants had dated, and all of them admitted to hiding it from their parents. The no-dating rule did not seem to exist in the moderately-involved group, but many of them nonetheless refrained from sexual contact due to religious ideals. Religion was a central justification for the structure of gender relations, but in a few cases, overlapping cultural considerations were also important. For instance, a highly-involved Somali female, aged 18, described her culture as difficult for women because it was assumed that all women were to conform to strict rules of sex segregation, otherwise rumours would spread about the girl and her family. In some instances, the female youth also have this structure emphasized by the community, as it tends to place her in a position where her actions not only represent herself, but that of her family and community members as well.

The *hijab* plays a central role in the structure of religious identity for the Salafist and the highly-involved female participants. All of the Salafist females (three) wore *hijab* as did 12 (out of 25) of the highly involved, and five of the other highly-involved females expressed a desire to wear the *hijab* in the future. This practice is therefore strongly correlated with intensity of practice and belief, and is not a matter of simple conformity to parental or community pressure.

Religious identification

For the Salafists and many of the highly-involved participants, religious identification is not closely tied to identification with a particular religious congregation. Many young Muslim women are not attached to a mosque as such, but rather construct their Muslim identities as individuals. Furthermore, amongst the youth interviewed, a predominant number of Salafists and highly-involved youth in effect considered themselves to be ardent fundamentalists. The results reveal that the fundamentalists tend to keep their style of Islam to themselves, or confine it institutionally to the university Muslim Student Association (MSA) or chat groups in cyberspace. The style of religion therefore does not already determine the institutional forms to which it will contribute. This group of participants has shown very little reliance on family members as a source of religious information or wisdom; they do not associate themselves with what they consider to be the cultural values of their parents and do not consider the mosque as the natural and prime place for the teaching of Islamic practice or philosophy. In fact, all members of the Salafist group had undertaken their own personal searches for the understanding of Islam and tended to separate the notion of ethnicity from the practice of Islam. These participants often criticized what they consider to be their parents' cultural practices, such as extravagant weddings, listening to music and encouraging career over marriage. They did not see their level of belief and practice of Islam as surpassing that of their parents; their Islam is 'purer' because it does not have these cultural attachments. A corollary of this attitude is that these participants feel completely integrated into Canadian society and do not feel tied to their parents' culture. One might say that they have cultivated a distinctive ethnicity, one that is truly Canadian and truly Islamic. Large numbers of these youth claim that they are able to practice their religion as freely as they would like living in Canada. They also consider themselves to be 'full and equal members of Canadian society'. About half of the highly-involved members have the same differences of opinion regarding parental culture, but the other half follow their parents' way of Islam and define themselves as belonging to both their parents culture as well as being fully Canadian.

The majority of the moderately-involved group tended to follow the practices of their parents, who are themselves moderately involved in terms of practice. There were a few participants from mixed marriages, and it seemed that some of them had actually learned to practice from other family members, such as cousins and aunts. The moderately-involved participants who had learned from other family members were actually practising their religion at a higher level than their parents. In general within this subgroup, there is little affiliation with religious institutions as they tend to go to mosques only for large functions such as Eid, breaking fast during Ramadan, or irregularly attend Friday *jum'ah* prayers. The moderately-involved group also tend to think of themselves as Canadian first because they do things that they consider are un-Islamic, but are considered 'Canadian' in context: some of them admit to drinking occasionally, smoking and dating. The impact of Canadian culture and the notion of religion, in this case Islam, play an important role in the formation of personal and community identities amongst this group.

Influences

Almost every single Muslim woman in the study agreed to have been shaped by their family's religious background. This influence affected the quality of the relationships they had with family members. All the Salafists and the majority of the highly-involved group acknowledged that they had inherited their religious values from their parents, but did not turn to them to discuss religious issues – this group tended to have differences of opinion with their parents as to what constituted 'authentic Islam'. The other highly-involved group saw their parents as role models for religious expression and had strong relationships with their parents. The moderately involved group argued with their parents much more regarding religious practice, or their lack of it. Most of the non-believers had poor relationships with their parents, particularly those whose parents continued practising the religion regularly.

For those who said that religion had a very high level of importance in their lives such as the Salafists and highly-involved participants, friendship networks played a large role in supporting their involvement. These networks could be found in school, in the MSA, in the mosque and on the internet. The Salafist women, in large part, had a majority (up to 90 per cent) if not all, friends who were Muslim, who shared their beliefs, behaviours and decisions. This trend did not follow through with the highly-involved group but many mentioned that their friends had many of the same values and family rules to follow. Institutional religion did not play such a large role. All the Salafist youth acknowledged that they attended Friday *jum'ah* services, but beyond that the mosque itself did not play a role in their lives. Two women noted that it was not obligatory for women to attend jum'ah services. A large number of highly-involved participants attended mosque on a regular basis but also went to religious classes on weekends or had tutors to learn to read *Quran* and *ahadith*, with the approval of their parents. Although this group does not attend mosque more often than the Salafists, more than half of the highly-involved group said that they would go the Imam of the mosque if they had religious questions. Only 12 of the 22 moderately-involved participants went to mosque, and it was usually for special occasions or sporadically to pray. Many of the female participants at all levels, when asked about mosque attendance, mentioned that it was not mandatory for women to attend mosque but many prayed with the family in the home.

In terms of personal faith, the internet has turned out to be of particular use in shaping individual religious identities. At least ten participants say they used the internet as a religious forum. All of the Salafist participants and some of the highly-involved group stated that they often used the internet and electronic chat rooms as sources for understanding Islamic values, practices, and as religious organizations. This practice added to the notion of eliminating cultural values in order to find a true understanding of Islam for themselves. Many of the Salafist and highly-involved members were encouraged by their parents to learn more about their faith on their own. Other highly-involved participants claimed to spend time reading religious articles and listening to lectures about Islam. A few of the participants, all highly-involved, also stated that religion was important for dealing with stress, anxiety and self-esteem. More than 15 of the Salafist and highly-involved youth interviewed stated that their religion was important for health and conducive to a good life. One female aged 21 stated that 'prayer is like breathing', and offered her a perfect way of life.

For the majority of the Muslim women interviewed, religion had a protective effect, in that it prohibited what could be considered problematic or delinquent behaviours. All of the Salafist and highly-involved participants stated that due to religious tenets, they could not smoke, drink, date, stay out late, or mix with the opposite sex. About six of the moderately-involved youth acknowledged that they drank, smoked or dated, but also stated that they hid these actions from their parents. Only one participant admitted to having premarital sex, but that was because she was in a committed relationship. Almost all of the moderately-involved individuals stated that these were values that had been passed down from their parents, and thought that it was due to both religious and cultural background.

Religious involvement

In terms of religious practice, more than 26 of the 58 participants stated that they tried to pray five times a day, and 11 others tried to pray at least once a day. The majority of the moderately-involved women said that they fasted during Ramadan, celebrated the two Eids and gave to charity, either individually or through the family. Highly-involved individuals claimed that doing good deeds and being honest were religious activities.

All of the Salafist and the majority of the highly-involved women were actively involved in the Muslim Student Associations on university campuses. Moderately-involved youth felt that treating people well, not hurting others and being environmentally conscious were forms of religious practice for them. All of the non-believers had been pushed to practice Islam when they were young, but had left the religion for different reasons. One woman said she stopped practising three years ago because she found the practices stifling and hypocritical. After attending university, she found that the teachings of Islam that she had learned in religious school were different from the academic setting and became cynical about religion. Another woman admitted that she had removed her hijab a month prior to the interview because of questions that were raised while in university. She still considered herself a Muslim and continued to pray regularly.

Role of the media

The media has also shaped the lives of many of the Muslim women interviewed. For the Salafist and highly-involved groups, media representations of Muslims after 9/11 had a correlating affect on identity. Many of these youth stated that the media made all Muslims seem like terrorists after 11 September 2001, and in reaction, many began 'wearing' their Islamic identity with pride and more openly. One woman stated that 9/11 played a large role in her deciding to wear the hijab and being more attentive to her religion. Another woman had started wearing hijab six months prior to the interview, but acknowledged that 9/11 made her want to learn more about her religion to answer constant questions. Moderately-identified Muslims also felt that the image of Islam had been tarnished after 9/11 and some acknowledged that they actually began studying Islam to better understand it and to explain it to others.

Religious morals

In terms of morality, many of the Salafist and highly-involved youth claimed that Islam was fundamental in their decision-making processes. Issues of right and wrong, good and bad, just and unjust were based on religious tenets. One female, aged 18, stated that 'honesty is a religious practice' for her. Another female, aged 20, declared that 'trauma' was a test of faith and patience, a test from God, and that all good deeds were acts of worship, therefore the intentions of all her actions were predicated on religious worthiness. A 21-year-old female stated, as others did, that the respectful treatment of parents was essential to Islam.

Many highly-involved participants stated that their career choices were dictated by their religious morals. Two participants wanted to work in underdeveloped Islamic countries, two were working for charity organizations like Amnesty International and one female was the host of an Islamic radio show. On the other hand, the Salafists felt that their parents' drive for careers pushed them away from religious ideals: they all stated that marriage and raising a family conformed to Islam more than making money. The majority of the moderately-involved participants said that they believed in the principles of Islam and thought being a good Muslim to be more of a spiritual journey than one of practice. Therefore many of them felt that being good to others, not hurting fellow human beings, and being respectful to their parents were forms of religious practice.

Not many of the Salafist or highly-involved youth participated in activities outside of their religion, or their religious values. Most of them stated that they spent time reading scripture and articles, listening to lectures and motivational speakers and participating in on-line chat groups in order to increase their spiritual development. Many of them affirmed that they thought about religion all the time. The moderately-involved group had more friends who were not Muslim, so would go out and spend time with their friends, and participated in Canadian activities. Two females from this group were dancers.

Conclusion

The development of faith for most of the Muslim youth interviewed seems to be based on individual searches: using the internet, reading articles and books, listening to scholars, etc. Even the moderately-involved participants who wanted to learn more about Islam were turning to academic books and the internet, rather than talking to Islamic authorities at their local mosques. Family and the mosque do not seem to be providing a foundation for this formation. But family does seem to play a large role in moral development: the idea of sexual segregation, not drinking, smoking and dating all stem from parental views and is backed by religious tenets. Social spheres are not considered to be separate from 'ecclesiastical oversight or theology' (Martin 2005: 146) but rather are negotiated with religion. Martin argues that religion is used as a way for immigrants to cope in a new society. First generation Muslim Canadians have worked hard to create a religious community that often is shaped by ethnic and national attachments in order to maintain a sense of group solidarity and communal identity. Through this research, it is evident that second generation immigrants do not need to do this as *this* is their society, their culture and their religion. It is not a process of assimilation, but rather of negotiation.

The majority of the youth interviewed were Sunni (36). The Salafist group tended to be young in age, ranging from ages 19–21. The highly-involved group was also young, ranging from 18–23: two were 26 years of age, and only one was at the highest age range of 27. The moderately-involved and non-believers had a wider range of age, from 18–26.

This conclusion applies especially to the highly diverse, the highly involved, ways in which the majority of these participants construct their personal identities and their Islam. Confirming conclusions reached from research among second generation Muslim youth in Europe (Vertovec and Rogers 1998), Canada's counterparts seem to be exhibiting a similar combination of greatly varied, very individualistic and for the most part very serious forms of doing their religion. They are not dependent on their elders, they do not rely on traditional sources of Islamic authority, and they are not in the least hesitant about creating their own *bricolages*.[5] These are not women who are just carrying on the traditions of their immigrant parents in a kind of exercise in religio-cultural preservation; nor are they women who are simply 'assimilating' to the dominant culture. Like most youth in Canada, they seem to feel it incumbent upon them to reconstruct their world for themselves and primarily on an individual basis, and in the process transforming their own religious identities within a wider Canadian context. Their Islam is innovative rather than imitative, individual rather than communitarian, and covers somewhat evenly a vast spectrum of attitudes and behaviours that some observers might be tempted to label as 'fundamentalist'.

References

Berns McGown, Rima, *Muslims in the Diaspora: The Somali Communities of London and Toronto* (Toronto: University of Toronto Press, 1999).
Beyer, Peter, 'Religious Identity and Educational Attainment among Recent Immigrants to Canada: Gender, Age, and Second Generation', *Journal of International Migration and Integration*, 6 (2005): 177–198.
Biles, John and Ibrahim, Humera, 'Religion and Public Policy: Immigration, Citizenship, and Multiculturalism – Guess Who's Coming to Dinner?', in Paul Bramadat and David Seljak (eds), *Religion and Ethnicity in Canada* (Toronto: Pearson Education Canada, 2005).
Bramadat, Paul and Seljak, David (eds), *Religion and Ethnicity in Canada* (Toronto: Pearson Longman, 2005).
Canadian Heritage. *Canadian Multiculturalism Act* (1988). http://www.pch.gc.ca/progs/multi/policy/act_e.cfm.
Coward, Harold and Goa, David, 'Religious Experience of the South Asian Diaspora in Canada', in M. Israel (ed.), *The South Asian Diaspora in Canada: Six Essays* (Toronto: Multicultural History Society of Ontario and Centre for South Asian Studies, 1987).

---

[5]   Thanks to Peter Beyer for the use of this term to best describe the 'do-it-yourself' assembly or creation of religion.

Coward, Harold, Hinnells, John and Williams, Raymond Brady (eds), *The South Asian Religious Diaspora in Britain, Canada, and the United States* (Albany, NY: SUNY Press, 2000).

Janhevich, Derek and Ibrahim, Humera, 'Muslims in Canada: An Illustrative and Demographic Profile', *Our Diverse Cities*, 1 (2004): 49–57.

Martin, David, 'Secularization and the Future of Christianity', *Journal of Contemporary Religion*, 20 (2005): 145–160.

McDonough, Sheila and Hoodfar, Homa, 'Muslim Groups in Canada: From Ethnic Groups to Religious Community', in Paul Bramadat and David Seljak (eds), *Religion and Ethnicity in Canada* (Toronto: Pearson Education Canada Inc., 2005).

McLellan, Janet, *Many Petals of the Lotus: Five Asian Buddhist Communities in Toronto* (Toronto: University of Toronto Press, 1999).

Roald, Anne Sofie, *Women in Islam: The Western Experience* (London: Routledge, 2001).

Rukmani, T.S. (ed.), *Hindu Diaspora: Global Perspectives* (Montreal: Concordia University Press, 1999).

Sanders, Åke, 'To What Extent is the Swedish Muslim Religious?', in Steven Vertovec and Ceri Peach (eds), *Islam in Europe: The Politics of Religion and Community* (Warwick: Centre for Research in Ethnic Relations, University of Warwick, 1997).

Shakeri, Esmail, 'Muslim Women in Canada: Their Role and Status as Revealed in the Hijab Controversy', in Yvonne Yazbeck Haddad and John L. Esposito (eds), *Muslims on the Americanization Path* (New York: Oxford University Press, 1998).

Statistics Canada, 'Religions in Canada', *2001 Census: Analysis Series* (2003). Accessed on 1 December 2006.

http://www12.statcan.ca/english/census01/Products/Analytic/Index.cfm.

Vertovec, Steven and Rogers, Alisdair (eds), *Muslim European Youth: Reproducing Ethnicity, Religion, Culture* (Aldershot: Ashgate, 1998).

Chapter 12

Being Seen by Many Eyes: Muslim Immigrant Women in the United States

Garbi Schmidt

Covering up?

On a Saturday afternoon in the mid-1990s I found my way to one of Chicago's largest mosques. My reason for visiting was to participate in a women's study group that always met on Saturdays. When I arrived, only one other woman was present in the room where the meeting normally took place. Waiting for the rest of the group to turn up, we spent some time talking about life as a Muslim woman and my fieldwork project on Muslims in Chicago. The woman was in her late 30s – at least that is my guess, as she was covered from head to toe in a black gown that hid most of her features. While we were talking, one of her sons came in and teased his mother by running off with one of the black gloves that she had left on the table. 'Oh, please give it back to me again', she pleaded. 'You know that I cannot walk out there [she pointed to the door] without my gloves.' Restricted dress

This episode could be read as a stereotypical way of describing Muslim women, regardless of where they live. However, in a chapter dealing with the interpretation and public manifestation of Islam within secular western nation states, I find it important to describe the diversity that these interpretations and manifestations represent. For that reason I take this incident as my starting point, as one end of a continuum of positions dealing with the questions of being a Muslim woman living in the United States. All these questions refer to the inter-referential aspects of moulding the self (subjectification, e.g. Foucault 1982, 1997; Jakobsen 2006) and being seen as something particular (objectification, e.g. Eickelman and Piscatori 1996: 38). To some the process of moulding the self implies covering up (yet not disappearing); to others, it means laying open even the most intimate details of their spiritual life.

Muslims are on their way to becoming the second largest religious community in the United States (Esposito 2000: 3). The country's first mosques were established almost a hundred years ago, and the community boasts a wealth of ethnic diversity and institutional entrepreneurship. The largest ethnic group within this religious community (or better, communities) consists of African-Americans (30–40 per cent), while people of other immigrant backgrounds comprise the rest (Nu'man 1992; Turner 1997: 12ff; Ba-Yunus and Siddiqui 1999). This chapter focuses mainly on the immigrant group, as the African-American community represents a particular historical and social experience that deserves to be described on its own.[1] All of my informants are of immigrant background, and interviews took place during two periods of fieldwork, one in Chicago (1995–1997) and one in Los Angeles (2001). Both fieldwork periods were completed prior to the terrorist attacks on New York and Washington in September 2001. During those seven years (1995–2001), a wide range of Muslim social and political initiatives developed. They focused both on the civil rights and social needs of Muslims nationally, and — not least given the embedded transnational perspective and experience of large segments of the community — sought to affect US foreign policy. From a historical perspective one can say that in the 1990s immigrant Muslim communities gained a national voice within public discourses, rather than being communities mainly talked about.

This chapter not only focuses on the role and agency of Muslim women, mainly in this specific period, but also draws lines to more recent developments in the Muslim American community. My description takes its starting point in questions of how, on the one hand, Muslim women participate in the wider community-based struggle for social inclusion and empowerment, and how on the other, they struggle for empowerment within their own faith-based communities. These two questions, as well as one central theme of this book – how various religions are manifested within western nations — has made me think in dimensions of space, visibility and mobility. My approach is inspired by the powerful image generated by Pnina Werbner in her contribution to Barbara Metcalf's *Making Muslim Space in North American and Europe* (1996). Werbner describes a procession of Muslim men in Birmingham (and other UK cities), marking the Milad ul-Nabi (birth and death of the Prophet Muhammad), a procession that 'not only purifies their hearts and souls, but also sacralizes and "Islamizes" the very earth, the buildings, the streets and neighbourhoods through which they march' (Werbner 1996: 167). Werbner convincingly underlines what human (ritual) interaction with space can do. Marching through the streets, and being seen as Muslim, the men make Muslim space. Being seen as occupying space can be a road to empowerment. Visibility is a statement of the right to presence. This perspective is important, as the women speaking in this chapter often refer to space and the right to mobility within certain spaces as crucial for their religious empowerment and rightful claiming of Muslim womanhood. The women's approach is particularly interesting because being visible as a Muslim woman — for example by wearing the *hijab* — is often viewed within the general public as a signal of gender-specific vulnerability, lack of rights and lack of power.

The imagery of the Muslim woman

Garbi: How do you see yourself as a Muslim woman in this society? What is Islam giving you as a woman?

Karima: As a Muslim woman? It is hard because first of all it is hard being a Muslim, period. But being a Muslim women, it doubles, because you have this notions, like 'Oh

---

[1]   For recent, ethnological descriptions of African-American Muslim women, see Rouse (2004) and Karim (2004).

your husband must beat you at home'. And a lot of times, I don't blame people from having these notions, because if you go back home, it is not rare at all, women are treated like scum a lot of places, like in the Middle East and in Muslim countries, and it is very disgusting. As a Muslim woman… for me, it means that I have to be twice as strong, twice as active and twice as out there. Because not only do I want people to respect me as a Muslim, but also as a Muslim woman.[2]

My interview with Karima took place in the outdoor cafeteria of a Los Angeles-based university campus. As was the case for most of the women I interviewed in the area, she was impeccably dressed in a colourful dress and wearing the *hijab*. Although my intention with the interview was primarily to learn more about Muslim youth organizations, our conversation soon turned into the question of women in Islam and the role of Muslim women in American society.

Karima's statement falls in line with this chapter's description of Muslim American women and their roads to, and strategies for, visibility and mobility within several social fields. She describes how being Muslim and being a woman is a source of exclusion in the society where she lives, and that how she counters this exclusion is to 'be active,' to be 'out there'. Rather than choosing a strategy of retreat, she stresses the very elements that make her different. Difference becomes a powerful way of marking identity in public spaces. The identity and political position she chooses to take within the United States equally compels her to position herself towards and even against other localities, for example the region that her parents came from. Within these diverse contexts, Islam becomes a means for protest and reform.

We need to remember that Karima's description of her religious identity does not exclusively mark her as different but rather includes its own fulfilment of the social norms upon which the United States is built. In the words of Raymond Brady Williams, 'religion [in the United States] is the social category with clearest meaning and acceptance' (Williams 1988: 29; see also Kurien 2001: 278ff). Using religious terminology, also in the field of politics, is not uncommon in the American context, and stating oneself as religious is thus neither dubious nor degrading but quite the contrary. By calling herself religious, Karima actually falls within the American mainstream. Like many other students at her university campus, she wears religious symbols and is affiliated with a religiously motivated youth organization. To that extent she is perfectly American.

Yet there is a difference between Karima and her peers. As is the case in (western) European countries, Islam carries negative connotations in the United States. The debate over Muslims as trustworthy citizens not only is linked to the fear of the Muslim, male terrorist but also focuses on the image of the oppressed *hijab*-wearing Muslim woman. The two typologies, detached as they are from individual features, are both dichotomous and interdependent. The male is the violent oppressor, the woman the violently oppressed. What the typologies share is how, within the public debate, they are seen as opposing and destabilizing mainstream American norms – in society as such. Some of this gendering may be understood as a result of a colonial past that the United States shares with western European countries. The sexualized image of the Oriental woman, paired with missionary impressions that women in the

---

2   Interview, 13 February 2001.

region were the weakest and thus most likely to convert, is important if we seek to understand the imagery of the Muslim women today (Haddad *et al.* 2006: 23–27).

In addition to the (post-) colonial perspective, positions in the debate are also affected by the domestication of Islam in western countries: Muslim women changed from being exotic 'objects' in strange countries to neighbours. In these contexts, Muslim women are just as much seen as provocative and intruding subjects as vulnerable and oppressed victims. Muslim women come to hold an identity of blurred categories that create both a burden and a catalyst of activism in various arenas, communal as well as national. As we shall see, Muslim women behave equally provocatively within these arenas, and visible expressions of gender become a way of challenging existing power structures, whether these structures are embedded in minority-majority relations or between men and women of faith.

The individual

Countering negative images (about Muslim women) by reversing them is a common rhetorical move among the women I interviewed, as illustrated by Aiysha, a young college student at a Chicago university:

> I think women in Islam are so liberated. When I wear my scarf and my hijab, and I go out, I feel that I demand respect from other people. I do not have to be anyone beside myself, beside my personality to be appreciated, to be liked, to get ahead in my education or career or whatever, as you see so many women do. I don't have to spend hours looking in the mirror. I am just myself. Coming out the way that God created me. I feel that he is giving us this protection. If I go out, get a job, apply for a job, I know it is for my skills, not for what I was wearing or how I looked. How my eye shadow matched my lipstick.[3]

In her statement, Aiysha portrays being a Muslim woman as a road to freedom, respect and success. Simultaneously, she deals with an implicit other that she portrays both as critical observer and as an illustration of failure: the non-Muslim woman blindly believes in her liberation but in reality is trapped in an enslaving search for identity that leads nowhere. Rather than dwelling on individual features, Aiysha stresses an overall image of ideal Muslim womanhood. One aspect of this image is women's visibility. The veil plays a significant role in creating and stating a visibility that is easy for both Muslims and non-Muslims to recognize. However, Muslim womanhood is not merely an external, objectified phenomenon but also one that highlights an inner process of subjectification. Aiysha's statement that she is 'coming out the way God created me' could at first glance be seen as promoting a static understanding of what it means to be Muslim. But her self-presentation makes room for other perspectives, as it underlines the *activating* of Muslim identity as being important. Being a Muslim woman is both something that one is and something that one strives for. To be a Muslim woman is to undergo a process of *becoming* and truly *realizing* what God has created one to be.

---

[3]   Interview, 9 February 1997.

Muslim women's activism

PROUD of Religion

Donning the veil is one strategy that some Muslim American women use to make visible the religious subjects they want to be seen as and whom they strive to be. The identity political statement of the veil, however, has strong consequences for those Muslim women for whom religion is a central aspect of their lives but who do not *Veil -* see the veil as an obligatory means of stating that identity. As Laila al-Mariyati, one *not oblig to* of America's most prominent Muslim female activists,[4] was quoted as saying in a *some* *Los Angeles Times* article discussing media images of Muslim women: '[Without *women* the *hijab*] we do not exist [in the media]. We are not allowed to be the face of Islam' (Sacirbey 2005). This quote illustrates not only how central the veil has become in marking and creating Muslim subjects, but also that other positions exist within the Muslim American community. Although these positions are perhaps less heard in, and less visible to, the surrounding society, they are not necessarily less committed to the enacting of an Islamic identity.

Female Muslim identity in America is a diverse phenomenon. The diversity is stated both as a matter of aesthetics and a matter of activism. In this respect we move from the focus on the individual statements to community statements, on local as well as national levels.

Changing marginalization within the mosque

Research reports from the threshold of the twenty-first century showed that women continued to have limited access to, for example, prayer facilities and women were remarkably absent in the leadership of mosques nationwide (Cainkar 2004; Bagby *et al.* 2001). Most of the women I interviewed in Chicago and Los Angeles argued that the marginalization of women within the mosque was wrong. In their view, no valid religious arguments existed for restricting women's spaces or potential for leadership in religious institutions. The strategies they chose for changing the situation differed, and some were consciously provocative. One example was Maryam, a young convert of Assyrian descent whom I met in a Muslim social service project on the southwest side of Chicago (Schmidt 2004: 44). Maryam saw the spatial restrictions of women as a prevailing problem in the Muslim community in which she worked, both within and beyond the mosque. She told me:

> Sometimes I walk in somewhere and just feel these eyes staring at me. And it is really unsafe, so to speak, because it is just — it is not necessarily meaning something physical will happen. I mean, just your being is questioned. Just the virtue of being a woman walking in there and it is kind of a 'what are you doing here?' look. And it is really an unsafe place for women to be, because, you know, what is that saying about women? What is that saying about who you are as a woman? If you walk in and people think that you shouldn't even be there. .. And that is, I think, what a lot of women struggle with religiously. [It] is finding those places where they can feel comfortable.[5]

---

[4] For more on Laila al-Marayati, see Bullock (2005: 103–110, 208) and Findley (2001: 100, 207).

[5] Interview (taped), 13 December 1997.

One way that Maryam chose to deal with the problem was to physically penetrate the borders that she believed religiously unjust. She once described how she sat down in the men's section of a mosque, arguing that this was where she could hear the *khutba*, the Islamic sermon. Maryam never told me whether her act was tolerated by the men who prayed around her. But her behaviour undoubtedly challenged the existing distribution of space between men and women inside the mosque, ultimately questioning the ideas of womanhood that the distribution promoted.

Other women chose different strategies for claiming their own gender specific spaces and niches of religious interpretation within the community and community mosques. One example was the women's study group to which I briefly referred in my introduction. The group was led by a Middle Eastern woman in her forties, Umm Khadijah, known and respected for her status as *hafiza*, a woman who knew the entire Quran by heart. The women participating in the group represented different ethnic backgrounds, and several were converts. Whenever the group met, Umm Khadijah started out with a short presentation of a religious topic, based on religious texts and exemplified by events in her own life as a wife and mother.

During group meetings, women – and their children – moved freely in and out of the crowded room. Just outside both men and other women rushed to and from the prayer hall and up and down the stairs to and from Sunday school for children on the second floor. Stressing the group's interconnectedness to activities outside the room was that none of the women removed their headscarves, an action that is otherwise permitted when women are among themselves and cannot be seen by males who are not members of their family. Yet, despite the possible gazes from the outside, the space that the women shared was their own. Within this room the women could present their own perspectives on what Islam was about, including the rights and plights that the religion put on their shoulders. I never heard the group contest the leadership of the mosque or the distribution of spaces within the mosque for men and women. Nonetheless, the women's independent use of this particular space challenged the existing distribution of power. Whereas men generally took upon themselves authoritative roles within the mosque, the women who gathered in this room interpreted Islam by themselves and for themselves – according to their own lives and everyday needs. No men participated actively in this process, because they stayed out of the room.

Mosques are by far not the only place where women meet to study their religion. Many groups also meet in private homes or on campus grounds. Both in terms of engaged localities and the interpretations that women undertake, women's study groups are a diverse phenomenon. However, one characteristic that the groups share in the US context is their allowing women to establish their own agendas on being women, Muslims and Americans at the same time. In that sense the rather private and secluded spaces that the groups create are crucial for the way(s) that Islam is manifested in public life. Returning to Umm Khadijah's group, we might ask whether these women's study groups in some sense challenged the stipulated dichotomy between private and public. Even when women kept their voices within the four walls of a conference room, their activities are – as illustrated by the women's refraining from removing their headgear – embedded in other activities taking place in the mosque.

Women taking action outside the mosque

Muslim women as political and academic actors

The activities of Muslims in the United States are not restricted to religious institutions. Over the last forty years a broad range of Muslim organizations have been formed on both national and local levels. Muslim students' associations were among the first to take the scene, superseded by professional organizations and, later, civil rights associations. Women frequently play central and active roles within these organizations. One prominent example is Ingrid Matson, an Islamic studies professor, who is the president of the Islamic Society of North America (ISNA). Within the spectrum of community organizations we also find several specifically representing the voices of Muslim women, including the Muslim Women's League (MWL)[6] and Karamah – Muslim Women Lawyers for Human Rights.[7] The two organizations, based in different corners of the country, share the ambition of supporting women within the community and building bridges to American society – activities based on a religious foundation. Improving the situation of women includes diverse perspectives on health and human rights, as well as dealing with complicated issues such as domestic violence and female genital mutilation.[8]

By participating in national activist organizations, Muslim women become central and even controversial representatives of the Muslim communities in American public and political life. Important here is that several Muslim American women hold positions as distinguished professors in Islamic or religious studies within American universities, for example Aminah Beverly McCloud, Ingrid Matson, Marcia Hermansen, Amina Wadud and Nimat Hafez Barazangi. These women (with several others) are explicit about their religious affiliation, while in their roles as academics they are scholars teaching this religion to a non-Muslim student audience. One prominent aspect of American Islam is exactly that of women taking the role of scholar-activists: of pairing the theories and position of an academic, and a profound knowledge of the Islamic scriptures and traditions, with a deep involvement in communal life, seeking to improve the situation of women within the community and the image of Islam within American society.

The impact that Muslim women – academics and activist – play at all levels of the community cannot be overestimated. Each in their own way, they challenge powerful representations of what Muslim womanhood is all about, both within the majority population and within segments of the Muslim minority. One example is Amina Wadud, who on 18 March 2005 led Friday prayer before a gender-mixed audience in New York. Traditionally, only men are seen as candidates for the position, and a woman can only lead prayer in a congregation of other women. Even before the event took place, it was heavily criticized by Muslims both within and outside the United States. Countering such criticism, the organizers of the event stated that:

---

[6]   http://www.mwlusa.org/.

[7]   http://www.karamah.org.

[8]   A comprehensive list of Muslim women's organizations in the United States can be found in Webb (2000: 249–257).

Fundamentally, this event is about Muslim women reclaiming their rightful place in Islam. It is not about any specific person or personality. Our sole agenda is to help create Muslim communities that reflect the egalitarian nature of Islam. This event is not a protest... Those who will gather for the prayer later this week will do so as a result of deeply held convictions that are rooted in our faith.[9]

The quote underlines two central aspects of ideas and practices of Muslim womanhood in the United States today, aspects that have prevailed in all the examples that I have presented so far. First, there is the issue of claiming or reclaiming space and mobility. Muslim women make such claims within arenas specific to their religious community and within the society around them, driven by the understanding that their gender is either excluded from or misrepresented within them. The strategy that the women apply within both arenas involves presenting an alternative, 'authentic' discourse of Islamic womanhood. Striking in this respect is the continuing reference to space. The organizers of the New York Friday prayer refer to women 'reclaiming their rightful space', Maryam talks about 'unsafe places' for women as a dichotomous reference to how an authentically Islamic distribution of space between genders should be. In some remarkable sense, everything becomes loaded with public significance within this discourse.

Second, all of the examples include perspectives on authentic, ideal Islamic womanhood. This model is presented as a constant, as something conveyed by divine intent, not subject to history (although humans, particularly men, have done their best throughout history to distort it). How this constant is placed *vis-à-vis* larger social dynamics varies. In some instances (e.g. the quote by Aiysha), ideal Islamic womanhood simply *is*, untouched by human history and strong enough to counterbalance the pressure of powerful others, such as the expectations of wider American society. In other instances (as exemplified by Maryam and the organizers of the New York Friday prayer), ideal Islamic womanhood is subject to historical conditions. Maryam talks about women struggling religiously to find a place where they feel comfortable, and the organizers of the New York event talk about women *re*-claiming their rightful place in Islam. In other words, the project becomes to return to the golden, truthful days of the first Islamic community. Although this quest is not exclusively gendered, it has powerful implications for women, as the idea of return influences what spaces and positions they – based on religion – find themselves able to occupy and pursue.

Muslim women taking action at local levels

The impact of Muslim women activists is also noticeable on local levels – within American cities and neighbourhoods. During my fieldwork in Chicago, women were at the forefront of social service projects such as IMAN (Inner-City Muslim Action Network), working on the southwest side of the city. Besides working to improve the conditions of Muslim children and youngsters – many with Palestinian refugee backgrounds – who were living in the neighbourhood, IMAN was driven by the

---

[9]   http://www.muslimwakeup.com/main/archives/2005/03/a_statement_fro_1.php.

ambition to empower the community's women and girls. The project established a girls' and a mothers' group, encouraging the women to establish their own networks and to develop their personal competencies – aspects that IMAN saw as main routes out of the isolation and abuse that some of the women faced.

Projects such as IMAN highlight the everyday, lived situation of less fortunate segments of the Muslim community. On the south side of Chicago, the lack of access to the wealth of the broader society – whether due to unemployment, substance abuse or the traumas of war-striven pasts – restricted women's mobility. From a religious perspective the leadership of IMAN found the painful circumstances of these women unacceptable, and project volunteers did their utmost to present models of Islamic womanhood that spoke for women's rights to participate in society. Maryam told me about young girls who, using quotes from the Quran, challenged their parents' rights to treat their sons and daughters differently. However, she also had to admit that the approach was not always successful:

> I haven't heard any feedback yet about trouble at home so I'm not sure if there is a conflict…. My problem is that I am teaching the girls these things—this is great. But if they're going to go back home and the dad is really abusive, he is still going to dictate what is going to happen to them.[10]

Local projects such as IMAN show how the struggle for women's rights and mobility within – and equally beyond – the borders of the community is not exclusively an intellectual pursuit. The diversity in viewpoints on how women are to participate in wider society, what their rights and plights as believing women are, stress the effects of social stratification, and the ways in which social deprivation frequently affected the lives of women (Muslim and non-Muslim) negatively. Within the more intellectual discourse the dichotomy is often portrayed as the fight between an authentic, knowledge-based and a traditional, non-evaluated form for Islam. When fathers tell their daughters to stay at home, their behaviour should be explained on the basis of their cultural heritage, and how culture has taken religion hostage, not according to the authentic and authoritative scripture. This model for explanation has both defensive and proactive implications. Given that gender roles within Muslim families are often presented as oppressive and backward by powerful public agents such as the press, a Muslim reference to authentic Islam can be a way of defensively resisting such possible linkage. Gender-specific inequality, according to this train of thought, is not a problem within 'real' Muslim families. However, the model can also be used proactively – as a means of reforming individual and communal attitudes. Here, oppression is seen as a disease prevalent within some Muslim families, with authentic Islam as the ultimate cure.

Sex and the Ummah

Within recent years, one movement growing out of the reformist, self-critical trail of American Muslim discourse has gained particular attention: the Progressive Muslims

---

[10] Interview (taped), 13 December 1997.

Movement. An important momentum in the early history of the movement was the publishing of the book *Progressive Muslims – on Justice, Gender and Pluralism* in 2003 (Safi 2003). Most of the contributors were prolific Muslim intellectuals living in the United States. The book included essays on feminism, gender justice and what one author called the 'need for a radical re-ordering of the Islamic discourse on women' (Simmons 2003). In his introduction, editor Omid Safi described the central characteristics of a progressive Muslim identity as occupied with aspects of social justice, gender justice and pluralism. Presenting a progressive Muslim stand on gender justice, Safi radically stressed that 'the Muslim community as a whole cannot achieve justice unless justice is guaranteed for Muslim women' (Safi 2003: 10).

Today, the progressive Muslims movement's most noticeable contribution is the 'Muslim WakeUp' homepage.[11] The homepage was launched by two former graduate students of UCLA, Ahmed Nassef and Jawad Ali, in the same year as the Progressive Muslim volume was published. One year later, the Progressive Muslims Union (PMU), was established.[12] Although the PMU – and particularly their homepage – is contested and criticized by other Muslims for being an 'un-Islamic' reform movement,[13] and the PMU has faced several internal conflicts,[14] the 'Muslim WakeUp' homepage is worth describing as another publicly visible example of how Muslim women in the United States teach and interpret Islam for and by themselves today.

The perspective of the 'Muslim WakeUp' homepage on gender is strongest in the section 'Sex and the Ummah'[15]. This title plays on a reference to the popular American TV show 'Sex and the City', which described the intimate life of four women best friends, all in their thirties. The project of 'Sex and the Ummah' is not to copy the TV show's focus but rather to see and promote sexuality as an integrated part of Muslim spiritual and family life. Mohja Kahf, the main columnist for 'Sex and the Ummah' and an associate professor at Rutgers University, about why and how the column was created:

> One, sex is positively valued in Islamic classical texts, most often in a male-centered, male-affirming way. I am expressing the same values but in a more woman-affirming way. Women's experiences simply interest me…. The second thing is that among the general Muslim populace, frank sex talk is usually done in family settings or single-sex venues. I am making it public rather than private discourse, and of course readers are a mixed-gender community.[16]

Mohja Kahf is careful not to describe 'Sex and the Ummah' as a break from tradition; rather she argues that the forum furthers a more complete understanding of what the Islamic tradition is all about: a more authentic vision of Islam. To reclaim authenticity women's perspectives are important because their voices have not been

---

[11]   http://www.muslimwakeup.com/.
[12]   http://www.pmuna.org/.
[13]   See e.g. http://almusawwir.org/progressivemuslims/?cat=3.
[14]   See e.g. http://en.wikipedia.org/wiki/Progressive_Muslim_Union.
[15]   'Ummah' is the Arabic term used for the community of Muslim believers.
[16]   http://www.muslimwakeup.com/main/archives/2005/04/002744print.php.

heard for centuries. Authentic Islam is presented both as a constant and as something developing according to human experiences. If Muslim women's experiences are left out of the picture, the vision of Islam cannot be complete.

Particularly interesting in this context is how Kahf envisions the project as inherently public. What is normally practiced and talked about in families (and perhaps not even there) is to be laid open for everyone to see and decide on. In 'Sex and the Ummah', the process of religious interpretation is intentionally unhierarchical and open, including its dealings with intimacy and sex. Well worth noticing is that the project is located on an open and well-visited Internet site, and thus implicitly public to Muslims and non-Muslims alike. The practice of Islam is stripped of its privacy, and the line between private and public is radically erased. Everything is public and everything is private.

Laying everything open?

In this chapter we have seen the multiple arenas in which Muslim women interpret their faith, ranging from women's study groups in mosques to Internet-based columns, and using diverse forms of expression, from social service to physical contestations of men's right to exclude women from certain spaces and functions. Some women use black veils and face veils to resist any contact with public space (while yet remaining visible); others describe and openly discuss the human body as a sexual-spiritual object.

In my analysis I have already pointed out the importance of women's using and re-claiming space by defining what being a Muslim woman is essentially about. I have also shown how the women are careful to present their project as located within Islamic tradition, as a way of accessing the authentic message of Islam rather than attempting to create something new. Religious reform is an archaeological process of getting back to the roots, carried out in current practice. Finishing this chapter, I find the significant role that American institutions play in this process worth briefly pointing out. Muslim women's holding positions within American academic institutions further their ability to hold positions as interpreters and reformers within their faith-based community. As a consequence the reform process is remarkably intellectually formulated. Although women within academia stress the importance of holding both a scholar and an activist identity, thereby acknowledging the needs of less privileged women in their community, the current status of things shows that some women have easier access to space, mobility and a voice than others.

Another factor worth noticing is the increased tendency towards portraying the intimate details of family life as an element of objectified religious identity. What is interesting from the perspective of this volume is how such developments contradict the notion that secularization – understood as religion relegated to, and secluded in, the private sphere – is speeding up in western societies. Examples such as 'Sex and the Ummah' show an intensified expression of private practices of religion in public spaces. This development results in large part from judgments being 'in the eye of the beholder' – of a religious minority under the scrutiny of a powerful majority, particularly after 11 September 2001. Whereas some members of the Muslim American community undoubtedly have drawn further back from public engagement, others have chosen the road of laying everything open. Being absolutely frank about practices, disagreements, vulnerabilities and even intimacies becomes a means of proving loyalty to the (secular) nation in which they live. The consequences of this development for different groups of individuals undoubtedly vary. But it states the potency of religion in the twenty first century: not as a private *or* public phenomenon, but as a phenomenon radically questioning the border zone between the two.

Muslim women play central roles in this process. By becoming public and visible activists, the women question the idea of women's religious practice as belonging to the private sphere that prevails within their own communities. And by going (provokingly) public with their practices of Islam, the women counter ideas of Muslim women as necessarily being suppressed, immobile and ignorant – ideas that prevail in the society around them. In that sense, bridging the gap between private and public in the field of religion becomes a strategic move for power and recognition.

References

Bagby, Ihsan, Perl, Paul and Froehle, Bryant, *The Mosque in America: A National Portrait* (Washington D.C.: Council on American-Islamic Relations, 2001).

Ba-Yunus, Ilyas and Siddiqui, Moin, *A Report on the Muslim Population in the United States* (New York: CAMRI, 1999).

Bullock, Kathrine (ed.), *Muslim Women Activists in North America: Speaking for Ourselves* (Austin: University of Texas Press, 2005).

Cainkar, Louise, *Assessing the Need, Addressing the Problem: Working with Disadvantaged Muslim Immigrant Families and Communities* (Atlanta: The leadership Center at Morehouse College, 2004).

Eickelman, Dale and Piscatori, James, *Muslim Politics* (Princeton: Princeton University Press, 1996).

Esposito, John, 'Introduction: Muslims in America or American Muslims?', in Yvonne Yazbeck Haddad and John Esposito (eds), *Muslims on the Americanization Path?* (New York: Oxford University Press, 2000).

Findley, Paul, *Silent No More: Confronting America's False Image of Islam* (Beltsville: Amana Publications, 2001).

Foucault, Michel, 'The Subject and Power', *Critical Inquiry*, 8(4) (1982): 777–795.

Foucault, Michel, 'Subjectivity and Truth', in Paul Rabinow (ed.), *Ethics, Subjectivity and Truth: Vol. 1 of Essential Works of Foucault, 1954–1984* (New York: New Press, 1997).

Haddad, Yvonne, Smith, Jane Idleman and Moore, Kathleen, *Muslim Women in America: The Challenge of Islamic Identity Today* (New York: Oxford University Press, 2006).

Jacobsen, Christine, *Staying on the Straight Path: Religious Identities and Practices among Young Muslims in Norway*, unpublished Ph.D. thesis (Bergen: University of Bergen, 2006).

Karim, Jamillah Ashira, *Negotiating Race and Class in the American Ummah: African American and South Asian Muslim Women in Chicago and Atlanta*, unpublished Ph.D. thesis (Durham: University of Durham, 2004).

Kurien, Prema, 'Religion, Ethnicity and Politics: Hindu and Muslim Indian Immigrants in the United States', *Ethnic and Racial Studies*, 24(2) (2001): 263–293.

Nu'man, Faree, *The Muslim Population in the United States: A Brief Statement* (Washington, D.C.: American Muslim Council, 1992).

Rouse, Carolyn Moxley, *Engaged Surrender: African American Women and Islam* (Berkeley: University of California Press, 2004).

Sacirbey, Omar, 'Uncovering the truth', *Los Angeles Times*, 15 September 2005.

Safi, Omid, *Progressive Muslims: On Justice, Gender and Pluralism* (New York: Oxford University Press, 2003).

Schmidt, Garbi, *Islam in Urban America: Sunni Muslims in Chicago* (Philadelphia: Temple University Press, 2004).

Simmons, Gwendolyn Zoharah, 'Are We up for the Challenge? The Need for a Radical Re-Ordering of the Islamic Discourse on Women', in Omid Safi (ed.), *Progressive Muslims: On Justice, Gender and Pluralism* (New York: Oxford University Press, 2003).

Turner, Richard, *Islam in the African-American Experience* (Indianapolis: Indiana University Press, 1997).

Webb, Gisela (ed.), *Windows of Faith: Muslim Women Scholar-Activists in North America* (Syracuse, NY: Syracuse University Press, 2000).

Werbner, Pnina, 'Stamping the Earth with the Name of Allah: Zikr and the Sacralization of Space among British Muslims', in Barbara Metcalf (ed.), *Making Muslim Space in North American and Europe* (Berkeley: University of California Press, 1996).

Williams, Raymond Brady, Religions of Immigrants from India and Pakistan: New Threads in the American Tapestry (New York: Cambridge University Press, 1988).

Afterword

Mary Jo Neitz

Understanding social change requires that we know where we are beginning, otherwise how can we assess what is different with the passage of time and under the changing conditions? Secularization theory assumes as a starting point a particular relationship between religious institutions and the state and that religion is publicly recognized and powerful. It also assumes that religion is internalized by ordinary people so that individuals are disposed toward piety, as indicated by holding orthodox beliefs, engaging in religious practices, living in a world in which the sacred can be experienced, and in religion is consequential in regard to the affairs of daily life. Secularization theory then posits a change over time in which religion lost power in the public sphere and plausibility in the private sphere, with an overall decrease in the importance of religion in modern society. What we are now thinking about is how that story might fit some people's experience and not other people's. The story, generated by elite white European male scholars, tells their understanding of the displacement of powerful state churches by secular authorities in the public realm, with a subsequent loss of status for the men who continued to lead those churches at all levels, and at the same time a migration of men like themselves out of the churches, and into other professions and institutions more highly regarded in modern societies. Of course, a loss of status for those who stayed or a choice to leave can only happen for those who had access or could imagine having access to such leadership roles in the first place. The public power of "religion" is also different depending on whether one is talking about state churches, sects, or outsiders. The secularization story is told from the vantage point of the unmarked mainstream, whose religion is mapped onto the dominant culture. Historians of the Moors in Spain, or the Jews of the Rhineland might tell a somewhat different story about modernization and the decline in the public power of religion, about exactly what changed and when and why. The US historian, Ann Braude, has observed that in telling the story of secularization in terms of decline, we tell a partial story of elite white men. In contrast, if we look at the story for women in the United States what we see that women were always the majority of participants, and become increasing involved in religious organizations. The question shifts, and Braude asks us to examine the reasons for women's prior exclusion and powerlessness (Braude 1997).

This collection of articles is important because it calls us to ask how secularization is gendered. Furthermore, it does not assume that there is a unitary category of "women" who all have the same location and experience of secularization. The various studies look at women in different countries, women who are affiliated with religious groups with different relationships to the state and to the dominant culture in their societies, women who have different ages and marital statuses. Reading across the chapters, one sees how differences in the locations of women help explain differences in their experience of secularization.

Particularly interesting in terms of how we think about secularization, is the way several of these chapters help us to think in a much more complicated way about what the *privatization* of religion means when we consider it in relation to women. Although women were certainly affected by the enveloping scope of religious institutions under state churches, at the same time most women were largely excluded from the public domains of religious activity. With modernization, more women moved into public arenas, including religious ones. Yet these chapters show that this formulation does not sufficiently capture the problematic nature of defining the boundary of public and private for women and understanding its relation to religious participation. Privatization does not capture the experiences of the Muslim women reported in several of the chapters here, for example. Sarah Bracke's discussion of Muslim women in Kazan, for example, report going beyond the private practices of their grandmothers, (their *babushkas*) to become in their words "real Muslims" for whom Islam is based in the pursuit of religious knowledge. In a different way, Garbi Schmidt shows the complicated negotiations of public and private engaged in by the Muslim immigrant women she studied in Chicago and Los Angeles. Living in a place where Islam is a minority religion, wearing the hijab marks a woman in such a way that being in public spaces is to be "active and out there" in the words of one informant. Her informants also challenged the marginalization of women within the mosque. In both instances, in both cases we see educated, urban women staking a claim to more public dimensions of religious practice. In these instances, we see religion as a site for blurring the boundaries between public and private, a "thirdspace", to use a term that the editors borrow from geographers.

In reading the chapters, one also begins to get a sense that the things that drive women away from religious identification may be different from those that secularization theorists have traditionally posited. In their introduction to this volume, the editors cite Callum Brown's claim that although men moved away from identifying with Christianity after 1800, women continued to be the main carriers of religion until the 1960s when women accepted feminism. In this volume Marler affirms the negative relationship between feminism and religiosity. What does this mean? In some chapters we see that religiously imposed restrictions on women's roles and women's sexuality became issues for some women. Sonya Sharma's discussion of the young Canadian women in Protestant churches suggests that some young unmarried women may leave their churches when they become sexually active. Aune's single women experienced marginality in the Evangelical church they attended, and they also were more likely to disaffiliate than married women. The editors note that the women who are least likely to be involved with religion are those who have full time and professional careers. They suggest that these women have the strongest boundaries between public and private and are least likely to inhabit "thirdspace".

When we turn to the question of what draws women to religion, a number of the chapters confirm the idea that home-centered women find reinforcement for their position in traditional religion. In seeking to explain the increasingly widespread interest in "spirituality" across western countries, Houtman and Aupers posit in their chapter in this volume that interest in spirituality, as opposed to either Christianity or rational secularism, is related to the decline in the plausibility of authoritative sources of meaning and identity of any kind: both men and women, especially the younger and more educated, look inside rather than outside for answers to questions about the meaning of life. Houtman and Aupers suggest, however, that this process of "detraditionalisation" is different for women and for men. They argue that women, especially women who are post-traditional, experience burdens and anxieties having to do with the difficulties, ambiguities and contradictions of negotiating their daily lives, and that it is these women who turn to spirituality rather than established Christian churches.

However, there is also the intriguing finding in a number of the chapters that what draws some women to religion is not simply the search for meaning, but some kind of experience of the sacred. Sian Reid finds women in goddess religions constructing their own woman-affirming, alternative religious identities in the context of widespread secularism. Giselle Vincett's fusers, are feminist women who are disaffected by Christian churches, even when they attend them, and at the same time seek they out alternative spiritualities which they combine with their Christian beliefs. Marta Trezbiatowska's Polish nuns make their unpopular choice, in part because they have, in Trezbiatowska's Bourdieuian analysis, developed an "appreciation of spiritual goods and have the appropriate spiritual capital to choose a convent".

It is not clear that we should think of this evidence of religion or spirituality as a "resacralization." Again, we need to know more about where and how men and women encounter the sacred in their daily lives, and the salience of those experiences. We need to know how experiences of the sacred fit with people's ordinary practices and what they mean. Ruth Frankenberg's interviews with 50 people from a diverse array of religions offer an attempt to explore the relationships between cultural framings and experiences of the sacred in everyday lives of both men and women for whom religion is highly salient (2005). In her study of religion and family among individuals in upstate New York, Penny Edgell found that for both women and men getting married and having children increased involvement in local congregations. For men, involvement in a congregation grows out of their definition of their family roles. For women, however, getting married and having children increases the subjective importance of religion itself, for example through a feeling of awe for the miracle of life (2006, pp. 49–50).

In looking at the questions of what draws women to religion and what pushes them away, it is clear that the answers will be specific to local places, traditions, and conditions. It is also clear that when considering how religious participation is gendered that the question of who has the power to include and who has the power to exclude continues to be important to where and how the sacred is experienced, and the extent to which religion consequential.

References

Braude, Ann, 'Women's History is Religious History.' In Thomas A. Tweed, *Retelling US Religious History* (87–107) (Berkeley: University of California Press, 1997).

Edgell, Penny, *Religion and Family in a Changing Society* (Princeton NJ: Princeton University Press, 2006).

Frankenberg, Ruth, *Living Spirit, Living Practice: Poetics, Politics, Epistemology* (Durham NC: Duke University Press, 2005).

Index